G000152604

THE 11:05 MURDERS

Volume 2 of the Inspector Sheehan Mysteries

By

BRIAN O'HARE

(Author of *The Doom Murders*)

Cover by **Marianna Hircakova**

Clock Illustration Provided By

Melanie Jeyakkumar

Published by

Crimson Cloak Publishing

©Brian O'Hare 2017 All Rights Reserved

ISBN 13: 978-1-68160-362-9

ISBN 10: 1-68160-362-4

This book is a work of Fiction. Names, characters, events or locations are fictitious or used fictitiously. Any resemblance to actual persons or events, living or dead, is entirely coincidental. This book is licensed for private, individual entertainment only. The book contained herein constitutes a copyrighted work and may not be reproduced, stored in or introduced into an information retrieval system or transmitted in any form by ANY means (electrical, mechanical, photographic, audio recording or otherwise) for any reason (excepting the uses permitted by the licensee by copyright law under terms of fair use) without the specific written permission of the author

Edited by Veronica Castle

Publishers Publication in Data

O'Hare, Brian

The 11:05 Murders

1. Fiction 2. Mystery 3. Paranormal 4. Murder 5. Crime

GLOSSARY

Northern Ireland is part of the UK and its police service has broadly similar ranks to its counterparts in England. The short glossary below, while not exhaustive, is offered to clarify for American readers the abbreviations used in this book.

RUC—The Royal Ulster Constabulary *now redundant and replaced, in 2001, by:*

PSNI—The Police Service of Northern Ireland *which is peopled by:*

CC—Chief Constable

DCC—Deputy Chief Constable

ACC—Assistant Chief Constable

CS—Chief Superintendent

Superintendent (tends not to be abbreviated)

DCI—Detective Chief Inspector

DI—Detective Inspector

DS—Detective Sergeant

DC—Detective Constable

SOCO—Scene of Crime Officer

Contents

PROLOGUE

October 2002

He was standing in a shadowed corner, his back to a wall, observing but not observed. His eyes, the only source of movement in an almost preternaturally still body, ranged the room. They came to rest on a laughing girl, mini-skirted, long blond hair, dancing in the middle of the floor with two of her friends. She was slim, beautiful. He stared at her for a long time, expressionless, studying her smiling face, her slender waist, her long, slightly-tanned legs.

There were some twenty students in the room, a large sitting room with all the furniture moved back to the walls to make room for dancing. The students were mostly from Queen's University but there were a few A-level students from one of the local grammar schools. He could identify them easily, overly made-up, suppressed excitement badly concealed behind a studied nonchalance that was supposed to pass for sophistication.

His gaze flicked to his two friends. Friends? The corner of his upper lip moved imperceptibly. Two guys he hung about with, maybe. Not friends. How could they be? Friends are intellectual equals. Nothing in his face moved, but somehow his expression had metamorphosed into contempt. He watched the two second-year under-grads sitting on a sofa, beers in their hands, giggling stupidly, poking and jostling each other. *Half-sozzled, and the party barely started.* He did not need to be a seer to decipher their thoughts. *Idiots!* Living in a drink-fuelled fantasy of sexual conquests to come, nodding and shoulder-pointing at the small group of female students at the music centre who were handing cd covers back and forth as they chose songs to play. *Yes, boys, point and nod all you want. But you'll drink yourselves into a stupor, go back to your digs and be sick, and attend lectures tomorrow with pounding heads and aching regret for opportunities yet again missed.* His gaze returned to the blond girl. The cold eyes seemed to glitter, but his expression and body remained motionless. *But not tonight, boys. Not tonight. This will be a night that you will not forget for a long time.*

He continued to study the girl, the way she moved, her body language. She was enjoying herself with her friends but, unlike them, she exuded a certain diffidence, a shyness that hinted at introversion. Decision flickered in the calculating eyes. *She's the one.* Minimum compulsion required. He recognised the type. *Shame will silence her.*

He eased himself from the wall and made his way to his two 'friends'. He did not move unnoticed. A number of girls seated at the walls stopped talking to watch the tall, handsome, strongly-built figure as he passed by. Some knew him, or at least they knew his public persona: captain of the Queen's University debating team, leading member of the drama society and, somewhat oddly, scrum half for the Queen's rugby team. He hunkered down in front of the two students on the sofa and put a hand on the outer shoulder of each. Leaning conspiratorially inwards, he spoke in low tones. "Boys, ease back on the booze. You want to be able to perform tonight, don't you?"

Two pairs of incredulous but extremely interested eyes stared at him. He gave them his charming grin, one that he had perfected before a mirror. He knew it made him look sincere when, in fact, he felt nothing. "Get yourselves upstairs and bag one of the bedrooms. I promised you something special tonight. Now's the time."

Excitement, fear, lust, puzzlement chased each other across the students' faces. "But who … what?"

"No questions. Get a bedroom. Make sure it has a key. I'll join you," he gave them a leering wink, "in about ten minutes. And I won't be alone."

The two friends jumped up from the sofa. He grabbed both their arms and hissed, "Calmly, you idiots. Act casual."

He watched as they left the room, tense with anticipation and almost sober again.

There was a small drinks table near the disc player, manned by a member of the rugby team. He went over, asked for a beer and chatted for a few moments with his teammate. While he was talking, he noted that one of the blond girl's friends had just left the room, presumably to use the toilet. He nodded a goodbye to the barman and followed the girl into the hall. There were two or three small groups standing there, glasses in their hands, laughing vacuously or arguing about matters of serious import affecting the future of the world. He followed the girl upstairs and found her on an empty landing, her head turning from side to side as she searched for the bathroom.

He glanced around. No one near. Silently he padded up behind her and hammered a fist into the side of her head, just above the ear. She crumpled immediately. He hooked a hand under each armpit and dragged her into a nearby broom cupboard. He had earlier made reconnaissance of the area and had left some rags there. With these he swiftly gagged and bound the still unconscious girl. One final furtive surveillance of the landing and he emerged from the cupboard, closing the door firmly behind him.

He wasted little time returning to the party. He walked over to the blond girl, who had now joined the group at the music centre, and touched her elbow. She turned and saw a handsome student on whose face was an expression of concern.

"Excuse me," he said. "Are you Lynda?"

She gave him a hesitant, "Yes?"

"Friend of Jacqueline?"

She began to share his concern now. "Yes."

He seemed unwilling to say what was wrong but forced himself to speak. "I don't think she's well. I was upstairs, and she collapsed on the landing as I was passing by. She sent me to get you."

Lynda turned to speak to one of the others, but he touched her shoulder. "She doesn't want to make a whole fuss about this," he said quietly. "She just wanted to know if you could just go up and be with her for a while."

She nodded quickly and went immediately to the door. He pretended to go back to his place in the corner of the room but, stopping to look at his watch, he clicked his fingers as if he had forgotten something and headed for the door as well. He caught up with her at the top of the stairs where she was standing looking right and left, still concerned but puzzled.

She saw him coming and said, "Where is she?"

"Just in here," he said, leading her to the bedroom at the end of the hall. He had seen the door of the room open a crack and knew that his friends were watching. He stood back as she walked in. The other two students, grinning gormlessly, were standing by the bed.

Lynda stopped, suddenly wary. "Who are you? Where's Jacqueline?"

The handsome one grabbed her by the shoulders, pulled her towards the bed and, with little effort, threw her on top of it. "Right boys," he commanded, "grab an arm each."

Instinctively they obeyed his command, seizing an arm each but clearly unsure about what they were supposed to do with them. The girl was struggling now, frightened. "What are you doing? What do you want?"

The handsome one stepped to the side of the bed and slapped her face hard. His features were distorted now with a sneer of contempt. "What do you think we want?" He stared at her for a moment. "You can do this the easy way or the hard way, but either way you are going to do it."

She struggled all the more and began to scream. Immediately he stuck a handkerchief into her mouth and began punching her even more roughly than before. Face, body, it didn't seem to matter.

"The harder way it is, then," he snarled with a sour grin. He hit the girl on the face again, very hard, this time drawing blood.

One of his companions, looking shocked, said, "Hey, steady on!"
He lifted a hand to silence him. "Patience, boys, patience. Plenty here for everybody." And he climbed onto the bottom of the bed, reaching for his belt-buckle.

ONE

October 2014

W oman Detective Sergeant Denise Stewart finally found her way to the Serious Crimes room that she was to share with a number of other detectives. She stared at the door and inhaled a deep breath. First time out of uniform, new job, new role, new station, a certain amount of tension was to be expected, but she had not anticipated that Strandtown Police Station would have been so large. It had taken some time to locate the room, but she had been hesitant to ask further directions, trying to make do with what she had been told at the information desk. She was not yet sure of the reception she might receive, particularly in view of the manner of her promotion, and was less than keen to draw any immediate attention to herself. *Some detective!* New to the job, maybe, but what kind of genius did she need to be to figure out that a station with a complement of two hundred and forty full-time officers and another forty-eight or so civilian workers was not going to be a two or three room affair?

Her hands were filled with a large cardboard box containing her "stuff," so she reversed into the detectives' room, pushing open the door with her back. She turned to examine the room wondering where she was supposed to sit. The room was quiet, almost fully unoccupied except for a fat, jowly detective who had been poring over some papers but who now looked up to see who had entered.

He leaned back on his chair, putting excessive demands on the buttons of his shirt, as he gazed at the newcomer. His gaze became an unashamed leer as he noted the trim figure, the blond hair, the exceptionally pretty face. Pushing himself awkwardly from the desk, he stood up. "Name's McCullough," he said, trying without success to suck in his gross paunch. He pointed at the box she was carrying. "Can I help you with that?"

She gave him a curt nod, irritated by his crude interest. "WDS Stewart," she said neutrally. "Thanks, but I can manage. Can you tell me where I might find Chief Inspector Sheehan, please?"

McCullough stepped back a bit and waved a vague hand in the direction of some offices at the far end of the large room. "Why don't you try his office," he said ungraciously.

The woman detective's lips tightened. *Is this guy for real? He's miffed because I'm not jumping all over him? With that comb-over? Good grief!* She carried her box to an office, which she could now see had "DCI J. Sheehan" painted on the door. She knocked and entered at the muffled "Come!" that issued from inside. She was struggling to support her box on one arm as she turned the handle but the chief inspector immediately came from behind his desk. He seemed to wince as he took the box from her but offered no explanation. He sat it on one of the chairs at the wall of the office and offered her another chair in front of his desk. "WDS Stewart?" he asked.

"Yes, sir. Reporting in."

"Welcome to B District."

She stared at the intense blue eyes, the darkly handsome face, and the genuinely friendly smile. Inwardly she relaxed. *I'll be able to work with this man for sure.* She gave him a tentative smile in return and said, "Thank you, sir."

He went back behind his desk. "Most of the guys are out, but you'll meet them later. A good bunch for the most part ..." He saw something in her eyes and grinned. "Ah, you've already met McCullough?"

She nodded, choosing to remain silent.

He grinned again. "Don't worry; he's not typical of the team." He leaned back in his chair and continued, "I'll show you to your desk in a minute." He stared at her, arms folded. She was remaining mute, waiting to hear what he would say next. He saw a very pretty woman in front of him, mid-twenties, but he saw also a woman in control of herself, a woman who was not intimidated by her situation or his status. He saw no arrogance, but he did sense a hint of concern, of apprehension. He'd read her file and knew what was troubling her. "Congratulations on your promotion to plain clothes, Sergeant."

Her lips compressed, but she said, "Thank you, sir. I hope I can fit in here. I'll certainly do my best."

"You'll be fine." He hesitated. "I have not yet told the squad about the circumstances of your promotion, but you're smart enough to know that word will filter through eventually. McCullough aside, though, you're unlikely to face any bile. McCullough's old school, a dinosaur. He doesn't like Catholics; he hates that he's PSNI and not RUC; he doesn't think women should be detectives. In fact, he embodies just about every prejudice Northern Ireland has to offer. He only holds onto his job because he has the wit to shut up when he's told. Bark at him a few times, and he'll leave you alone."

Stewart listened as the CDI was talking and thought that he was unlike any of the bosses she had worked for before. Apart from the fact that she had heard that he had not long been married, she was sufficiently experienced to recognise that he was not trying to come on to her, that he was being genuinely friendly. She had also heard someone say that Jim Sheehan represented the human face of management in the upper echelons of the force. She could already see why he had earned that approbation. She was thus emboldened to ask, "What have you heard about my promotion, sir?"

"Well, you know there's nothing secret in the ranks of the PSNI, Sergeant, but there's always the question of interpretation."

She raised her eyes ceilingwards and shook her head slightly from side to side.

"Depends on whom one talks to," Sheehan went on, "but you got promoted either for betraying a colleague, or ridding the force of a corrupt police-officer."

"I have had some stick about it, sir."

"Sergeant, you've nothing to be ashamed of. You discovered the corruption in your station, you ferreted out the culprit, and you were unafraid to bring your findings to your superiors. Good detective work allied to integrity. Any cop who questions your actions would need to look into his own heart. When are you testifying?"

"Tomorrow, sir. But I have a meeting with the Crown Prosecutor this afternoon."

"Right. I knew it was soon. Okay, we'll not put you on duty until you've got that business squared away." He hesitated. "I think I'll go round the members of the squad individually and see that they get the truth about you. Don't want any uncertainty cluttering up the place." He stood up. Again, that slight awkwardness. *He must be in pain with something*, she thought. "But come on out to the room now, and you can unload that box on to, or into, your desk." He lifted the box from the chair. She stood up and waited at the door for him to pass, but he said, "Ladies first, Sergeant."

The feminist in her wasn't sure how to react to that, but here was a man she could forgive easily. She gave him a quick smile and went out before him although she had to wait immediately for him to lead her to the desk that had been cleared for her, fortunately a comfortable distance away from McCullough's.

As the chief inspector was setting the box on Stewart's desk, the door opened, and a tall, well-built young detective came into the room. "Oh, Tom," Sheehan called to him. "I'd like you to meet our new colleague, Detective Sergeant Denise Stewart."

Detective Allen came over, hand proffered while he was still a few steps away. "Tom Allen," he said. "Welcome to the squad, Sergeant." Then, with a grin, he added, "You'll certainly brighten up this dreary place."

Denise accepted the handshake but said, unsmiling, "I'm not altogether sure that that is my role here, Detective."

The young detective's handsome face reddened, "Of course, Sergeant," he stammered. "I didn't mean ..." He waved his hands defensively. "I'm sorry." He backed away, embarrassed, and went to his own desk.

Seeing the young detective's confusion, Denise felt a moment of guilt. If he had been less good-looking, would she have reacted differently? She caught Sheehan's somewhat puzzled eye and said, "Shouldn't have said that, sir. Instinctive reaction. I get that sort of thing a lot, and I'm a bit fed up with it."

Sheehan nodded. "Okay, Sergeant, but keep it outside. Morale in the squad-room is important to me. You're going to have to get along."

"Sorry, sir. I will."

Sergeant McCullough, an interested spectator, looked at Tom and raised his eyebrows. Tom made a face, and with a quick glance at the new team member to see that he was unobserved, he mouthed the word, "Prickly."

The chief inspector went back to his office as Denise unpacked the cardboard box and made her desk habitable. She heard a low voice and looked up. Tom Allen was speaking into a desk phone. His eyes were on her, but he looked away hastily when she caught his gaze. Denise hesitated. She would need to get to her appointment with the crown prosecutor, but ... She looked at Tom Allen again. Even with this slight acquaintance she sensed something straight and honest about him. The last thing she was looking for right now was any kind of relationship, but perhaps she had been unnecessarily harsh in response to his welcome.

Pursing her lips and straightening the rather formal jacket she had worn for her first meeting with the DCI, she walked over to the young detective's desk as he was putting the phone back on its cradle. Young detective? He was no younger than she was. "Excuse me, Tom." She hesitated. "I might have been a bit brusque earlier. Thank you for your welcome. I hope we can work together."

Allen's face showed surprise, but he quickly recovered and said with a quiet smile, "Not a problem, Sergeant. DCI Sheehan wouldn't have had you on his team if he didn't respect you. Welcome again."

Not quite smiling, she replied, "Thank you." She turned back to the door, acknowledging McCullough with a brief inclination of her head as she left. Tom Allen's eyes never left her retreating back until the door was closed.

TWO

"**W**oman Detective Sergeant Denise Stewart?"

Denise had been sitting for over an hour against one of the marble panelled walls in the central hall of the Courts of Justice in Chichester Street, Belfast. With so much movement in the hall as counsel and clients met, negotiated, separated, she almost missed the call. The repeated shout eventually caught her attention. "WDS Denise Stewart?"

She raised a hand and stood up. "Here!"

The clerk nodded and went back into court number four, assuming that she was following him. Stewart had testified in the Crown Courts many times before, but this time she experienced a frisson of anxiety. This time she was not testifying against an ordinary perp but against a senior colleague. Instinctively straightening to military bearing, she marched behind the clerk to the witness stand. She was sworn in and stood in the box. For a second she stared straight ahead, but inevitably her eyes were drawn to the visitors' gallery. As she suspected, a number of her erstwhile colleagues, many in off-duty plain clothes, were among the spectators, their stares resentful, their faces hostile.

Her eyes flitted briefly to the defendant, seated at the defendant's table with his legal team. Mid-forties, but already showing signs of a too-indulgent lifestyle, Inspector Richard Kerley stared back at her. His face remained expressionless, but his eyes were filled with a cold animosity that almost unnerved the young detective despite her anticipation of his malevolence and her determination to ignore it. She held his gaze for a few seconds showing no reaction, and turned her head to the crown prosecutor. He smiled his encouragement.

Even in his wig and gown, among a number of others in wigs and gowns, Crown Prosecutor Robert Turner was a man apart. Early thirties, charismatic, and handsome, he was a figure that drew eyes, and his bearing reflected the easy confidence that comes with success. At their meeting the previous afternoon, he had warned Stewart not to allow herself to be disturbed by the resentment that she would inevitably experience from her erstwhile colleagues. "Cops tend to be a boys' club," he had said, "and Kerley was a popular inspector who had mingled easily with his men. He will retain the support of many of his men, older officers in particular, who would find it galling that ..." Turner had grinned and lifted his hands to indicate that what he was saying was the opinion of others. "... a pushy young WPC had been instrumental in destabilising the status quo."

As she stared down now at the prosecutor from the witness stand, Stewart remembered how courteous and attentive he had been to her in his office. She had wondered if perhaps the young barrister had harboured some previous animosity towards Kerley and that his cordiality towards her stemmed from the simple fact that she had been instrumental in bringing the corrupt inspector to justice. But she thought she had also detected something else. Given the prosecutor's attractiveness, however, the experience had been no great hardship. Now, as she looked across at him, he was smiling and mouthing the words, "You'll be fine."

The prosecutor stared at some notes on the desk in front of him while the clerk asked Stewart to state her name and address for the record. Then he looked up and said affably, "Good afternoon, Sergeant Stewart. Could you tell the court where you are currently stationed, please?"

"I have just been appointed to serve at Strandtown Police Station in Belfast 'B' District."

Turner nodded. "Of course. But prior to that you were stationed at ...?"

"Lisburn City Police Station, 'D' District," Stewart finished for him.

"Thank you." The prosecutor appeared to study his notes again. "You worked there with the defendant, Inspector Richard Kerley, did you not?"

"Yes!"

"In what capacity?"

"I was a uniformed police constable attached to Crime Branch. I would carry out door-to-door enquiries on behalf of inspectors, make phone enquiries, do occasional research, just basic legwork."

"Did you do any detective work?"

"No, sir, I mean, yes, sir. Well ..."

Turner smiled and held up a hand. "Take your time, Detective. I understand the complexities here. You were not a detective but circumstances led ..."

"Objection!" This from the defendant's table. "Leading the witness."

"Sustained." Judge Walters looked over his spectacles at the prosecutor. "I'm sure the witness is sufficiently intelligent to explain the complexities herself."

"Of course, your honour," Turner said, unfazed. He turned again to WDS Stewart. "Perhaps you can unravel the confusion of your last response for us? Did you mean 'yes' or did you mean 'no'?"

"I was not a detective. I had no duties in that regard. It was just that I noticed some anomalies in events leading up to this case and I decided to look into them. In that sense I did do some unofficial detective work."

"Anomalies?"

The defending barrister was on his feet again. "Your honour, the prosecutor is asking an untrained, unqualified constable to identify alleged anomalies in a case that she had only peripheral involvement in and thus limited knowledge of any details. I ask, my lord, that her earlier response be stricken from the record and this whole ludicrous line of enquiry be disallowed."

The judge turned to the prosecutor. "Mr. Turner?"

Turner smiled easily and said, "Your honour, the defence is using semantics to cloud the issue here. Whether Sergeant Stewart is trained or untrained, whether or not her involvement in the case was peripheral, her efforts led to the exposure of significant malfeasance. I intend soon to establish that as a fact, your honour. Right now, I'm simply asking the witness to explain what roused her early suspicions."

"Objection overruled," the judge declared. He turned to the witness and said encouragingly, "Please go on, Sergeant Stewart."

Stewart glanced briefly at Turner as she gathered her thoughts. He was smiling at her. *Must be something to do with the fact that she was the star witness, his star witness.*

Aloud, she said, "For the past couple of years there has been a UK-wide investigation into a Chinese prostitution ring. Part of what they were doing was putting job advertisements in UK newspapers and duping the women who answered them into coming to Northern Ireland. When they arrive in Northern Ireland expecting to find jobs, usually Belfast or Derry, they are kidnapped and forced into prostitution."

"Human trafficking?" Turner asked.

"Yes, sir."

"All very interesting, my lord, I'm sure," the defendant's barrister drawled, "but is there a point to this? And might I warn the witness, my lord, no unfounded opinion."

"If she needs such a warning, Mr. McCahey," the judge snapped, "I'll see that she gets it." He turned to the prosecutor. "Where is the witness going with this, Mr. Turner?"

"A little latitude, your honour, and all will become clear."

The judge harrumphed. "Well, move it along, please."

Turner smiled again at the witness. "Sergeant Stewart, did this investigation involve the Lisburn Police Station in any way?"

"Only peripherally insofar as we received intel a few months ago that the ring had started operating out of a house in Lisburn. We organised a raid on the property, but the premises were empty when the police searched it."

"Oh? Who led that raid?"

"Inspector Kerley."

"The defendant?"

"Yes, sir."

"How did he feel about the failure to make arrests?"

"Objection!" It was McCahey again. "Calls for a conclusion on the part of the witness."

"I'll rephrase," Turner said quickly. "Did Inspector Kerley say anything about the fact that the premises were found empty?"

"He was angry and made several derogatory remarks about our confidential informant."

"Who was your informant?"

"A person that I had cultivated myself, sir, in relation to much smaller crimes. I kept his identity secret, but his information was always reliable."

"He wasn't very reliable this time."

"Apparently not, sir."

"Did you find that odd?"

"I did, sir."

"Did you speak subsequently to the informant?"

"I made a point of doing so. He was as surprised as I was that the raid failed. He said he knew for a fact that there were prostitutes working in the premises and that some Chinese woman was running the house."

"And what conclusion do you draw from that?"

"Objection!"

Turner held up a hand. "Your honour, I am simply asking the witness to report factually on a conclusion she drew during her conversation with the police informant. I am not asking her to draw a conclusion here in court."

"Overruled. Witness may answer the question."

Turner nodded at Stewart to continue.

"Given the informant's usual reliability, I wondered if perhaps the traffickers might have had prior information about the raid."

"From whom?"

"I had no idea at that time, sir. I just had a general suspicion that it had to be someone on the force since these raids are usually kept secret until they take place."

The defending barrister was on his feet immediately, exasperated, "Your honour?"

The prosecutor raised his hands. "Sergeant Stewart is just reporting on a general suspicion she had. That is the extent of her testimony at this time."

The judge nodded. "Overruled," he stated.

"So what happened next?"

"Not much, sir, until a couple of months later when we got further information that the ring was operating again out of a new house in a different part of town."

"Did you plan another raid?"

"Well, I didn't, but Inspector Kerley did. I was part of that team."

"Was this raid any more successful than the first?"

"No, sir. The same thing happened. Empty house when we got there. No sign of the traffickers nor any clues that the house was ever used for prostitution."

"So your confidential informant was, as they might say in America, batting zero?"

"That's how it looked, sir."

"And what did Inspector Kerley do?"

"He was very angry again. He swore that the informant was simply making stuff up to get paid. He gave me instructions to dump the informant."

"Did you?"

"I had to, sir. I had no choice."

"Why didn't Inspector Kerley deal with him himself?"

"He didn't know who the informant was. I would always meet him somewhere away from the station."

"Why you?"

"The informant had helped out on an earlier case, choosing to come to me, a lowly constable. He has a record and prefers to avoid the brass, I mean, the higher ranked officers. He was also useful in a couple of subsequent cases, but he tended always to deal with me. As far as Inspector Kerley was concerned, the informant was mine."

"And did you speak to him again after you sacked him?"

"Yes, sir. I arranged to meet with him at a local pub. I was dressed in plain clothes and we pretended to be a couple having a drink together."

Turner said, "Why would you have done that?"

"I had brought photographs with me of a number of officers who had been on the two raids. I wanted to see if he recognised any of them."

"And did he?"

"Yes, sir. He identified one of the officers and said that he had seen that man with the Chinese woman on a few occasions."

"Did he know why they were meeting?"

"Objection! The informant would have no knowledge of that. He would be speculating."

The judge looked at Turner.

Turner said, "In the interests of confidentiality, your honour, and, indeed, in the interests of the informant's safety, we cannot say too much in open court about him, but I can say that at Sergeant Stewart's request the informant had been able to secure a small role within the organisation where he worked undercover. That was how he was able to provide the information to Detective Stewart."

"Answer the question, Sergeant Stewart," the judge instructed her.

"The informant was pretty sure that the person in the photograph was laundering money for the organisation through his own bank account."

"Who was the person in the photograph?"

"Inspector Kerley."

Turner turned to take a long look at the defendant. Then, without taking his eyes from him, he said, "The defendant?"

"Yes, sir."

"And what did you do then?"

"There was nothing I could do, sir. I was way down the line with no authority, and I did not know who in the station I could trust with this information. I thought about it for a long time and then I knew I had no option but to ask for a meeting with the Assistant Chief Constable. I explained the situation to him, presented him with the informant's statement and the photographs, and left it for him to deal with."

Turner said, "Thank you, Detective Sergeant Stewart. That's all I need from you. The Assistant Chief Constable will take up the story from there."

The judge looked at the defence's barrister. "Do you wish to cross-examine, Mr. McCahey?"

THREE

W hen WDS Stewart arrived at her desk the following morning, Tom Allen was brewing coffee at a table in a corner of the Serious Crimes Room. He nodded to her and came over to her desk with coffee in a cup that was too delicate and elegant to be a mug but was large enough to hold a sizeable quantity of coffee. He offered the cup to her with a half-smile. "Coffee?"

"Thank you, Detective Allen."

"Tom."

Denise gave him a sideways glance, and with a half-smile of her own, said, "Thank you, Tom."

"Black? White? Sugar? No sugar?"

"Black, no sugar."

"That's what we've got here, so no problems." He hesitated. "The mug is new and it's yours."

"Oh? You didn't need to go to that trouble."

The young detective grinned and said, "Ah well, you see, now that you have your own cup, you won't be tempted to drink out of mine when I'm not here."

Denise grinned and sat down. She placed the coffee to one side of her desk and began taking some papers out of a drawer. Tom stood above her, slightly diffident, but instead of leaving her desk, he said, "How did it go yesterday?"

She stared at the young man, for a moment unsure about the motivation behind the question. But he seemed interested in hearing her answer or, perhaps, interested in spending a few moments longer in her company. Either way, she could sense no threat in the question. *I'm going to need friends,* she thought, *and this fellow seems nice.* "I had no problem with the prosecutor. Mr. Turner was very supportive."

"Bet you can't say the same for McCahey. He's a bulldog. I faced him once and I don't know how I stopped myself from jumping down and thumping him."

Denise laughed a trifle ruefully. "I know exactly how you feel. He went after me hammer and tongs yesterday."

Tom's face expressed surprise. "From what DCI Sheehan told me, your evidence had to be pretty straightforward and the Assistant Chief Constable is said to have found all sorts of questionable dealings in the defendant's bank account, large deposits and withdrawals that he couldn't account for. What could McCahey have come at you about?"

"Yes, my testimony was sound and there was little he could successfully challenge in it. So he went after me."

Tom raised his eyebrows. "After you?"

"Yes. Started off by demanding to know by what right I, a lowly untrained constable, could take it upon myself to investigate a superior officer. He made it sound that what I had done was very questionable and underhanded. It was hard to fob that one off. Then he tried to make out that there was something twisted and off-colour about my meeting an informant in a pub, wearing plain clothes. I tried to point out that what I did, I did in my own time and that it wasn't illegal. So he changed tack and practically called me a brown-nosed bitch who would shop her own mother to get a promotion." She stopped speaking and looked at Tom to see how he responded to that. She was faintly amused to see that Tom

28

actually looked annoyed, apparently angry that the defence should have treated her in this manner.

"That's disgraceful," he said. "What did the judge say?"

"Well, Mr.Turner objected that McCahey was badgering the witness and the judge sustained the objection. I think at that point, actually, McCahey felt that abusing me was losing him credibility with the jury. I noticed him eyeing them a couple of times. After that objection, he excused me. It was with a nasty dismissive wave of his hand and a disgusted expression on his face, but at least that was me finished and out of there."

Tom started to ask another question, "Did you hear …?"

He was cut short by a knock on the door, which was followed by the appearance of a skinny youth carrying a large bunch of flowers.

"Is there a WDS Stewart here?" he asked the room at large.

Denise said, "Over here."

He walked over to her desk and handed her the flowers without any ceremony. "These are for you," he said.

Surprised, Denise accepted the flowers and said, "Oh, thank you."

The youth uttered a hollow laugh. "They're not from me. I'm only the messenger." As he turned to leave he pointed to a small envelope lodged among the blooms. "But there's a card."

Denise reached for the envelope and extracted the ornate card that was inside. Tom had backed away a pace or so from the desk, but she felt obliged to share the contents with him. "It's from Mr. Turner," she said as she read the message. "Thank you for your excellent testimony yesterday. We'll do dinner when Kerley is behind bars. Robert."

Tom's expression was hard to read but he said, "Flowers? Dinner? Nobody bought me flowers or dinner the last time I testified at the Crown Courts."

Denise's instinctive grin quickly faded as she wondered now if the barrister fancied her. *Goodness. I swear off men and here's a good-looking young detective hanging over my desk, and a charismatic barrister sending flowers and talking about dinner.* But the wounds of her recent breakup were still raw and she was not sure that she wanted to entertain either of them.

When she took her eyes off the card, Tom was backing away, a wry smile on his face. "Nice flowers." He waved his right hand, a small movement from the wrist. "Enjoy the dinner." He went back to his desk, and with one final surreptitious glance at the flowers, he settled down to work.

FOUR

C hief Inspector Jim Sheehan negotiated the lights and several traffic lanes at the Sydenham Bypass, heading for Kyle Street and then home. *Home?* His mouth turned upwards in a bemused grin. Home was Margaret's house. There had been some talk about her selling up and both of them moving elsewhere. Margaret had lived in the bungalow at Connsbrook Drive with her husband while he was alive. After their recent marriage she had suggested to Jim that if he felt awkward about living there they could find somewhere else. There had been no question of them moving to Jim's place, a small, purely functional apartment very obviously designed to accommodate one person.

It took little time, however, to realise that the still-inflated prices in Belfast, despite the fall caused by the recent recession, had made the purchase of a new house a senseless proposition. They could have sold Margaret's house, of course, but it still carried a hefty mortgage, one, unfortunately, that was in negative equity. Jim told her that he didn't care where he lived so long as it was with her. So they stayed at Connsbrook Drive and already it was, indeed, becoming home for him.

He turned into the cul-de-sac at the end of the road and pulled into the driveway. Margaret heard his key in the lock, and met him in the hall. She gave him a welcoming hug, and had to cling to him as he stumbled awkwardly. "Sciatica acting up again?"

"Yeah," he said, lips compressed. "It's been driving me nuts all day."

"You really should get a cushion for that chair in your office."

"No way. I'm not gonna be seen with stuff like that."

"Okay. Suffer for your pride. So, how was your day otherwise?"

"Boring. Just paperwork."

"Well, at least nobody was killed or injured," she said, smiling.

Jim grinned back. "Terrible, isn't it? Somebody has to be murdered or robbed to make life interesting for me."

Margaret smiled again. "Go and wash your hands. Dinner's almost ready."

Massaging his right hip as he went into the hall cloakroom, Jim said over his shoulder, "My new sergeant arrived today, Sergeant Stewart."

Margaret went into the kitchen to serve the meal and when Jim came in and sat at the small table, she said, "Well, what's he like?"

Jim looked at her from under his eyebrows. "He's about five seven, blond, has a fantastic figure, and is seriously pretty. His name's Denise."

Margaret gave him a bemused look before her face cleared. "He's female?"

Jim laughed. "That he is."

Margaret put her hands on her hips and gave him a tight-lipped "Hummmph!" Then she said, grinning, "Am I going to get all sorts of phone calls now about having to work late at the office or whatever?"

Jim got up and put his arms around his wife. "She's not my type. My type's right here."

She hugged him back then punched him lightly on the shoulder. "And don't you forget that. Sit down, and I'll put out your soup."

"I think she might be more Tom Allen's type," he said as he sat down. "His eyes were half out on stalks most of the morning."

"Oh? A budding romance there, do you think?"

Jim put a table napkin on his knees. His grin faded slightly. "I'm not sure. Doubt it. Allen clearly liked her but she's as prickly as a cactus. Bit his nose off for saying she'd brighten up the place."

"Gosh. That was a bit rough."

"Aye! Though I must say, she was pleasant enough when I welcomed her. I think she might have been hurt by a man sometime, and I know she had a really tough time at Lisburn from a few dinosaurs there, but I had to tell her to leave it outside the squad room." He sipped a spoonful of soup and then said, "Still, she was man enough to apologise. I think she'll make a good sergeant; she's ambitious, bright and her instincts are right."

FIVE

Two men in business suits were engaged in conversation as they lunched in the Piano Bar on the first floor of the Europa Hotel. Although the age difference was less than ten years, the younger of the two, probably early twenties, seemed awed by his more sophisticated companion. He had little interest in the view of the bustling Great Victoria Street below, focused as he was on what he was hearing.

"Thirty grand last month," the older man was saying, "and all it took was a stroke of a pen." He forked some lasagne into his mouth and leaned back complacently. Mid-thirties, dark-haired, tall, heavily built, possibly running to fat, he might have been handsome but for a self-satisfied smirk that seemed permanently etched on his features.

The younger man's expression was one of envy. "All I get is my salary. How do you get into that end of things?"

"Well, the obvious answer is hard work, promotions and such. But you need a certain mind-set." He paused to eat again and, still chewing, went on, "Calling in loans is no place for the faint-hearted." He pointed his fork at his companion. "You'll hear all sorts of sob stories. They'll promise you the earth and come up with all sorts of seemingly brilliant schemes to repay their debt. You can't listen to any of that stuff." He wiped a corner of his mouth with a napkin. "There are two reasons for that. The first is that most of the time they're talking crap, and secondly," this with an arch look, "you're throwing your bonus out the window if you give them any leeway."

"Thirty grand is a hell of a bonus," the younger man said, still envious. "It's more than my whole year's salary."

His companion smiled. "You'll get there one day, with the right attitude."

"How'd you manage it, a big bonus like that, I mean?"

"I spend a lot of time going over the loans, particularly the larger ones. Some of them have interesting restrictions on them. That's where any astute banker can make himself a few pounds." He pushed his empty plate an inch or two forward. "A while back my bank had given a loan facility to two brothers in the property business. Just before the crunch they were flying, doing really great. They had purchased a large, three-storey building in the city and were converting it into small separate business premises for lease. They had borrowed about three million and were paying it back with rent they were earning from another large property in the city that they had rented to a shirt-making company. They were getting about eighty grand a year for that. But that company went out of business, and the eighty grand cheque that should have appeared in the brothers' loan account a couple of months ago, didn't appear."

"I'm not quite with you."

"Well, you see, I told you that some of these loans come with interesting restrictions, and I'm a guy who does his homework. I know every dot and comma of the larger loan arrangements. I study them constantly. I knew the loan these two guys had arranged had a *repay-on-demand* clause. They were crazy to sign it, but they were doing so well before the crunch, as were so many others, that they could not foresee any problems."

"So, if they defaulted on the eighty grand annual repayment, you could legitimately ask them to repay the three million loan immediately."

"Exactly. You catch on sharp. Maybe you'll be in my place one day."

"But did the bank not give them a bit of time to sort things out?"

"Well, they came in and said that they were about to sell some property or other and they were going to get a large lease on another building and if we gave them a month and, etc., etc. It's the same thing all the time. Bottom line, they didn't have the eighty grand and they were not likely to get it any time soon."

"So what did you do?"

"I showed them the loan agreement, sympathised with them all over the place, but had to tell them business was business. So I called in the loan."

"Three million?"

"Yep!"

"So what did they do?"

"What could they do? They didn't have it. I reported the situation to my superiors and the bank took over their properties in lieu of cash. Anytime I cancel a loan like that, I have to dress it up and make it look like I am really looking after the bank's interests. I get one per cent of the amount called in."

The younger man shook his head, envy still leaking from every pore. "And one per cent of three million is thirty grand?"

His friend smirked and lifted his hands in a *there-you-go* gesture. "They're not all as good as that," he admitted. "But there are still a few nice juicy ones I have my eye on. This credit crunch is bad for some, but for guys like us," he reached forward and patted the younger man's arm, "it's a wee goldmine."

"How did those two guys feel after …?"

"How do you think they felt? Pretty miffed. But you can't let yourself, I mean, it's a dog-eat-dog world. You gotta look out for yourself, right?"

"I suppose."

"You suppose? Wait till I tell you. A mate of mine, same job, bigger bank, called in forty-six mil a couple of months ago."

The younger man emitted a silent whistle. "Forty six million? Holy shit! That's …" He did a quick mental calculation. "That's a four hundred and sixty thousand pound bonus."

"Exactly. Makes my thirty grand look a bit piddlin', doesn't it?" He raised his left arm and looked at the heavy platinum watch on his wrist. "Right, I'm going to have to go." He smirked again. "Small matter to be dealt with in a room a couple of floors above."

The younger man looked sharply at him. "You're not still …?"

His companion grinned.

"You really need to be careful, James," his younger companion warned. "Her husband might be legit now, on the surface at least, but he still has all his old contacts. What if he should find out?"

James shrugged. "What's life without a little bit of risk? Where's the excitement?"

"What about Pauline?"

"Huh! What she doesn't know won't hurt her."

He eased his chair back from the table.

The restaurant assistant manager noticed the gesture and eased over to the pair. "I trust everything was to your satisfaction, Mr. Fitzpatrick?"

"Perfect, as always, Thomas." He proffered a credit card. "Take for the two meals out of this and," he gestured to his companion, "bring Mr. Magill a cappuccino."

The younger man demurred but James Fitzpatrick waved a dismissive hand. "Take your time, Oliver. Relax and enjoy your coffee. You've half an hour yet. I need to get on." Then he winked and grinned lasciviously. "Pun intended. Get it?" And he left laughing.

SIX

Pauline Fitzpatrick looked at her watch and sighed. Then she looked at the half-finished cocktail in her hand. She raised the glass and said, "I'm going to have to go, Kathy." Then, grinning, she added, "But only after I finish this."

Kathy Gibbons, friend of her childhood, made a face. "What's the hurry? It's not as if he'll even notice whether you're home or not."

The two women were enjoying a girls' night out at Tedfords, one of Belfast's trendy haunts. They had been here before, many times, and had never been disappointed, except on the single occasion when they had forgotten to reserve a table. The restaurant was housed in a well-kept historic building, dating from the middle of the nineteenth century. They loved its warm friendly atmosphere, the muted décor with its gold drapes on the windows. On this occasion, they had opted to eat in a first floor room that reflected all the elegance and style of a luxury liner, having earlier enjoyed an excellent meal from the *à la carte* menu. Now they were sampling one or two or even five of the bar's unique cocktails.

Pauline, an attractive woman, late twenties, dark hair parted in the middle, longish but not quite reaching her shoulders, said, "James says he's doing it for us. He's trying to ensure that we'll have a comfortable retirement and that he has to work his pants off to make that happen."

"Humph!" Kathy, plump where Pauline was slim, made no effort to hide her scorn. Kathy was usually scornful where men were concerned. Her frizzy red hair seemed to be as uncontrollable as her expression. "From what you're telling me that's something he'd need to work a bit harder at. You love children, Pauline. It's time you had one of your own."

Pauline was momentarily puzzled, missing the connection. Then she grinned ruefully. "God forgive you! He does work hard. He's tired all the time. He's only fit for sleeping when he gets home." She finished her drink. "Almost midnight. You'd need to get home as well or Stephen will have the police out looking for you."

Kathy said, "Hmmph! Stephen's happy when I'm out enjoying myself." But she began to gather her things. "Share a taxi, all right?"

"Of course."

The taxi left Kathy off first and dropped Pauline at the gate of her house sometime around twenty past twelve. She lived in an exclusive residential area in Piney Way and the house, a large two-storey, detached building, walls partly covered in ivy, was set back from the road some thirty or forty yards, partly concealed behind a high, thick hedge. There were no lights anywhere and Pauline assumed that James had already gone to bed. She walked up the drive and let herself in quietly. She reached for the vestibule light switch just inside the front door and pressed. It clicked but no light came on. Initially puzzled, she remained uncertainly in the vestibule, an unease beginning to grow in her. *Don't be silly. It's just a fuse.* She edged forward in the darkness, hand feeling along the wall, to where there was a light switch for the inside hall. She found it and pressed. Again there was a click, but again no light came on.

Her uneasiness increased and she called in a quavering voice, "James …"

There was no answer. She called again, louder but no less nervously, "James. Are you home?"

No answer and she began to sense an almost preternatural stillness about the house. It was her own home. She should feel at ease here. But her foreboding was palpable now. The dark silence seemed possessed of menace and she began to reverse backwards towards the front door, frightened, but still ridiculing herself internally for such a spineless response to what was probably a simple electrical fault.

She hurried back down the drive, relieved to notice light in a lower window of her neighbour's house. She rang the bell and after a few moments Frank Darcy, elderly, wearing a dressing gown over pajamas, opened the door somewhat hesitantly. When he saw Pauline, he pulled the door wider and exclaimed, surprised, "Pauline. Is everything all right?"

"Sorry for getting you up this late at night, Frank," Pauline said, breathless from nerves, "but the light switches are not working in our house and James doesn't seem to be in. I was wondering if you knew anything about fixing fuses?"

Frank opened the door still further. "Come in, Pauline; come in." He led her to a door. "Sit there in the living room. I'll only be a minute. I'll just get changed and find a torch."

Pauline could not sit and paced restlessly until Frank returned.

"Okay!" Frank said. "Let's go and see what the problem is."

They entered the house again, Frank shining his torch around, somewhat pointlessly, on the walls and ceiling as well as the floor. He tried the light switch in the hall even though Pauline had told him it was not working. "Is your fuse box in the garage, same as ours?" he asked.

"I think so. At least, that's where the guy who reads the meter goes."

"All right. Let's go and fix it. I have fuse wires with me."

The meter was just inside the garage door, low on the left. Frank shone his light on it and realised right away that the problem wasn't a fuse. The electricity supply switch had been turned off. "Somebody's messin' here," he muttered and switched the electricity back on. They could see light immediately flooding the hall and the front living room.

"Thank God for that," Pauline breathed.

"I'll go back in with you, Pauline," Frank offered, "y'know, just to make sure everything's all right."

"Would you, please?" Pauline said, relieved. She was not quite ready to go back into the house on her own.

Frank led the way, entering the house two or three steps ahead of Pauline. He walked through the hall and into the front living room. What he saw there stopped him dead. He sucked in a shocked breath as he turned to Pauline and, taking her by the arm, scarcely able to enunciate the words, he said, "We have to go back out, Pauline."

Pauline, sensing something was seriously wrong, struggled to get past him into the room but Frank kept pulling at her arm. "No, Pauline. You can't go in there. Something's wrong. Please, come on back out. We have to phone the police."

SEVEN

WDS Stewart was on late duty in the Serious Crimes Room of Strandtown Police Station. Close to one in the morning, the room was empty, cheerless. She put her desk in order, tidying some folders, notices and memos. She was making sure that everything in the drawers was neat, tidy and accessible, working slowly to allow time to pass. She almost jumped when the phone rang. She snatched it up and said, "Serious Crimes, Duty Officer Denise Stewart here."

As she listened to the disembodied voice for a moment, her grip on the phone tightened and the colour left her face. She reached for a pen and pulled a notepad towards her. Trying to keep her voice from shaking, she said, "What was that address again?" She wrote for a few moments and then asked, "Has Chief Inspector Sheehan been informed?" She nodded at the answer, put the phone down carefully and stood up, uncertain and ill at ease. Then she lifted the phone and rang the front desk, explaining that the Serious Crimes Room was temporarily unmanned. She batted away a nervy inner *'or un-womanned'* and ran to the coat rack. *No need for panic* she rebuked herself as she grabbed at her coat and almost ran from the room.

EIGHT

DCI Sheehan reached the Fitzpatrick residence some moments before his sergeant. Already some squad cars were lighting up the dark street with their flashing lights while uniformed officers were closing off the area with lengths of yellow crime scene tape. The chief inspector noted the medical examiner's car parked nearby as he made his way along the narrow corridor of yellow tape leading towards the house, hopping on one foot from time to time as he struggled into a white hooded coverall and matching shoe covers. What he did not note, nor did any of the officials milling around note, was the powerful car that had just turned into the street, its lights off, its expensive engine so quiet that its purr was barely discernible. The car's driver, however, was immediately aware of the police activity in the street and reacted with something approaching shock. He braked immediately and studied the scene with a sense of puzzlement. Confused, but conscious of his own security, he reversed quietly into a nearby driveway, turned, and sped from the scene.

A uniformed officer met the chief inspector at the front of the house and led him inside. He pointed to a door at the left of the hall. "In there, sir."

Sheehan nodded his thanks and stood for a moment at the door. He was in a large, well-appointed room with elegant furnishings and expensive wall-papering. Beige and chocolate drapes floated at the three large windows, and a cream-coloured leather, four-piece suite was set squarely in the room with almost geometrical precision. *No shortage of money here,* he surmised, as his gaze moved past three busy white-suited forensic officers to the body on the floor. A police photographer was already taking a last couple of shots while a colleague was completing a video recording of the scene.

The victim was a white male. Sheehan did not have a full view of the body or what injuries there might be because Dr. Richard Campbell, Deputy State Forensic Pathologist, was kneeling over it and another man standing over him, observing. The observer was a good-looking black man, very tall, with a cast of features that suggested one of his parents might have been Caucasian.

Although Sheehan's view of the corpse was somewhat obstructed he did note that the lower clothes were disturbed and that a lot of blood was ruining the thick beige carpet. As he eased forward, he was suddenly conscious of movement behind him and turned to hear Sergeant Stewart say, "Came as soon as I heard, sir."

Sheehan moved slightly to allow the sergeant to witness the body. At that moment the pathologist was probing the victim's mouth with small forceps. He paused to secure something, withdrew the forceps, and turning slightly towards Sheehan, held aloft a fleshy, slug-like object.

"Ah!" he said. "I wondered where that had gone."

"What is it?" Sheehan asked.

"Ah, Jim, thought you'd be here." He pointed to the man standing beside them. "Meet Doctor Andrew Jones, new Assistant State Pathologist."

Jones nodded, his expression serious.

"You've no idea of the trouble I had to go to," the pathologist went on, talking seemingly to the object he was holding in the air, "to get the authorities to appoint new help. Just breaking him in."

"Pleased to meet you," Sheehan said, somewhat perfunctorily. Then he gestured to the object in Dick's hand, eyes questioning.

"It's the victim's penis, which, if you care to observe the body, is no longer where it should be."

"In the name of God! Who the hell does that sort of …?"

Sheehan was distracted by a muffled noise at his right shoulder and sudden movement. He turned to see Detective Sergeant Stewart leaving the room at some pace, bent over, one hand across her mouth.

Dr. Campbell glanced at Sheehan, poker-faced. "She didn't stay long."

Sheehan said, "She's new. What about this penis-in-the-mouth business? What's the killer trying to tell us?"

Doctor Jones stared at the two men, unsure of what to make of their banter but he never allowed his attention to waver as he listened to every word his boss was saying.

Responding to the chief inspector's question, Campbell said, "As I so often have to remind you, Jim, I simply find these things. You're the detective; you make the deductions. But," he held up a didactic finger, "I can tell you that this is nothing new. Cutting off an enemy's penis happens all through history, more recently Vietnam and Afghanistan. Every captured Russian soldier lost his penis to Afghan women. There's always a message of some sort in it. Perhaps there's one here, too."

Sheehan, a lapsed Catholic, had lately found himself wandering in and out of his faith. He had not yet developed the habit of prayer but in extreme circumstances he was wont to speak to the Lord. Now he was thinking, *How can you allow this evil in the world, God?* And, as always, a little voice, whether it was his own, or God's, or even Monsignor Keenan's, would sound in his head. *Free will, Jim. Free will. My hands are tied.* Sheehan pulled his mind back to Dr. Campbell. "Thank you, Encyclopaedia Britannica. Was it done post-mortem?"

"Ante-mortem." He shuddered slightly, empathy inevitable. "Lots of blood. Pretty vicious. Must have been a lot of hate there, maybe even rage. I don't know if the victim was fully conscious at the time, I hope he wasn't, but ..." He pulled a face and waggled a hand in mid-air, indicating doubt.

"What are you getting at?"

Campbell pointed to small burn marks on the left side of the victim's neck. Sheehan bent closer to observe, straightening again almost immediately as his sciatic hip sent a message of protest. "Taser marks," the medical examiner explained. "The victim was rendered helpless before any killing was done. But from what little I know about tasers, I think that while the strongest of them can incapacitate, they don't really render the victim unconscious. I think this victim was meant to suffer." He lifted the body slightly. "Hands tied behind the body with strong cord, stuff you can get in any hardware store."

"And this means?"

"Jim, how would I know? But, a rough guess, the killer might have wanted to talk to the guy or rant at him. He obviously tied the victim up so that he couldn't get the jump on him. I don't know why he was delaying. Maybe he wanted the victim to know precisely why he was being killed. Your guess is as good as mine. No, far better, you're the highly-lauded chief inspector."

Sheehan threw him a frosty look. "Cause of death?"

The pathologist pointed to the deep, bloodied cut on the victim's throat.

"This might give you a clue, although the answer may not quite be as obvious as you think."

Sheehan suspected that he was not going to get the abbreviated version. "Keep the lecture short, Dick."

"Don't be so hasty, Jim. You might learn something about the killer in the details." He sat back on his heels, still kneeling. "There are three possible causes of death when the throat is cut." He held up a finger of his right hand. "One, the most likely is exsanguination. If the external jugular vein, or internal jugular vein, or carotid artery, are cut, the person will bleed to death." He pointed to the cut. "The interesting thing here is that the killer was hesitant, which doesn't sit with the violence to the nether region."

"What are you saying, Dick?"

"Just what I said, Jim. I would have expected a harder, more brutal slash, given the nastiness of what happened below. But this cut is almost tentative."

Jones spoke for the first time. His voice was deep, down-in-his-boots deep. Sheehan, influenced by his love of opera, couldn't help thinking, 'basso profundo'. "Perhaps the perpetrator simply didn't know what he was doing and made a hash of the cut. It looks like a very amateurish effort."

Campbell nodded. "Perhaps. Whether the killer didn't know what he was doing or what, I don't know. But unless the slit is from ear to ear and not simply the front of the throat, then the jugular vein and carotid arteries aren't involved. To truly ensure death by," he made quote marks in the air with two fingers of each hand, "slitting the throat, as they say, one has to make the cut," he accompanied this word with a slashing movement, "to include the carotid artery. If the carotid is only nicked, pressure will build and there'll be a huge swoosh of blood, and even if it's properly cut there will still be a thick geyser of sorts. Either way, death will not occur for three to five minutes until the victim bleeds out. But it's possible to slit the victim's throat and miss the vital spot. That's what seems to have happened here."

"So, no arterial spray?"

The pathologist looked at Jim, amused. "So you have been listening to my little talks. Good for you, Jim."

"No, I wasn't. I saw that on TV."

The doctor scowled at him and held up a second finger. "Another possibility is the occurrence of an embolism, if air enters either of the jugular veins. Death can come rapidly because there is no intake of oxygen."

"Is that what happened here?"

"No." He held up a third finger. "It is also possible, if the throat has also been cut open, for the victim to choke to death on the blood. That, together with the loss of blood below, made death inevitable."

Sergeant Stewart returned to the crime scene, looking pale but determined. "Sorry about that, sir."

"Yeah, well, it's a pretty gruesome introduction to serious crime." He indicated Doctor Jones and said, "This is Doctor Andrew Jones, new Assistant State Pathologist." Looking at Jones, he flicked a hand at the sergeant. "Sergeant Denise Stewart."

Jones rumbled a deep, "How do you do?" but remained unsmiling.

Stewart noted the doctor's handsome looks and experienced a tremor as the deep voice all but enveloped her. She smiled a silent greeting.

Sheehan pointed to the victim, gestured to the blood all over the floor, and said. "This is vicious, nasty, brutal. Probably lots of rage here. Yet the doc tells me that the attempt to slit the throat was hesitant. Any thoughts?"

Jones studied the body. "Were there two of them? An alpha and an acolyte? The dominant one orders the submissive one to slit the throat but he makes a mess of it?"

"Good thought," Sheehan said. He turned to the medical examiner. "Well?"

Campbell looked again at the body and up at Jones before saying, "Can't see any evidence to support that. I'm pretty sure it was the one killer."

"Maybe he missed the mark? Maybe the victim was still struggling?" Sergeant Stewart kept her eyes resolutely on her superior as she was speaking.

"Hardly, if he was tasered." Sheehan replied. "Maybe the perp didn't want to get blood all over his clothes. Or maybe something disturbed him. Lot of maybes."

The pathologist held up a finger. "Interesting you should say he was afraid to get his clothes stained. Look around. All blood spatter splashes are intact, no disruptions to the flow. And no footprints or any other indicators of the perpetrator. He was definitely careful, even fastidious."

"Or maybe he was standing, or kneeling, behind the victim when he slit his throat," Sheehan mused.

Campbell nodded with an upward twist of one eyebrow. "Good thought, Jim. They'll make a detective of you yet."

Sheehan pretended not to hear Campbell's remark. He stood slightly aside to allow Stewart, who had finally forced herself to look at the body, to make a closer inspection. She stared, lips in a tight, thin line. For a moment her face was expressionless but puzzlement began to replace her grim control.

"What is it?" Sheehan asked.

"You say there's a lot of rage here? Why did the perpetrator leave the face so unmarked? You'd think if there was rage he would have wanted to beat him up."

Sheehan noted that the corpse's face was, indeed, completely free from any bruising. He nodded slowly. "Good point, Stewart. Any observations, Dick?"

The pathologist shrugged. "Might have been cold rage."

"So the killer had no trouble whacking off this poor guy's manhood, starts to lose it a bit when it came to cutting the throat and, despite indicators of hate and anger, never laid a hand on the victim when he had him tied up. That about right?"

The doctor spread his hands slightly and raised his shoulders to indicate agreement.

"Interesting little anomalies here," Sheehan mused. "The killer has cleaned up after himself, leaving no clues, but he's telling us, maybe inadvertently, something about himself."

"What would that be, sir?" Stewart asked.

Sheehan emitted a mirthless grunt. Then he added, "That's the sixty-four thousand dollar question. We still have to figure that out. But he has left us something, however vague and minute, to think about."

He strolled over to one of the SOCOs who was testing the doors and furniture for prints. "Find anything?"

"Nothing really. Few prints. Pretty sure they belong to the place. No fibres, no hairs, but …" He held forward a gloved hand, showing Sheehan the face section of a broken cufflink. It was polished-brown with gold marbling. "I found this under an armchair."

"What do you make of it?"

"I just assume it belongs to the guy who owns the house, the dead guy. I mean, a killer is not going to commit murder dressed up to the nines, is he?"

"Guess not, unless it fell out of his pocket or something."

The officer's expression indicated what he thought of that possibility.

"All right. Give it to the exhibits officer anyway. I needn't ask if there was any sign of a weapon?"

"No. Almost certainly took it with him."

"Killer wearing coveralls, do you think?" Sheehan asked.

"Could have been. There's nothing here that looks out of place at all."

A couple of officers came from another room, presumably a den or study, carrying plastic bags of correspondence, a laptop and other paraphernalia belonging to the deceased.

"Either of you two guys find anything?" he called to them

The two SOCOs shook their heads in unison. Bill Larkin, Exhibits Officer, appeared just behind them. "We're just bagging and labelling stuff from his work-room, Chief," he said, "but there doesn't seem to be anything out of the ordinary. Maybe there's something on the laptop."

"Okay, Bill. Stay with these boys and protect the chain of evidence."

"Don't worry, Chief," Larkin cut in, half-smiling. "They don't call me a nit-picky obsessive for nothing."

Sheehan returned his grin and said, "Any idea how he got in?"

"Back door," Larkin replied. "He came prepared, used a glass circle cutter. Quite a neat little circle in the back window just above the door lock."

Sheehan grimaced. *Criminals are getting more and more savvy these days.*

"All right, thanks Bill." He pointed to the SOCO at the door. "This officer has something for you."

The SOCO handed the broken cufflink to Larkin and Sheehan went on, "Make sure that stuff is conveyed to forensics as soon as possible. Oh, and organise the usual appeals for witnesses, radio ..."

"Yeah, I know, Chief," Larkin cut in, slightly miffed. "Radio, TV, newspapers ..."

"All right, Bill. All right. Just do it." He glanced at his sergeant. Almost lost in the voluminous coveralls, she was standing to attention, hands clasped behind her back, eyes straight ahead. *Tough first case, but she'll get used to it.* He strolled back to the corpse. It seemed oddly flaccid to him.

"Have you a time of death, Dick?" he asked.

"Five minutes past eleven." This with some nonchalance.

"Aye, right!"

"Five past eleven, Jim," Doctor Campbell said with more forcefulness.

"Come on, Dick. You're always giving me four or five-hour windows. Where is this exactitude coming from?"

"Exactitude? I like that. Okay! Check the watch. It's stopped at eleven-o-five. Maybe it got broken in the struggle."

"Or maybe it was already broken."

"Well, the body was found less than an hour ago, no smell yet, and rigor mortis has barely started. The time on the watch would pretty much match the time of death, I would guess."

Jim bent, lifted the corpse's wrist and examined the watch, a gold Rolex. "Expensive taste." He looked closer, puzzled. "This watch isn't broken, Dick. The winder has been pulled out to ensure that it stopped at this particular time." He put the winder back in and the second hand began to move. He pulled the winder back out and left it. He braced himself to stand again, anticipating the inevitable twinge from his sciatic right hip. He set his face to reveal nothing of the pain to his colleagues. It was a weakness that embarrassed him. Still staring at the watch, he muttered, "Now, isn't that convenient. Killer wants us to know the exact time of death." He stared at the pathologist. "What's that about?"

The doctor clambered awkwardly to his own feet and, stripping off his rubber gloves, said, "No idea. I'm away to wash. You two can figure out what's going on here." Jones left with him, acknowledging the two detectives with a brief nod.

Sheehan, watching them leave, muttered, "Your man, Jones, doesn't say much, does he? Hope he's more forthcoming if we have to meet him in the mortuary." He brought his eyes back to the corpse. "Well, Stewart, what do you think?"

Stewart stood immediately to attention and said uncertainly, "Think, sir?"

Sheehan turned to face her. "This is not a word you're familiar with?"

Stewart, flustered, said, "Yes, sir. Thoughts, sir." Her face was suddenly set in concentration but, though her lips were moving, no words emerged.

"I don't want a whole, carefully worked-out scenario, Stewart. Just give the first thought that comes into your head."

"The appendage, sir. It was in his mouth."

"I noticed that."

"I mean, why was it there, sir?"

Sheehan waited.

"Could it be that he had been putting it somewhere he shouldn't and somebody got mad and chopped it off?"

"Uh huh."

"Or maybe the killer is impotent. Maybe he feels emasculated in life and wants his victim to be the same way in death."

"Deep, Stewart. Deep. And you surmise this because …?"

"No idea, sir. Just thinking out loud, sir."

"All right, all right. Will you quit with the feckin' 'sirs'. Anything else?"

"Could it be a deliberate ploy? Maybe a misdirection of some kind. Maybe it doesn't mean anything."

Sheehan stared at the body, an expression akin to disgust on his face. "I don't think so, Sergeant. This is too up close and personal. Whatever it means, it means something. It says something, something about the victim and probably something about the perp as well. Still, there's no real point in speculating at this time without evidence. Start guessing too much and the next thing you know, you're looking for facts to support the guess and you sail right past something significant. We'll wait and see what facts we find and we'll go from there."

"What do you think about the cufflink, sir … er … boss?"

Sheehan mused. "I'm puzzled by it. Makes no sense that a perp this careful would drop that."

"It was found under a chair, sir. Could have been there a few days. Dropped by a visitor or friend maybe."

"Maybe." He was silent for a moment, lost in thought. "No. I don't get it. It's a definite anomaly. I mean, it's half a cufflink. Yes, it could have broken off and rolled under the chair but …" He shook his head, frustrated. "Crime scenes are bloody puzzling sometimes."

Dr. Campbell, dressed in his overcoat, returned with Jones and two mortuary attendants. "Okay, men. You can take the body away now." Pulling on a pair of leather gloves, he said to Sheehan, "I'm off now, Jim …" He held up an arresting hand as Sheehan made to speak. "No, definitely no. Don't come near me tomorrow or the next day. I might have some sort of report ready for you after that."

As they stood back to let the newcomers lift the body on to a stretcher, Sheehan raised his hands. "I never opened my mouth."

"No, but you were going to." He nodded to Stewart as he and Jones left the room, chivvying the two attendants with non-stop cautions and instructions.

Sheehan caught his sergeant's bemused stare. "Dick and I go way back. He knows what I'm going to say before I say it. But we'll be in his mortuary day after tomorrow for an update and he knows that, too."

He began to divest himself of his coveralls and Stewart, staring at the retreating mortuary attendants as she rid herself of hers, said, "What about the throat, si ... si ... boss? Why so diffident after the violence to ... to the other part of his body?"

Sheehan took a moment to reply, staring at the chalked outline on the floor. "Have you ever tried to cut anyone's throat, Sergeant?"

"Me? No, sir."

"Me, neither. But from talking to Dr. Campbell over the years I picked up a few things." He lowered his eyebrows and stared down at her. "Don't tell him I said that. He's bad enough as it is. Anyway, as I understand it, a throat is very difficult to cut properly. It needs a fair bit of strength and persistence. It could be that the killer didn't quite know what he was doing and just made a mess of the effort, or maybe he did indeed suddenly lose his nerve. Or, as you say, maybe he simply wanted to give the impression he didn't know what he was doing. But why?"

"Maybe, as you say, he was cutting from behind and found it awkward. Maybe he was disturbed. Could he have still been here when the wife's car lights showed through the window?"

"An hour after he started? Seems like a long time to hang about."

"He could have got away while she was round fetching the neighbour?"

"Lot of 'could haves' and 'maybes' without any evidence."

"Where do we start to find out, sir ... Chief?"

A fleeting grin caught the edge of Sheehan's lips. "At the beginning, Stewart. We start with the victim. We have to find out everything we can about him, from the neighbours, from his work colleagues, from his social circle, from anybody who had even five minutes' contact with him whether today, yesterday, last month, last year, or years ago. Are you up for that, Sergeant?"

Stewart looked stunned.

"Detection is not about amazing hunches and clever deductions, Stewart. It's about chasing leads, even the most tenuous, and it's hard, hard work. We have to suss out scraps of information from his connections, from his emails, his phone records, his credit card transactions and follow them up. Slow and laborious. But by the time we're finished, we're going to know more about this guy than he knew about himself. Okay?"

Stewart nodded and tried to look purposeful.

"It's okay, Stewart, you won't be on your own. We have a whole team. There'll be plenty of debriefs and discussion. Once we set up the Incident Room and brief the men, we divide up the work. You'll have plenty to do but you won't be expected to do it all by yourself." He sighed heavily. "Have you got your notebook? Right now we'd better go and have a word with the wife ... widow. Prepare yourself, Sergeant. This is never pleasant."

NINE

Sheehan and Stewart, directed by a uniformed policeman on duty at the crime scene periphery, found Mrs. Fitzpatrick in the living room of the neighbour's house. She was sitting on a sofa in a large, comfortable room which had an arch leading through to a dining annex. The neighbour, Frank, was sitting in an armchair beside her, looking anxious and helpless in equal measure. He stood up when the detectives introduced themselves and shook their hands. "Frank Darcy, neighbour. This is Mrs. Fitzpatrick, Pauline, wife of James."

Sheehan shook the proffered hand and introduced himself and his sergeant. He studied Mrs. Fitzpatrick, clearly a very good-looking, young woman but right now haggard and very pale from the shock of discovering her murdered husband. She had been watching them as they came into the room but had remained very still, unmoving, almost as if she was removed from what was happening around her. She seemed, however, to have control of her emotions and, if there had been tears, they were dried up now. Sheehan sat, leaning forward, on an empty armchair on the other side of the woman while Stewart moved back out of her eye line, surreptitiously opening her notebook.

"Mrs. Fitzpatrick, I understand this has been a terrible shock for you, and I am truly sorry for your loss. Unfortunately it is extremely important to get our investigation off the ground as quickly as possible, and we need you to answer a few early questions right now. Can you cope with that?"

Pauline gazed directly at him, emitting a tired breath, and said, "What would you like to know?"

"Just some basic information, Mrs. Fitzpatrick. Did your husband have any enemies, or do you know if he has offended someone enough for them to want to hurt him?"

The woman's face crumpled for a moment, but she said softly, "No, James worked in a bank. As far as I know, he got on well with all his colleagues and has had several promotions. I can't imagine who might want to harm him."

"What does he do socially? Does he play golf, squash, go to the gym?"

Mrs. Fitzpatrick seemed somewhat at a loss, surprising Sheehan. "He's very busy. His work keeps him out all hours. He does have golf clubs, but I don't think he has played in some time."

"Do you know if your husband owns a pair of cufflinks, brown with gold marbling?"

"Cufflinks?" It was almost as she didn't understand the word.

"Yes."

"No … no. James didn't use cufflinks. He had this Rolex watch he was very proud of. He always made sure his shirt sleeve didn't hide it."

"Might someone have bought him cufflinks as a present at any time?"

"I don't think so. I have never seen cufflinks on the bedroom dresser or anywhere else."

"All right. Do you know where he spent this evening?"

"He was working overtime again. He says he is having a lot of problems lately with clients not keeping up with their loan repayments." Her hands, which had been clasped together on her knees, move slightly. "The recession. It seems to be affecting lots of people."

"You were out tonight yourself?"

"Yes, most Tuesday evenings I would have a meal with my friend, Kathy Gibbons. We went to Tedford's this evening just after eight o'clock." Stewart noted the place and the time. "I got back just after midnight and when I entered the house ..."

"Would many people know that you're out most Tuesdays?"

"I've no idea. I've never tried to keep it a secret." She started and her head came up. "Do you think the killer knew that James would be alone tonight? If I'd been here, would he ...?"

Her face tightened and she bowed her head, seeking to control herself. Sheehan admired her courage. Many women in this situation allowed themselves to lose control, weeping incessantly and being generally incoherent. "Take your time, Mrs. Fitzpatrick. I know this is very difficult for you."

Frank butted in. "When she got home, Chief Inspector, all of the lights were off and none of the switches were working. She came and got me, and I found that the meter switch in the garage had been turned off."

Sheehan sucked in a breath. "Did you touch it?"

"Course I did," the older man said sharply, miffed at the implication that he had been careless. "How the hell else was I goin' to get the lights back on?"

"Of course. It's just that there might have been prints."

"Aye! And if somebody had told me there was a murder next door, I might have known to be more careful."

Pauline's hands went to her face. Frank was immediately contrite but still found time to glare at Sheehan. "Sorry, Pauline," he said. "I didn't mean ..."

"Don't worry about it, Mr. Darcy," Sheehan said, attempting to appease the older man. "From the state of the crime scene, it's almost a certainty that the perpetrator would not have been careless enough to leave any prints on the meter. You didn't notice anything out of place there, did you?"

"Nope! The switch was just down at OFF. I just turned it back on again and went back to the house."

"Is the garage usually kept open, Mrs. Fitzpatrick?"

Pauline was shaking her head before she spoke. "No. The door is generally pulled down. But I suppose it is easy to pull it back up. It does have a lock but we rarely use it."

"Do many people know you don't lock it?"

She stared at Frank for support. He raised his shoulders but didn't speak. She then said tentatively, "I don't know. It's nothing we ever talked about. I'm sure most people wouldn't have known it wasn't locked."

"Would James have had any colleagues from work, or any other friends, home with him some time in the past who might have seen him opening the garage door?"

Pauline showed signs of distress. Her hands were pulling anxiously at the handkerchief she was holding. "I … I … don't know."

Sheehan backed off. Too much pressure too soon. "It's all right, Mrs. Fitzpatrick. That'll do for now. Maybe something will occur to you and if it does, you can always get me at one or other of these numbers." He handed her his card as he stood up and signalled to Stewart that they should leave. Turning to Frank he said, "Just before we go. You didn't happen to notice any strangers in the area recently taking an interest in this house?"

The old man's head cranked up and his eyes widened. "Do you think somebody was casing the joint?"

In deference to Pauline's grief, Sheehan fought hard to restrain the chuckle that almost overwhelmed him. "Casing the joint? Yes, casing the joint." He rubbed a hand over the lower half of his face to conceal the grin that refused to acknowledge his control. "Did you see anyone?"

Frank's face screwed in thought but there was no enlightenment. "I don't rightly remember off hand, but if I think of anything …"

"Yes, please do." He offered the old man his hand. "Thank you, Mr. Darcy. You have been very helpful."

Pleased, the old man took the hand and said, "I'll chat with Pauline over the next few days and see if we can come up with any names or something."

"That would be great, Frank. Thanks." He turned to the woman who had remained unmoving on the sofa. "Thank you for your time, Mrs. Fitzpatrick, and please accept our deepest sympathies for your loss."

Stewart added her sympathies and both made to leave.

"I'll see you out," Frank said, heading for the door. When they were out of earshot, he said, "Pauline's a lovely woman, as nice as they come, but James was an arrogant bastard. God forgive me for speaking ill of the dead, but there were plenty around here who didn't like him. I'll try to get some names for you. Could you give me one of those cards? I'll contact you if I hear anything."

"Thanks, Frank." Sheehan handed him a card. "That would be very helpful."

TEN

When the first debriefing session began, Bill 'Larko' Larkin was already working on the white board at the 'Incident Room', set up for convenience in the Serious Crimes Room. Photographs of the victim, taken from different angles, adorned the board. There were some photographs, too, of the crime scene, but at this point of the investigation there was little else. There was a large television with a video player nearby. Sheehan's voice cut through the murmured conversations and called the session to order.

"All right," he said. "This is what we know." Using the photographs on the board and replaying the video taken by the police photographer at the scene, he took them through the murder of James Fitzpatrick, breaking off only once to glare at Sergeant McCullough who seemed to find amusement in the revelation that the victim's penis had been cut off and stuffed into his mouth. Whatever witticism McCullough had intended to utter died as a cough in his throat as he suddenly discovered something fascinating about the hands clasped across his ample paunch.

"Normally we would have some leads, however tenuous at this stage," Sheehan went on, "but our perp is clever. Preliminary knocking on neighbouring doors has produced zilch. CCTV in neighbouring streets has also given us nothing. The witness appeals in the media have also come up blank so far. Nobody saw anything, nobody heard anything, and, apart from the broken cufflink which may very well mean nothing, the crime scene was clean as a whistle." He paused for comment.

Tom Allen said, "We need to take the victim's background apart."

"Yes, that's all we have right now." He turned to Larkin., "Action book ready?"

Larkin nodded, preparing to enter into a simple duplicate book notes on what courses of action were to be taken, who would do them, and the expected time frame for each action. After the meeting, top copies of the agreed actions would be given to the relevant officers.

Sheehan briefly consulted some handwritten notes he had in front of him. "Sergeant Stewart has some technical skills, so she's going to spend time with Fitzpatrick's laptop. Allen, you and McNeill will go to the bank where he worked and see what you can find out about him there."

Geoff McNeill, prone to stuttering when in the spotlight, said quietly, "Aw-aw-all right, boss."

"We've lost Gerry Loftus to Manchester," Sheehan went on, "and Fred's on indefinite leave in England, as you know—"

"What's Loftus doing in Manchester?" McCullough interrupted.

"His wife's from there," Sheehan said. "She's been wanting to go back home for some time. Loftus applied to the Greater Manchester Police and sailed into a job."

"Good on him," Allen said. "Couldn't have been easy."

"Gerry's bright and ... ah ... someone wrote him a glowing reference."

Everybody smiled.

"Any word from Fred, sir?" interjected Simon Miller, slight, neat, generally unobtrusive but sharp, and Sheehan knew that.

"Yes, Simon. I had a brief phone call yesterday. He's well improved. He's stopped the drinking now that, with a little influence from a certain PSNI DCI," this with a modest smile, "he has special privileges to visit his son every day. Said the lad had been terrified, but he's a lot better now that he sees his dad regularly. Fred says the good thing is that once the boy's out, he'll never deal drugs again. I'm guessing that both of them will come through this."

There were a few murmurs and nods of approval. Sergeant Fred McCammon had been a popular colleague but recently he had been drinking himself almost to the point of incapacity, worrying about his son in a London prison. The leave of absence was granted as much on health as on compassionate grounds.

Sheehan went back to his notes. "So, we're two men down but we'll manage. In the absence of his usual partner, Sergeant McCoy will take Connors with him and dig into Fitzpatrick's past life. Find out where he went to school, what college education he had if any, and anything you can find out about his private life. You know better than I what to do. Look into his social connections, people he was close to, people he made enemies of, and everyone in between."

McCoy, stout, red-faced, nearing retirement, nodded acquiescence and glanced at Connors sitting nearby. He grinned and said, "It'll make a change to have a big gorilla with me. It'll make any witnesses think twice before messing with me."

Everybody chuckled. Declan Connors was at least six foot six and built like a rugby player. Now he was pretending to be annoyed. "Who's gonna protect you from me, Oliver, huh?"

More laughter.

"All right, all right," Sheehan cut the banter short. "That leaves Miller and McCullough." He pretended not to notice Miller's eyes flicker skywards and his head droop. "There's a neighbour, a Mr.Darcy, who seems to know a lot about our victim. Pump him and squeeze as much as you can out of him. And don't try to bully him, McCullough."

McCullough's injured, 'Who me?' expression fooled nobody.

"He's feisty. You'll get far more out by letting him know he's a useful source." Sheehan put his pen back in his pocket. "Oh, and try some of the other neighbours as well. The uniforms might have missed something."

Miller said, "We could call in some uniforms to stop traffic in the neighbourhood about the time of the murder. Some of the regulars on that route might have seen something that hasn't registered with them. A cop questioning them might trigger something."

"Yes, set that up, Simon. And I'd also like the two of you to visit all the jewellers' shops in the city with the cufflink. It looks expensive. Somebody might recognise it."

ELEVEN

WDS Denise Stewart stared at herself in a large mirror in the ladies' cloakroom on the ground floor of the Hilton Hotel. All she saw were worried eyes. She was not conscious of the shining blond hair, newly shampooed earlier that day and tastefully styled by her hairdresser, not quite shoulder length but thick, wavy and long enough to frame a face that could only be described as beautiful. Nor did she give any attention to the elegant black dress she was wearing, perhaps not too daring but definitely short of her knees. Neither was she seeing the thin, gold chain around her neck with its single white pearl. Her thoughts were entirely elsewhere. Staring into her own eyes she wondered, *What have I let myself in for? How did I allow myself to be roped into this?*

She gave herself a mental shake. *It's just two colleagues meeting to celebrate a great victory*, he had said. *It's a beautiful place,* he had enthused, *an idyllic location on the banks of the Lagan River with lovely river views which we can enjoy while we're dining.* "So, just a celebratory meal," she murmured. And then her eyes caught the dress, the hair, the necklace. "God," she muttered, "why did I have to dress like this? This is way over the top. He's bound to think …" She stared at herself again, remembering the huge, modern entrance hall, the ultramodern décor with large, pink pillars supporting the low circular ceiling that ran above the long,

65

glass-topped reception area, class oozing out of every cranny. *Aye, like I could have bowled in here in jeans and trainers.*

She blew air out of puffed cheeks. "Well, I'm here and he's waiting. Better get back to the table." She checked her lipstick, gave her hair a couple of unconscious pats, straightened her dress, and marched to the door, feeling for all the world that she was heading out ... to do what? To do battle? *God, I hope I don't have to spend the whole meal fighting him off.*

She had spent endless hours debating whether or not to accept Robert Turner's dinner invitation. She supposed that it was flattering in a way, a good-looking, wealthy young barrister paying her this kind of attention. No doubt most of the girls in the city would have fallen over themselves for such an invite. And, of course, friendship with so prominent a public figure couldn't do her career any harm. But the last thing she wanted at this point in her life was to dive helter-skelter into another relationship. The scars from the last one were not even remotely healed. But perhaps she was being super-sensitive. Was Robert necessarily looking for a relationship? With her? Maybe he was just hyper about closing down that den of bastards that had the nerve to call themselves policemen and wanted to celebrate like he said. He hadn't actually tried to hit on her and, in his dealings with her, he was politeness personified. *Well, we'll see.* Thank God she'd had the wit to insist on celebrating on her afternoon off. That took care of any awkwardness about coffee afterwards in her flat or any other ideas that might be prompted by darkness, by streetlights, by raindrops on the windscreen window. No thanks. *I've had more than my share of that.*

She reached the Sonoma Restaurant with its floor-to-ceiling windows and as soon as he saw her, Turner was on his feet and pulling back her chair. She passed a table where two male diners made no secret of the fact that they found her an object of serious interest and she sat down with a hesitant smile. She began immediately to fiddle with her napkin as Turner sat opposite her and said, "May I say how beautiful you look." His tone was calm, almost matter-of-fact, simply stating a truth. "That pearl is just perfect against the black background of your dress."

Denise smiled briefly, "Thank you. It's the only one I've got." *God, where did that come from? Are you trying to win the idiot of the year award?*

"I'm sure in time you'll have many more," he said smoothly, and pointing towards the windows, he added, "Aren't the views magnificent?"

She looked through the large windows that ran along the restaurant. The views were indeed wonderful. The trees outside were still green, but the autumnal browns and reds and yellows were beginning to make their appearance, and the October sun endowed them with a glowing luminescence that held the eye in thrall. Glorious, too, were the distant hills, sweeping across the horizon in a never-ending panorama, an infinite harmony of greens, steeped in the splendour of the October sunlight. Stewart was stunned.

"Spectacular," she breathed, lost for a moment in admiration. "Truly marvellous." Drawing her eyes, almost reluctantly, away from the windows, she glanced briefly at the other tables. The restaurant wasn't crowded, but many of the tables were occupied, some by couples, one or two with young families. A small girl seated with her father and mother to her left subjected her to a disarming, if frank, stare. She smiled briefly at the child before turning to Turner to say, "I've never been here before."

"Well, then, you're in for a treat," Turner replied, leaning back slightly as a waiter appeared and handed them menus. Turner ordered a bottle of wine and said as he opened his menu, "I'm not sure where your tastes lie but the Samona Restaurant prides itself on classic Irish and British cuisine, from rump of Irish lamb to pan-fried sea bass."

"You must come here a lot."

He laughed. "No, I'm just quoting from the brochure on the table that I was reading while you were in the ladies' room."

Denise couldn't help but grin back at him. *Maybe this guy's half-human after all.* She lowered her eyes, slightly discomforted by the hold his eyes were having on her. "I must say the menu looks interesting ..." A vaguely pat response and not at all in keeping with the natural control she usually exercised. It was seldom that she was made to feel inadequate. Why was she letting this guy get to her?

Choices made, the waiter, who had just arrived with the wine, took their order. Turner filled their wine glasses. He held his aloft towards Denise who instinctively raised her glass to touch his. He was holding his drink in his left hand, leaving his other hand free to take hold of the hand Denise had left resting on the table. Immediately her diffidence disappeared.

"So we're holding hands now?" she said frostily.

He smiled easily and, still clasping her hand, he raised it a few inches and said, "Don't be silly, Denise. This is what is known as a victory hand clasp." He touched her glass again and raising their hands a little higher, he said, "To a great victory, and may there be many more of them."

Denise raised her glass again and replied, "To victory." Smiling, she retrieved her hand and added, "Something I'm sure you have become very accustomed to."

He shrugged. "I've had my share, but you're just on the threshold of a great career. More victories like the exposure and conviction of rotten apples like Kerley will propel you up the ranks." He raised his glass again. "And I will help you all I can. You deserve that."

"That's kind of you. I appreciate that," she replied.

Their food arrived, and they ate quietly for some minutes. Turner then began to regale her with stories of some of his past prosecutions and, in that mode, she found him interesting. The meal passed quickly, and by the time their coffee had arrived, she was telling him that she had now been drafted into a team with whom she would be working her first homicide.

"That sounds like a fascinating case," he said, showing considerable interest. "I wouldn't mind prosecuting that one. Must put out a few feelers."

"Well, I'm sure you won't have too much difficulty swinging it your way," Denise said with a somewhat knowing smile.

He raised an eyebrow, pretending ignorance. "What do you mean?"

"I've heard it said that you and the Deputy Director of Public Prosecutions are great golfing buddies. That's bound to be useful."

He laughed. "With your observational skills and quick wits, you'll probably have the murderer identified in no time."

Denise uttered a self-deprecating chuckle. "Some chance. At this point, I have absolutely no idea what I'm doing." Then she continued, with a deal of unconscious enthusiasm in her voice, "But thank God for Chief Inspector Sheehan. He's brilliant and easy to work with. All I have to do is follow his lead."

Turner said encouragingly, "You underestimate yourself, Denise. Once you get into the case and start finding clues, you'll surprise them all." He raised his arm to signal the waiter for the bill. "Mind if I drop into the Incident Room occasionally to see how things are going?"

"I can't see that as being a problem. The chief inspector has to keep you, well, the Public Prosecutions Service, informed about the investigation, does he not?"

"Oh, yes. We'll receive a full file when the investigation is complete so that we can decide whether the case is strong enough for prosecution, what the correct charges should be and," he grinned again, "who is responsible for prosecuting the case in court."

She smiled. "Well, as they say on TV, it's a slam dunk then."

The waiter arrived with the bill and after paying him, Turner said, "That was a nice celebration, Denise. I must say I enjoyed your company. We must do this again sometime."

Denise clenched inwardly. "Thank you very much for inviting me, Robert. It was a lovely meal. If there are any more great victories, I would be delighted to celebrate them with you."

"We have to wait for victories?"

Denise hesitated. "Robert, I hope I am not being presumptuous when I say this but for personal reasons I am not ready to start any kind of relationship just now."

Turner's smile faded, but he rallied quickly. "Good heavens! Where did that come from? I'm sorry if I gave you the wrong impression, although," he fed her a disarming grin, "I can see how you might have misunderstood my intentions." He gestured vaguely at the table, at the room. "This is purely a professional courtesy, a 'thank you' for your help in the courtroom. And I know how the boys in blue like to close ranks. That can sometimes lead to a feeling of isolation. I just want you to know that you still have friends."

"Sorry, Robert. I'm just a bit ... Look, let's forget I said that. Thanks again for the meal. I enjoyed it very much." She stood up, reaching for her handbag. "And now I'm going to go shopping. No doubt we'll meet again soon. I'll just get my coat."

Turner stood up as well. "Can I give you a lift into town?"

"No thanks. We're quite close to the city centre here. The walk'll do me good." She reached forward awkwardly and shook his hand. "'Bye! Thanks again."

He nodded a wordless response and his eyes followed her as she crossed the restaurant and headed for the ladies' cloakroom.

TWELVE

As Tom Allen prepared to leave his apartment on University Road, he stopped to glance back over it, just to be sure. *Aye, just to be sure that it doesn't look like a student's flat after a Hallowe'en party, like* my *student flat after a Hallowe'en party. God, we really were pigs then.* Just to be sure. Just to be sure that it's presentable enough not to let him down should someone happen to visit with him. His eyes quickly ranged the one-roomed studio. It was large enough for him, bright, clean, and yes, tidy. Neat little kitchen, decent sized bed, and not too far from the city centre. Nice place to bring a girl home to, if there was a girl to bring home. There had been one or two brief dalliances since Amy, but nothing serious enough to warrant an invitation back to the flat. His expression darkened. *Dammit, Amy. Why did you have to ...? Bloody hell, a restraining order?* It still stung. All those unanswered phone calls. He didn't get it. All he had wanted to do was talk to her. I mean, they were so deeply in love one minute, talking for hours about nothing, about everything, engaged to be married, and the next ... the engagement ring in a registered envelope and days, weeks, months of solitary pain.

All right, all right. He'd been over this and over this and over this. Time to close the book. *Best way to forget a girl is get another one, right?* He uttered a dry chuckle as he closed the door behind him. *Aye! I'll just take my pick of all the ones that are throwing themselves at me.*

71

He headed down the stairs to the street door, unaware that the subtle sadness in his mien, his obvious lack of interest in pursuing any kind of relationship with girls he met, were the real reason for his solitary existence. There were many who had been drawn to his blond good looks, his easy charm, but none could penetrate the invisible barrier that Tom himself didn't know was there. And so had come a pattern that was beginning to baffle him - a drink, a laugh and a goodbye.

He stepped into his car, parked handily at the kerb outside the entrance door. One good thing about the apartment was the street parking that was part of the deal. He looked at his watch. Just time to pick Geoff up at the police station in Dundela Avenue and make the 9:30 am appointment with the bank manager in Donegal Square.

As he negotiated his way through Shaftesbury Square, his mind drifted to the new sergeant. *Very good looking but, God, is she wound tight. Wonder what her problem is?* He hummed along with the radio, letting his thoughts wander. They didn't wander far. Maybe she had a tough time in Lisburn? Largely male force, half of them crooks, kowtowing to a toe rag like Kerley. Just a woman constable. She'd have needed chain-mail to get through a day there. *No wonder she's built a wall around herself. And yet, she had seemed anxious to repair the damage to my nose after she almost bit it off, and she was friendly enough when she was telling me about the court case. Aye, friendly enough but....But what?* Distant, sort of. Untouchable, maybe. She didn't even seem pleased about that huge bunch of flowers. Something in him lightened at the thought. His mind drifted to the card that had come with the flowers. From Prosecutor Turner. *Big league. Bloody lady-killer. Wonder did she accept that invite to dinner?* Whatever had lightened in him, darkened again. *Shit! He'll eat her alive.*

As he approached the station he saw McNeill waving at him from the footpath in front of the gate. No need to park then. He slowed long enough for Geoff to jump in and headed for the city centre.

They parked on a double yellow line outside the bank's imposing façade - Greek colonnade, arches, patronising, calculated to make most clients feel inferior. Geoff got a police-on-duty card from the boot and threw it on the dashboard.

As they entered the building, Allen sucked in a deep breath. He was sensing the intimidating power of the place, but he resisted the urge to tread quietly as Geoff was doing. Almost marching, he strode to the reception desk, heels clacking on the marble floor. The dark-haired girl at the counter was pleasant and, after asking them what they wanted, she phoned someone, keeping her head down and speaking almost inaudibly. There was a brief discussion during which Allen surmised that the manager was being obstructive. Eventually the receptionist looked up and said, "If you would just sit over there in the waiting area." She pointed at some easy chairs and a magazine table in a corner of the lobby. "The manager will try to be with you in about ten minutes."

It was nearer twenty-five minutes by the time the girl came over to them and invited them to follow her. Just as well. Allen was at the end of his patience. McNeill already had to stop him twice from barging back over to the girl and demanding to be brought to the manager's office immediately. She led them through a door and up a small flight of stairs. Following her, Allen was tight-lipped and unusually silent. Normally he'd be flirting with the girl by now but their appointment had been for nine-thirty and it was now just after ten o'clock. The receptionist knocked diffidently at a door on the second-floor corridor and, hearing a muffled, "Come," she stood back and ushered the two policemen into the office.

The room they entered was airy, devoid of clutter. There was a large oak desk, bare of papers or files except for a large leather-bound blotter and an expensive pen lying beside it. There was also a mahogany nameplate at the desk's front edge displaying in gold letters the name, 'M.J Henley, Mgr'. In front of the desk were two chairs.

Mr. Henley had been standing beside the large window staring down into Donegal Street but when the visitors entered, he strode immediately behind his desk, sat down, and gestured to the two policemen to do likewise. Elegant in a charcoal grey suit, white shirt, red silk tie, Mr. Henley was small, neat and economical in his movements. Even his head wasted no time getting from where it was to where it needed to be. The result was a strangely jerky movement as he looked from one policeman to the other. Typical of some arrogant small men, he tilted his head back so that he could look down his nose at the visitors, not easy considering Allen's six-two frame.

Even as he sat, Henley was already speaking. "How can I help you?"

"We're pursuing some enquiries about Mr. Fitzpatrick," Allen said curtly, not in any way pacified by the manager's attitude.

Mr. Henley joined his hands on the desk, fingers spliced. "Ah yes. Sad business." He waited for the policemen to speak further.

"We would need to talk to some of Mr. Fitzpatrick's colleagues," Allen said, "members of staff he worked closely with, and take a look at some of the files he was working on."

The manager stared at them for a moment, eyebrows down. "Don't you need a court order for that?"

"No." Allen was getting miffed. *This guy wants laconic, I'll give him laconic.* He let the word hang in the air, forcing the banker to speak.

Henley's eventual response wasn't exactly profuse. "Explain."

Allen's lips tightened. He glanced at his partner with an imperceptible nod. The manager's head darted towards McNeill.

Geoff said, "It's t-t-true that under the Data Protection Act we are not allowed to see personal information held on paper which is not organised or indexed or st-structured in any way, but we are entitled to seek access to collections of f-f-files or papers or computer organised data organised in a way that makes it easy to find information about a p-p-particular individual. This would include files which are indexed or arranged by reference to the name of the person concerned."

The manager's lips tightened. His head jerked back to Allen again.

Allen said, "We'll need a room where we can talk to members of staff and spend some time with these files."

The manager's head jerked downwards. He seemed to be seeking inspiration from his blotter. Eventually his head moved upwards again with a brief twitch. "See Jenny."

"Jenny?" Allen said.

"Receptionist. She'll sort you out."

He stood quickly, one sudden movement, and offered the policemen his hand. His handshake with McNeill was perfunctory, but Allen deliberately held the man's hand in a momentary clamp, experiencing a perverse satisfaction from seeing him struggling to conceal a wince. "Thank you for your help, sir," he said. "We'll go and see Jenny."

On the way down to the reception area, Allen said, "Bloody hell! Squeezing words out of that guy was like pulling hen's teeth."

McNeill chuckled. "Hardly surprising. He moves like a b-b-bloody hen. Did you see the way his h-head kept bobbin' about?"

"I'd hate to work for that guy. I wouldn't be able to resist wringing his scrawny neck."

"That's how they k-kill hens, isn't it?"

"For crying out loud, Geoff, will you quit with the bloody chickens." They had reached the first floor again. "Right, there's Jenny. Let's get this show on the road."

Jenny was efficiency personified. She soon found them an empty office and provided them with the internal extension numbers of staff members that seemed to fit their requirements. Allen, by now mollified and aware of Jenny's prettiness, gave her a wide thank-you smile and said, "You'll throw those files into us when you can?"

Jenny smiled back at him, eyes sparkling. "Certainly Detective, but it'll take a little time to put them together."

"No rush, Jenny. We have to interview the staff members first anyway."

She gave him a coy nod and left the office. Allen showed no haste in taking his eyes off her retreating back, the tightness of her uniform skirt, the little flat ballet shoes.

McNeill gave him a look. "You never quit, do you?"

"Quit what?"

"Never m-m-mind. Let's get one of these interviews started. Who's first?"

THIRTEEN

T he morning dragged for the two policemen. The staff they interviewed tried to be helpful, some slightly nervous, others seemingly reluctant to speak ill of the dead. A picture of sorts did begin to emerge, however. Fitzpatrick was one of the bank's bright lights, a man whose ambition was obvious to all and who seemed to have the talent to further that ambition. There were some staff who, despite their reserve, were unable to avoid giving the policemen the unmistakeable impression that they had resented Fitzpatrick's brashness, his greed for promotion. None, on the other hand, gave the impression that the man had been particularly well liked.

One older colleague did say, "Nothing wrong with a bit of ambition but it shouldn't be hanging out there naked for the whole world to see."

"Oh?" Allen said, "So he wasn't particularly popular, then?"

"I'm not saying that. I hardly knew the fellow. It was just well known that he was very ambitious, and nothing and nobody was going to get in his way."

"Did his ambitions get in the way of the ambitions of other colleagues?"

The man sat back, almost raising his hands to defend himself from this line of questioning. "I don't know anything about that. You'd need to ask the manager."

"All right. Do you happen to know if he was particularly friendly with any other member of staff?"

The man gave the question a moment's thought. "He wasn't the type to have friends as such but I do believe that he lunched occasionally with a younger teller in his department. I think his name is Magill, maybe Owen or Oliver or something like that."

While Geoff noted the name, Allen dismissed the man. "Thank you, sir. That will be all. You've been very helpful."

When the man had left, Allen searched the list of extensions Jenny had given him, "I'll check if the guy's name's on here." He turned a page. "Here he is, Oliver Magill. All right, Geoff. Give his extension a ring and get him in here. This has been bloody frustrating. Maybe he'll be a bit more forthcoming than the lot we've had in so far."

Oliver Magill took the seat near the two detectives. Tall, mid-twenties, dressed in a dark suit, he seemed the sort of man who would normally be capable and confident. Right now he looked distinctly uneasy. The detectives read nothing into that. Murder enquiries usually put even the totally innocent on the defensive.

"Thank you for agreeing to talk to us, Mr. Magill," Allen said easily. Watching closely to gauge the man's reaction, he added casually, "I understand that you were friendly with Mr. Fitzpatrick?"

Magill's eyes watched as McNeill opened his notebook and took the top off his pen. "I ... I'm not sure that we could be described as friends, but I did have lunch with him a few times."

Allen smiled. "That's what friends do, isn't it?"

"I suppose." He searched for something to add but seemed unable to find anything. Again his eyes darted to McNeill's notebook.

This guy's pretty nervous, Allen was thinking. *It's different from the others. What's he so worried about?* "So how did you end up lunching with him? He was a lot senior to you, I take it?"

"Yes. I suppose I was useful to him in the department. We'd occasionally have lunch and talk things over."

"Your job is what exactly, Mr. Magill?"

"I'm a senior teller."

"And Mr. Fitzpatrick was in charge of loans and acquisitions?"

"Y ... yes."

"No disrespect meant, Mr. Magill, but how would your work overlap with that of an Acquisitions Manager?"

Magill seemed uncertain as to how he should answer the question. Then he said, "Often, James, Mr. Fitzpatrick, would ask me to go through client accounts, search for anomalies ..."

Again that uneasiness that Allen couldn't quite understand. It resembled something close to guilt. What exactly was this man hiding? *Time for the heavy hand. If this guy knows anything, he's far too nervous to conceal it.* Sitting up and adopting an expression of extreme seriousness, he said, "Mr. Magill, I'm sure you are aware that this is a murder enquiry. If we discover later that you have been withholding information that might have been useful to us ... well, you know there will be consequences."

The young teller paled, swallowed and said, "I don't know anything about the murder."

"Perhaps not. But you know something about the victim. Whatever you know, you have to tell us now. And don't worry. Your input will be kept confidential."

Magill licked his lips, his mind casting about for somewhere to start. Allen waited patiently, but his expression was stern. "Well, initially I simply had lunch with James."

"Initially?"

"Yes. It was a bit strange. I'd be heading out of the bank for lunch, and James would appear behind me and invite me to join him. He always paid. Wouldn't let me put my hand in my pocket."

"Did that not strike you as odd?"

"It did, but I was, I suppose, flattered. I mean, he was a big shot and I was just, well, a teller."

"I presume there had to come some kind of payoff?"

The man nodded, his lips tightening. "Yes. One afternoon he asked me to take any calls that might come in for him. He said he was taking the afternoon off, but I was supposed to tell the caller that Mr. Fitzpatrick was in conference and that I'd arrange for him to return the call at the earliest opportunity. Then I was supposed to call James on his mobile and let him know that there had been a call."

"Wouldn't he get plenty of calls if he was a ... a big shot?"

"Ah, yes. I was to handle any ordinary business calls myself. I was supposed to report any calls that seemed strange or out of the ordinary."

"Were there any such calls?"

"No ..." Magill was hesitant again. "Although I covered for him several times like this there were no out-of-the-ordinary calls. I think I was there just in case, but he wasn't really expecting to ..."

Allen said bluntly, "What was going on? Were you supposed to fob off the wife or something?"

"Well, no, not the wife."

"So what was it, then?"

Magill said in a rush, "He was having an affair with the wife of an ex-loyalist paramilitary. The man's supposed to be legitimate now but there are rumours. He's still very dangerous. James wanted to be sure he had an alibi if this guy ever came enquiring after him. I warned him that the guy has a seriously bad reputation."

"Who are we talking about?"

"Ronnie Weir."

Both policemen sat back in their chairs, shocked. Allen almost squawked, "The Bat?"

Ronnie 'The Bat' Weir earned his cognomen by virtue of an aluminium baseball bat he had carried everywhere with him during his paramilitary days. He used it for punishment beatings, and reports of his violence were legendary. No victim's knees, ankles, elbows, wrists or hands escaped horrific abuse when 'The Bat' meted out his punishment. For those victims whose treachery was viewed as particularly serious, special treatment was reserved for the head, ensuring a lifetime of mental incapacity if, indeed, the victim survived.

"Yes," Magill said. "When I found out who James was worried about I told him he was crazy, but he laughed me off. I think he liked living on the edge."

Both policemen stared at the teller, tension evident now in their bearing. Here was motive with a capital M. Allen was about to dismiss the teller but the man seemed to have something else to say. What could he possibly have to add after that bombshell?

"Was there something else, Mr. Magill?"

"You might want to study some of the accounts he was working on."

Allen blinked. Accounts? What could they possibly find there? "We'll be doing that. What should we be looking for?"

"I've been doing a lot of thinking about this after I heard about James ..." He stared at the floor, lost briefly in memories. Then he said, "James was pretty ruthless with some of his clients. He would search client contracts for clauses that would allow him to call in huge loans without giving the clients any leeway. More than one major business has hit the wall as a result of James's—"

"Why would he want to do that?" Allen cut in, looking mystified. "Was it just sheer bloodymindedness?"

"Not really. James was on a one per cent bonus for every so-called 'questionable' loan he was able to call in. The last one he told me about was a three million loan. That left a couple of very angry partners losing everything."

McNeill had been doing the mathematics. "Thirty grand for one transaction," he breathed.

Magill nodded, almost comfortable now that he was able to get all of this off his chest. "Yes, and he was combing the files for others. I was thinking that he might have made a few enemies that way."

This guy's a mine of information, Allen was thinking. Anxious to get a look at the files, he handed the teller his card. "Thank you, Mr. Magill. This is all very helpful. If you think of anything else, please give me a call, day or night. We'll probably want to talk to you again, anyway, so please, don't leave town." He uttered the old cliché with a disarming grin, but Magill wasn't comforted. Looking shaken, he left the office.

Allen turned to McNeill. "Bloody hell! 'The Bat' Weir's missus? Was he insane? And driving wealthy clients to bankruptcy? This guy was a dead man walkin'."

"The chief needs to know about this stuff right away," McNeill said, feeling the weight of what they had just learned. "And we'll have to subpoena those files. They'll need more s-s-study than we can give them."

FOURTEEN

Sergeant Stewart headed for the Serious Crimes Room. The corridor she was walking down was empty but she gave that no thought. She was carrying James Fitzpatrick's laptop and, though she had spent a great deal of the previous evening trying to pry open its secrets, she had met with little success. She was planning how best to present her findings to the team when two men exited from a door some twenty feet in front of her. One was smallish, thin, sallow, and dark-haired. The other was more robust, red-faced and balding. Stewart recognised them immediately, two of her erstwhile colleagues from the Lisburn station.

"Well, well, if it isn't the tout herself," the red-faced man said, an ugly sneer crossing his face.

Stewart's lips tightened, the old feelings of vulnerability and helplessness that she had lived with in Lisburn suddenly threatening to overwhelm her again. Allowing none of this to show, she kept walking, attempting to pass the two men. The sallow one, his sneer as ugly as his companion's, stepped sideways to bar her path.

"No time for your old pals, Denise?" he said. "Can't even pass the time of day?"

Stewart, forced to stop, stared hard at him. "Move aside, Chambers."

"Or what?" he smirked. "You'll report us?"

The larger man came closer, leering into Stewart's face. "Of course she will. The slag's good at that." Then, his face darkening and his voice rasping with menace, he said, "Are you not ashamed of yourself for putting a first-class cop in prison?" He moved closer so that he was looking down at her. "How can you live with yourself?"

Stewart struggled to maintain her ground. "First-class?" she spat. "He was bent, so bent that he was … kyphotic." She continued to glare. "And you two thugs are no better. Now get out of my way, Wilson, and let me pass."

Chambers moved closer but stepped back a pace when he was forced to raise his head so that he could look directly at her. "What's that you said?" He looked at his companion. "What did the lying bitch just say?"

Wilson continued to press forward, his face now filled with anger. Stewart was forced to give ground but she continued to glare defiantly at the two men. At that point a door at the end of the corridor opened and Tom Allen came in carrying a bunch of files under his arm. He sensed rather than understood the threat and walked quickly to the trio.

"Everything okay, Sergeant?" he said to Stewart.

Wilson's face seemed to become even redder. "Move along, son," he said. "We're just having a quiet conversation here."

Allen was not stupid. He quickly figured that these two were probably old colleagues of the sergeant and, judging from their demeanour, were bullies still filled with resentment about the past. He stared at the trio for a moment and then raised his head slightly, sniffing. "Sergeant," he said to Stewart, "do you smell anything?" Stewart just stared at him. Allen continued to sniff. "Something nasty … like rotten eggs." He moved his head close to the two men, still sniffing. "God, I think it's these two …"

Chambers said, "Watch it, son. Both of us have sergeant's stripes. You want to find yourself up for insubordination?"

Allen's play-acting ended. Scowling now, he said, "You two get the fuck outa here right this minute, or you'll find yourselves with a lot more than your sergeant's stripes stuck up your arses." He flicked a finger towards the end of the corridor. "Now, get lost."

Wilson tried to brazen it out. "You're asking for trouble, son."

"No," Allen cut in. "You are. Two bent bastards like you are not going to draw attention to themselves by reporting anybody." He placed himself between Stewart and the visitors, hissing, "You have five seconds."

Despite his youth, Tom Allen's build and obvious strength were intimidating. Chambers backed away but his companion tried to bluster, "We'll get you, you wee prick."

"No," Allen said, poking the guy forcibly in the chest with a forefinger the size of a carrot. "If I decide to come after you, you'll rue the day you were ever born. Now get the hell out of this building."

Both men now backed away, Wilson shouting, "This isn't over."

Allen said, "It had better be. Don't make me come looking for you."

The men shuffled down the corridor with as much dignity as they could muster while Allen turned to Stewart. "Are you okay?" he asked solicitously.

Stewart's expression had not changed during the entire exchange but now she said, her eyes firing sparks at the young detective, "Why did you interfere? I could have handled those two by myself. Did you think I was some sort of damsel in distress or what?"

She turned on her heel, stalking angrily away. Allen stared after her, his mouth almost agape, puzzled at first, then feeling annoyance surge through him. Three quick strides and he was standing in front of the sergeant, his eyes as angry as her own. "Listen you to me, Sergeant …" He spat out the last word as if it were something soiling his mouth. What followed was delivered with little less force. "I know something of your history at Lisburn, and I understand why you feel the need to be so damned self-sufficient." He bent closer. "But you need to understand one thing about where you are now …"

Stewart saw the anger in his eyes and, surprised by it, stepped back a pace, fearing suddenly that her experiences in Lisburn were about to be repeated. But no. As she stared into Allen's eyes, she could see that this anger was different. This anger was … what? Was she sensing an element of hurt? *No, that doesn't make sense.*

She heard him continue, the words spilling from his mouth. "You are with a team now. Team? Do you understand that word? We all have each other's backs here. It wouldn't have mattered if those two greaseballs were threatening any member of the team, the chief himself, or even McCullough, I would have done exactly the same thing." He continued to glare, breathing heavily for reasons he couldn't understand. "Lady, you have one serious chip on your shoulder and if you want to fit in here, you'd better get rid of it, and fast."

He turned away immediately, stalking towards the Incident Room. Stewart didn't move after him. She had been shaken, badly shaken. She was reluctant to admit to herself that the menacing behaviour of the two Lisburn policemen had frightened her, and she was even more reluctant to acknowledge the relief she had felt when Tom Allen had intervened. Nor could she understand why she had been so ungracious to him unless, perhaps, she felt that somehow she had lost face because he deemed that she had needed help. Well, dammit, she had served two years in Lisburn with bullying, sexist coppers all around her and survived. She could easily have survived this latest episode without Tom Allen's interference. Tightening her grip on the laptop, she followed Allen into the Serious Crimes Room.

FIFTEEN

A s she entered the Serious Crimes Room, Stewart flicked a glance at Allen's desk. He was already seated, ignoring everyone, his glare burning holes in an inoffensive file folder. When she sat down at her own desk, she also noticed Robert Turner chatting with the chief inspector. He caught her glance and gave her a small wave of acknowledgement. *God! Just what I need right now*, she thought, as she gave him a half-smile in return. However, he did not make any attempt to move towards her.

The room was pretty full and, as far as she could see, the whole investigation team was there. Sheehan said something to Turner who nodded in response and found himself a chair near the whiteboard towards which Sheehan was striding.

"All right, team," Sheehan said, "we've a lot to get through, so let's get started. Sergeant McCullough, how did you and Miller get on with Mr. Darcy?" Sheehan's voice was level, neutral. He had little time for McCullough, a lazy cop, soured by outdated and pointless prejudices, but it was Sheehan's practice to give everybody respect where possible, one of the traits that made his team so loyal to him.

McCullough, attempting to look important, thumbed his notebook while clearing his throat. "The truth is, Chief, he had plenty to say but little of any import." He looked up to see how the team received that rather neat little phrase. He had been working on it for quite a while. No one seemed to notice, so he harrumphed and went on. "One thing he did say was that a day or two before the murder he had noticed a car reversing into Fitzpatrick's driveway. He just assumed it was turning to get back out of the cul-de-sac, so he didn't pay it much attention."

"Any kind of a description?" Allen asked, still glaring, thus causing the hapless sergeant some mystification. He gave Allen a puzzled glance before returning to his notes.

"Yes, a vague one. He said he thought it was a large, expensive car, dark-coloured, but he couldn't remember if it was black, dark grey, or navy blue."

"Well, it's worth taking a note of," Sheehan said. "If we unearth a suspect with a dark, expensive car, it might help to narrow things down a bit. Anything else, Sergeant?"

"Well, he says he remembered hearing the garage opening earlier in the evening but he just assumed it was Fitzpatrick coming home. He didn't bother to look out but was pretty positive that it was about ten fifteen because he was watching the UTV News, and it was about halfway through. Doesn't help much but it seems to conform to Doc Campbell's time of death."

Sheehan was already nodding. "Any of the neighbours notice anything?"

"Not really. We knocked on a few of the doors either side of the house on both sides of the street but nobody saw anything. Our perp was obviously very careful and anyway, you know what it's like when people are locked in for the night. Somebody would've had to have been out with the bins or something, but we couldn't find anyone who was outside at that time."

"Anything from the traffic stops?"

Miller said, "It was quiet that time of the night, sir. We did stop one or two cars heading home a bit late, but they hadn't been out on Tuesday evening so they were unable to offer any help."

Sheehan sighed. "It was worth a try. Any luck with the cufflink?"

McCullough said, "No. We hit all the major jewellers in town over the last two days, but so far we have not met one who recognises the cufflink or can even tell us who might have manufactured it. We have a few more to try, and we'll get on to that right away."

"All right, Sergeant, thank you." He turned to Sergeant McCoy. "Right, Oliver. Can yourself and Connors shed any light on the life and times of our victim?"

McCoy, comfortable now that he was near retirement and lacking all ambition, sat back, arms folded, his ruddy countenance wreathed in a complacent grin. "Ach, Chief, I'll let young Connors report back on this. To tell you the truth, he did most of the work."

Sheehan couldn't help grinning back, but he said, "You're not retired yet, Sergeant."

McCoy leaned forward a little and said, perhaps a little hastily, but still grinning, "Oh, I did help, Chief. Just thought I'd give the lad a wee chance to show his mettle."

"What have you got for us, Connors?"

"Nothing remarkable, Chief. Fitzpatrick went to Methody, the Methodist College here in Belfast. Seems he was popular enough there, played rugby for the college with some distinction and got good grades in his A levels. Went on to Queens …" He checked his notes. "He did a degree in accountancy from 2001 to 2004. Graduated with 2.1 honours and spent a couple of years as an intern with Ernst and Young. Apparently he lost interest in that particular career route. I had a sense of something a wee bit fishy, but nobody was talking. One young woman there told us that she had heard rumours, which she couldn't confirm, that there might have been a sexual harassment episode which was hushed up, but Fitzpatrick was asked to resign. He applied to the Ulster Bank and has been working there ever since."

"Social life?" Sheehan asked.

"Yeah. Seems to have gone quiet. He used to play squash twice a week with some friends from the bank, but that stopped a couple of years ago, shortly after he got married, I suppose. If he has any social contacts, other than what he and the wife share together, we haven't been able to find out anything about them."

McNeill grinned knowingly at Allen but refrained from comment. Allen gave him a slight, poker-faced nod.

"Enemies?" Sheehan asked.

"The few people we talked to seemed generally agreed that Fitzpatrick was not particularly well liked. Too arrogant, too self-centred, but they couldn't think of anyone who might want to harm him. And there didn't seem to be any couples socialising with them. He and the wife generally went out alone to eat, to the theatre or whatever."

"Okay." Sheehan turned to Stewart who was working with a PowerPoint link to her computer. "Anything on the laptop, Stewart?"

"Not a lot, Chief. There were a few locked files, but he wasn't very original with passwords, various combinations of his own and his wife's dates of birth, probably because they are easy to remember." She risked a quick glance at Allen. His eyes were focused on her but, although his expression was serious, the anger seemed gone. She quickly reviewed her notes and went on, "One or two of the files were encrypted and it took a while to break into them. I had to—"

Sheehan held up his hand. "We accept your skills, Sergeant, but you'll only confuse us if you go into the technical details. Just tell us what you found."

"Oh, all right. A few of these files were a bit bland, rather surprised me that they were encrypted. They were mostly about loans, repayment periods and agreement details. I couldn't really see anything significant in them. But a couple of files did puzzle me. One was this old photograph." She touched a couple of keys on the laptop and a photograph appeared on the whiteboard. It showed three male students standing at the front gate of Queen's University, two with their arm around each other's shoulder, one to the side, arms folded, slightly aloof. "I think the guy standing to the side is our victim. The strange thing is that this is the only photograph of his student days. I was wondering what was so significant about this photograph that he had to keep it."

She turned back to her laptop. "The other anomaly is a newspaper clipping I found ..." The photograph disappeared from the whiteboard while she talked, fiddling with her computer. "It's just a death notice, dated about twelve years ago about a young girl who committed suicide. There are no notes with it or any kind of commentary. It's a bit odd. I mean, who keeps a newspaper clipping in their files for twelve years? I'll put it up on the board." She fiddled with some keys on the computer and an image appeared on a blank part of the whiteboard.

The funeral took place today of Ms. Lynda Bell, 22, late of Wellbrook Avenue, Dungannon. Ms. Bell had been ill for some time. The coroner's report states that she took her own life while suffering from clinical depression. Her death is deeply regretted by her sorrowing parents and extended family. The family asks for privacy at this time and requests that small donations be offered to charity in lieu of flowers and wreaths.

The team stared at the board, reading the notice, mystification on their faces.

Sheehan was the first to speak. "Did you highlight this simply because it seemed to be an anomaly in the computer files, or do you have any thoughts on it in connection with our murder?"

"Both, sir." Her eyes were drawn to Turner who had seemed to move forward in his seat. She noted that his eyes were fixed on the whiteboard. "Well, I'm not really sure that I can say it has any connection with the murder, but I have been thinking about it. All I have really is conjecture. I haven't had time to follow this up or find out any more about it."

"Okay! Give us your thoughts, Sergeant."

"I'm thinking that I need to find out who this girl is, what might have been the source of her depression, and why she committed suicide. I believe the answers to those questions could be very significant, but only if there is, in fact, a connection to our victim." She turned off the PowerPoint. "Our victim kept this small notice in a locked file on his computer for twelve years. It is hard to avoid the conclusion that he at least knew the girl. More than that, that she probably had meaning for him in some way. I'd like to know what and why. What if he not only knew her but had some involvement in her depression or even her suicide? That might lead us to someone seeking revenge ..." Her voice petered out as she realised her entire commentary was grossly speculative.

Sheehan raised a finger in the air. "No ... no ... Don't feel that you have to be apologetic for this contribution. We all say what we think here no matter how off-the-wall we might think it is. Actually I am drawn to your line of thinking. It might not be quite as speculative as you seem to think."

Turner turned away from the board to address the group. Waving an arm in Stewart's direction, he said, "I have to commend Sergeant Stewart on her perspicacity." McCullough raised one eyebrow and looked around for someone to explain. No one did. "I believe she may, indeed, have come across something significant here ..." He smiled at Stewart and turned back to the team again. "Sergeant Stewart definitely has to pursue this."

Stewart kept her eyes fixed on her keyboard, determined not to blush. She was afraid that this effusive praise from the crown prosecutor was more likely to earn her acrimony than admiration and she had just about enough of that during her time at Lisburn. Because she had her eyes down, she didn't notice the look of disdain Allen threw in Turner's direction.

"I think we need to find out who they are, and why Fitzpatrick kept that photograph," Sheehan said. "Can you follow up on that, Stewart?"

She nodded. "I'll see what I can find."

Sheehan turned to Allen and McNeill. "Right, you two. You intimated that you were going to blow the socks off us at the debrief. So, what's the big bombshell?"

"Well, those are great leads that Sergeant Stewart has found," Allen said, "but McNeill and myself learnt a few startling facts that might cast a different light on things." Now it was his turn to hold the room's attention. "We have uncovered two very serious lines of enquiry. One, Fitzpatrick was targeting bank clients with large loans who were having difficulty keeping up their payments." He waved a hand roughly in the direction of the whiteboard. "That would explain the files that Sergeant Stewart found on the laptop. He was calling these loans in, mercilessly bankrupting the clients in the process in order to pick up a one per cent bonus each time he did so. He actually boasted about this to a bank colleague. The last bonus he earned was thirty thousand quid, meaning that this client lost three million. And this client, actually two clients, brothers, were not the only ones to suffer like that at Fitzpatrick's hands."

"You're saying that a disgruntled client, having lost everything, decided to take it out of Fitzpatrick's hide?" Miller asked.

"It's feasible," Allen replied.

There were nods of agreement in the room. Sheehan wasn't quite so sure. "I suppose it is, but how does this link in with the penis in the mouth and the implications of that?"

"Who knows what somebody in loathing and desperation might do?" Allen replied.

"I take it you have some names to follow up on?" Sheehan asked.

"Yeah, including those two guys that lost the three mill. We'll be onto them right away."

"Fair enough. What's your second lead?"

"Fitzpatrick was banging 'The Bat' Weir's wife on the side," Allen said bluntly. There was commotion in the room. Several expletives could be heard as the team tried to get their heads around this latest revelation.

"Holy shit."

"Fuckin' idiot."

"Was he mad in the head?"

"All right. All right," Sheehan shouted, calling the room back to order although he looked every bit as stunned as the others. "That's a helluva bombshell, Tom. What's your justification for making that assertion?"

"We got it off a young teller Fitzpatrick bef-f-friended at the bank," McNeill said. "Tom scared the life out of him with t-t-talk about accessory after the fact for withholding information. The guy spilled everything, and we're a h-h-hundred per cent sure that what he said was genuine."

Sheehan leaned back, a breath exploding from his lips. "Bloody hell. That does put a different complexion on matters."

"And the penis fits, obviously," Allen added, then grinned as he became suddenly aware of the *double entendre*.

"Oh aye, it seems to have fitted all right," McCoy shouted, with his ruddy face creased in a big grin.

"That's enough, Oliver. This is serious," Sheehan said, "and the implications are scary. Are we going to go after this guy? Weir is legit now, or so he claims, and we have no evidence to the contrary. But he is one remorseless villain, and killing a cop that was annoying him wouldn't cost him a thought. He's done it before, but we've never been able to pin anything on him."

"Of course we're going after him," Allen declared. "This crime has his fingerprints all over it."

"We'll certainly have to investigate him," Sheehan agreed. "But with finesse. Not like a bull at a gate, Tom. That could get you killed or seriously damaged."

"And there's another very s-s-serious issue," McNeill interjected. "What if Weir isn't the killer and he didn't know about the affair between f-f-Fitzpatrick and his wife? If our questioning him about it is the f-f-first he's heard of it, he'll kill her for sure and it'll b-be our fault."

The bustle in the room ceased, replaced by a sudden and pervasive sense of unease. Turner was the first to break the silence.

"You make a frightening point, Detective McNeill, and there's no doubt that the danger you spell out for Mrs. Weir is very real. How do you propose to handle this part of the investigation?"

Allen said, "We're going to have to find out his whereabouts on the night in question without actually telling him why we want to know."

Connors said, "That guy's got some sort of radar. Couldn't have kept his skin whole this long without it. The slightest sense that something is off and he's all over it until he ferrets out the truth."

"And there's the fact that it doesn't matter where he was that night," Miller added. "He doesn't get his hands dirty anymore. He could have got one of his henchmen to do it, probably did."

"This is a fraught situation," Turner said. "Very delicate. I think, Chief Inspector, someone of your skill and experience will have to handle this. It could go terribly wrong."

"What about contacting the wife first?" Stewart suggested. "Tell her what is going on and get her to a safe place until we can figure out what we can do to get her away from him?"

"Good point," Sheehan replied. "But apart from the complexities of that, there is the cost involved. I don't know how we could pay for such protection. Still, in general, it seems like the way to go. We could talk to her first anyway and see what she herself says." He stood up. "Right, men, that'll do. Sergeant McCullough will keep looking for the cufflink. Allen and McNeill will follow up on the bankrupts. Stewart and I will figure out what do to about Mrs. Weir." He turned to Turner. "And I'd like to thank the crown prosecutor for taking an interest in this case."

Turner smiled and nodded as the men got up to go to their desks or undertake other duties. He made his way towards the chief inspector's office, giving Stewart a small wave *en route*. She nodded a brief acknowledgement. Tom Allen had noticed the gesture and immediately glanced at the sergeant to see how she had received it. But her head was already down and he learned nothing. After a moment's hesitation, his expression cleared, became resolute. He left his desk and stood in front of Stewart who was bent over her laptop, disconnecting the PowerPoint. She stood up when she saw him.

His face was expressionless and, as he spoke, his voice was almost robotic. "Sergeant, I wish to apologise for my outburst earlier. Apart from the bad manners, it was a breach of protocol, you being a sergeant and all. You have every right to report me."

Surprised, but suddenly glad of this opportunity to clear the air, she said, "Look, just forget it, Tom. Emotions were running high." She began to turn back to her laptop but stopped to add, her expression softening, "And thanks. Those two bastards really were annoying me."

Something flickered in Tom's eyes but his expression didn't change. Instead he simply said as he turned back to his desk, "Thank you, Sergeant."

Voices distracted her. She glanced over to see that Turner had retrieved his overcoat from the chief's office and that Sheehan was accompanying him to the door. As he was leaving, Turner said, "That was interesting, Chief Inspector. Your team is effective. But you're going to be scurrying all over the place chasing these leads."

"That's police work. We're used to it."

"Impressive. Demanding, though. What do you do to de-stress?"

Sheehan grinned. "I'm only recently married. Life's good. We share a love of music, attend concerts. I must say I hadn't realised how important it is to have a stable home life to offset the rigors of police work."

"And the frustrations, I'd bet."

Sheehan grinned again. "Tell me about it. You married yourself?"

"No. Too busy."

"You should think about it. So what do you do to relax?"

"Well, I have a cottage on the shore of Lough Neagh. Try to get there the odd weekend to do some boating. Blows the cobwebs away." He threw an amused glance at the chief. "You should get one."

Sheehan laughed aloud. "On a policeman's salary? Aye, right."

As he shook hands preparatory to leaving, Turner said, "Your new sergeant seems to be fitting in. Bright girl, that."

"Early days, but I like her attitude."

"She'll go far." Seeing the detective's quizzical look, he added. "I worked with her on the Kerley case."

Light dawned in Sheehan's eyes. "Of course. It was you who prosecuted that case."

"Yes, and Sergeant Stewart was a brilliant witness. Solid as a rock on the stand." Then he added with a grin, "I think she broke McCahey's heart."

"Oh, him," Sheehan's tone was disparaging. "Deserves all he gets. He doesn't care who he defends."

"He's good. That's why the rich flock to him." He began buttoning his overcoat. "Well, thanks again, Chief Inspector. Enjoyed the experience today. Might come back another time, if you wouldn't mind."

"Any time," Sheehan said as he closed the door behind him.

SIXTEEN

Sergeant Stewart pulled on a pair of leather gloves and tightened the belt of her beige raincoat as she left the station to go home. She glanced back at the gateway as she left, not yet fully accustomed to its grim exterior, its high, redbrick walls and the tall wire fencing on top of them. Absolutely necessary for protection, she knew, but so unsightly. Still, there were too many dissidents still trying to kill police officers and every precaution was necessary. She made her way past the grey and, frankly, quite ugly additional protection around the side of the gate and headed towards her home.

She had chosen to live within walking distance of her work. Apart from the expense of running a car, with its attendant parking costs, this also enabled her to eliminate daily commuter costs. For her, these were necessary economies to help with the mortgage that ate heavily into her monthly salary. But she couldn't have countenanced renting, couldn't see any sense in allowing a significant monthly sum disappear into some kind of financial ether.

The October evening was chilly and she pulled the collar of her raincoat up around her ears. As she did so she was conscious of a nervous prickle at the back of her neck. *Was someone watching her?* She stopped and turned to look behind her but, apart from an innocent couple walking their dog, she saw no one.

She turned and walked briskly along Dundela Avenue, sheltered a little from the wind by the road's unkempt hedging. Again she had that feeling that someone was following her. She tried to ignore it, walking quite fast now with her head buried in her coat collar.

As she turned right into North Road where her new house was, she threw another quick glance over her shoulder. There was a car parked some yards behind her but she could not tell if it had been moving or if there was anyone sitting in it. She stared at it for a few seconds, angry as much as disturbed, and continued into the North Road Estate.

There were a number of houses here, detached, semi-detached, large, small, all neat and well cared for. It was a pleasant area, one that had appealed to her the moment she first walked into it. She had been fortunate to find a tidy little two-storey semi, just past a row of high redbrick terrace houses, at a price she could just about afford. It took most of her savings to cover the deposit but she felt that it was worth it. The house had a small driveway, bordered by a neat hedge about five feet high, a decorative bay window, and red bricks that would not need much maintenance. All in all, it suited her needs perfectly.

Almost running, she got to her front door and let herself in. She turned immediately as she entered the hall and peered through the curtained glass window that formed the top part of the door but saw nothing and no one. She bit her lip in frustration. *Bet it's those two bloody bastards that were hassling me today,* she thought. "Well, bring it on, you swine," she muttered aloud. "See what it gets you. I've got real friends now." She was thinking of Chief Inspector Sheehan, but somehow an image of Tom Allen slipped into her mind. *What am I doing thinking about him?* she asked herself, throwing her coat over an armchair in the small sitting room as she passed through it on her way to the kitchen. Halted by the image, she stood in the middle of the room, hands on hips, staring at the floor. *Must be because he tackled those two pigs on my behalf,* she reasoned.

Replaying the incident in her mind, conscious of no emotions around it, she wondered why she had turned so defensively on the young detective. He had only been trying to help. And he had looked so hurt. *What was that all about?* She shrugged, pulled a bemused face at the kitchen, and began to prepare a small meal. No dinner tonight. Toast, with cheese and a banana, would fill her. She wanted the eating out of the way so that she could do some research on the net in the hope of finding some information about Lynda Bell. She had to admit, though, that he was quite good-looking. She shook her head. *Where did that come from? You're being silly, girl. No fraternising, and anyway, I thought you'd had your fill of men after Dermot?* Her stomach clenched and she experienced again the mix anger and heartache that was an inevitable accompaniment to any thoughts of him, however unbidden. *Men! They're all ...* She stopped the judgement. *Come on now, you can't tar all men with that bastard's brush.* She again shook the thoughts from her head. *This is silly. Eat, girl. We need to get down to work and see what the net can tell us.*

After her sparse meal, she settled herself at the small table in the corner of the sitting room, a table that served as a desk and on which her laptop more or less permanently resided. As she was booting up the computer, the phone on the kitchen bench rang. She got up to answer it, wondering who it might be. She had given her new number to very few people.

"Hello?"

"Is that Sergeant Denise Stewart?" The voice sounded weird, electronic, obviously disguised.

"Who is this?"

"A friend."

The strange voice set her on edge. "How did you get this number?"

"That's not important. I have information for you."

Still on edge but wondering if the caller was some kind of informant, she asked, "What information?"

"About the murder of James Fitzpatrick."

She sucked in a breath. This might be important. She decided to play along and evaluate later what she was about to hear. "What do you know?"

"Are you a person of your word?"

"What?"

"Are you a person of your word?"

What the hell is this? She offered a tentative answer. "Well, I like to think so."

"Not good enough. Are you a person of your word?"

She was getting angry now. "Yes, I'm a person of my word."

"Do you promise to tell no one where you got the information I am about to give you?"

"I don't know who you are. How could I tell anyone?"

"Tell no one you have an informant. Let people assume that you discovered this by yourself, as well other things I might tell you. Do you promise?"

"Look, what's all this about?"

"Do you promise?"

"All right! All right! I promise."

"Did you look at his laptop?"

"I am not at liberty to comment on that. I thought you were giving me information?"

"Quit messin' with me. Did you look at the laptop?"

She hesitated, unsure how to respond.

The metallic voice rasped into the silence. "You have five seconds and then I'm gone. Do you want the info or not?"

"All right. I looked at Fitzpatrick's laptop."

"Did you find an old newspaper clipping announcing the death of Lynda Bell?"

Again she was reluctant to answer but, afraid to lose the caller, she said, "I did."

"Did you find an old photograph of three university students?"

"Yes, I did."

"They're connected."

Stewart felt the blood rising towards her skin, and her arms prickled with tension. This could be a significant lead. She tried to respond calmly. "In what way?"

"Lynda Bell was a student at Queen's in 2002, around the same time as the students in that photograph. She dropped out at the end of her first year."

"So what's the connection?"

"Twelve years ago there were rumours after Lynda Bell left Queen's, that she had been sexually molested." The weird voice droned on, lacking inflection or emphasis but sounding all the more convincing because of that. "This was never confirmed, but Lynda went into chronic depression after she left, did the whole anorexia thing, before taking her own life."

"How do you know all this?"

"Doesn't matter."

"Do you know who the students in the phot ..."

A click on the line, followed by silence, stopped her. The caller had hung up. She quietly replaced the phone, her mind racing. Connors had told the team at the debriefing that Fitzpatrick was at Queen's from 2001 to 2004, and now she was hearing that Lynda was there in 2002. She did not notice her empathic use of the girl's Christian name. The newspaper cutting had been on the victim's computer for twelve years, definitely unusual. So was the photograph. The aloof student to the side of the photograph was definitely Fitzpatrick, but who were the other two, and what was their connection to Lynda, to Fitzpatrick? If she read the caller's implication correctly, there was a possibility that these three boys had something to do with the ... what did he say it was … sexual molestation. Was it rape? How did they get away with it? Did Lynda not report it? She shook her head, exasperated. It wouldn't be the first time an assault like that had gone unreported. Shame, embarrassment, self-disgust, and the fear that somehow she had prompted the attack herself would silence an innocent, introspective girl. Was Lynda one of those? It was a story that was all too common, one that Stewart had come across more than once during her time as a policewoman.

She felt a rising anger as she considered the poor girl's plight. *Why in the name of God couldn't she have reported it, or at least got proper counselling?* She rubbed her face in her hands and sat at the desk again, speaking aloud through clenched teeth. "I'm going to find out everything I can about this, Lynda, and I will make damn' sure the bastards who did this to you will not go unpunished."

Her mind turned to the strange caller. Who was he? Why was he helping her? Did he have a connection to Lynda? How did he know about the laptop? This last thought stopped her flow of questions. She repeated the question slowly, mystified. How, indeed, did he know about the laptop, and what she had found on it? Could it be someone connected with the case? There are all those SOCOs, uniforms, our own team, interviewees, lots of people connected to the murder, or on the fringes of it. Could it be one of them? But why does he crave anonymity? Or is it a 'she'? Those electronic voices sound the same for either gender. She paused as she wondered if there was some way she could narrow the list down by figuring out just how much any of the people on it were likely to know about the details of the case. Then she shook her head. That would be very time consuming and, anyway, how could she do it without raising people's suspicions. But how does he know so much?
Her mind went blank. She had no clue and couldn't even begin to hazard an answer.

SEVENTEEN

S tewart's phone rang again at eight o'clock the following morning while she was cleaning her teeth. "Good timing," she spluttered. Rinsing her mouth, she was conscious of tension. Was it the weird caller again? She ran to the phone and said, "Hello?"

"Good morning, Sergeant. DCI Sheehan here. Would you get a car from the compound, please, when you come in this morning? We're going to the mortuary."

"The mortuary, sir?"

"Yes. At the Royal Victoria Hospital. It's Friday. I don't want to have to wait until after the weekend for Dick's report."

"Oh, yes. Sorry, sir."

There was a brief pause at the other end as Sheehan remembered that she was still new. "Don't worry about it, Stewart. All this will be old hat to you in a few months."

"Thank you, sir. Where do you want me to pick you up?"

"I'll be at the front of the station at nine o'clock."

"I'll be there, sir."

As her boss hung up, Stewart was thinking that the early call was actually considerate. He was ensuring that she would still have plenty of time to get herself ready. *Nice man. That pig she worked for in Lisburn would hardly have given her two minutes notice, and then he would have ranted at her for being late.*

She arrived at the gate with an unmarked police car at nine o'clock exactly. Sheehan was just coming out of the front office. As he got into the car, Stewart wasted no time on small talk. She elected to say nothing about the incident in the corridor or her suspicions about being followed home. The last impression she wanted to give her new boss was one of a wimpy female running to him for help at the first sign of trouble. Shackled to her promise to the mystery caller, despite the fact that she neither knew him (or her?) nor owed him anything, she said nothing about the strange phone call either.

Sheehan remained silent while she eased her way out on to the M3. He seemed lost in his thoughts and, since her own mind was whirling, she was happy to drive in silence. She paused as she negotiated her way onto Servia Street.

He noticed her hesitating as she studied the road. "Just turn right here," he said, "and we're at the hospital." She made the turn and drove along the hospital entrance road. Then he said, "Just drive into the car park. We'll walk from there."

They arrived at the door to the mortuary at the same time as Dr. Jones. Sheehan's eyes were drawn to the well-tailored dark grey suit, the white shirt immaculate against Jones's dark skin, the maroon striped tie, the quarter inch of cuff with a small gold cufflink showing at each sleeve. "Good morning, Doctor Jones," he said.

Jones's return greeting seemed to rumble from somewhere in the depths of his stomach. "Good morning, Chief Inspector. Good morning, Sergeant."

Stewart, who again had to struggle to restrain a half-sensual, half- amused tremor in response to the seductive voice, gave him a nod and a friendly smile.

Sheehan said, somewhat dryly, "Your clients must appreciate the way you dress for work?"

Jones's serious expression remained unchanged. "I have an important meeting in a couple of hours," was all the explanation he offered as he unlocked the door and led them into the mortuary. He said nothing more but left them standing at the door while he put on a white lab coat and went to one of the huge refrigerated drawers in the far wall. As he was pulling it out, he said, "I take it you're here to talk about Mr. Fitzpatrick's post-mortem?" His tone remained serious, if slightly impatient.

Doesn't quite have Dick's whimsy, Sheehan thought, as he stared at the body, at the repaired throat, at the huge, roughly stitched Y-cut in the chest area. "You got anything for us?"

"Pretty much what we had at the crime scene. There were no extra or unusual circumstances surrounding the death."

"So, the cut to the throat …?"

"I can confirm now that the victim choked on his own blood. That, together with the loss of blood in the nether region, made death inevitable."

"Did you come to any more conclusions about the nature of the cut or whether we can learn anything from it about the perpetrator?" Sheehan asked.

Jones led them to his desk where there were some large coloured photographs of the body at the crime scene. "Let me go over it with you," He pointed to an enlarged shot of the throat on one of the photographs. "Take a look here. As Doctor Campbell pointed out at the scene of the crime, the cut is jagged and unfinished. The jagged edge means that the throat was slack when it was cut."

"Slack?" Sheehan wasn't getting it.

"Yes, meaning that the killer might have some expertise in this area."

"Expertise? How does jagged indicate expertise?"

"You would be more impressed by straight and clean?"

"Well, I suppose, yes."

"I can see why. Just about any time you watch someone getting his throat cut in the movies or on television, the killer grabs his hair or his forehead and pulls the head back."

"So the throat becomes taut, right?" Sheehan said. "And because the throat is taut, the cut is straight and neat. No jagged lines. Right?"

"Guess our perpetrator didn't watch much television," Stewart said. "Looks like he didn't know what he was doing."

Jones stared at her for a moment, eyes intent. "Interesting you should say that." Stewart thought she could feel the floor vibrating as the man spoke. "Actually, someone who knew what they were doing wouldn't pull the head back. The muscles taut like that would be much harder to cut. Someone who didn't know what he was doing would instinctively pull the head back to get a better angle on the throat, not realising that he was making the task much more difficult for himself."

Sheehan said, "So the killer actually did know what he was doing? Is it likely that he had military training?"

"I have no idea. He might just as easily have had medical training, that is, if he did know what he was doing."

Sheehan was feeling confused. "What … what are you saying now? That he didn't know what he was doing?"

Jones shrugged as he straightened up. "You heard Doctor Campbell at the crime scene. The cut was poorly executed. Maybe it didn't even occur to the killer to pull the head back."

Sheehan stared at him thinking, *Come back, Dick, all is forgiven.*

Stewart, looking as puzzled as Sheehan felt, said, "So, what, if anything, can we deduce from the nature of this cut?"

Jones went to a basin and washed his hands. He seemed to be pondering her question. Drying his hands, he moved back towards them and rumbled in his deep voice, "I would suggest you do not try to deduce anything at this stage. The facts are open to contradictory conclusions."

"No chance that the killer actually did know what he was doing but is trying to confuse the investigation ..." He stopped talking as Jones turned to give him a withering look.

"Chief Inspector," he said. "You are moving into seriously hypothetical territory now and I can't offer answers to these questions. Frankly, I think you're wasting your time with them. I do not think that focusing on this cut will make any significant contribution to your investigation."

EIGHTEEN

A *phone rings.*

"Hello?"

"Hi, Pete!"

"Hi ... uh ... who's that?"

"Finbar."

"Finbar? Oh, Finn! How are you? Long time, no see."

"Aye! How's it goin'?"

"Well, you know how it is; same old, same old."

"Still teaching?"

"Yeah, workin' away. Yourself?"

"Aye! Thinking about applying for a job in a grammar school. These wee secondary school buggers are driving me nuts. No home discipline."

"Tell me about it."

A pause.

Pete says, "So, is there something I can help you with, Finn?"

"Suppose you heard about James?"

"Yes." His voice is tense now. "Messy business."

"You don't think ....?"

Pete's response was immediate, perhaps too immediate. "No. No. Not after all these years. Definitely not."

"Yeah, I suppose."

"You know what he's like, was like, Finn. Always getting up people's noses. Obviously he got up the wrong nose this time."

"I suppose you're right. Has me thinking about the old days. Why don't we meet for a drink and catch up?"

"Yeah, I'd like that."

"Good. I'll give you a ring in a day or two and organise something."

"Look forward to it. Good talking to you again."

"Yes, Pete. Talk to you in a day or two, okay?"

"Great. 'Bye, Finn."

"'Bye, Pete."

NINETEEN

"**S**he's seriously terrified," Stewart remarked, as they pulled out of the long driveway.

Sheehan nodded. "Strange sort of a marriage when a wife is that scared of her husband."

"Will she run, do you think?"

"Hard to say. She's like a rabbit caught in headlights. She knows she's likely to be found out once we interview her husband, but she seems incapable of taking any action that could save her life."

They were silent for a moment, each reflecting on their visit with Mrs. Weir. She had calmly ushered them into her lounge when they identified themselves, clearly unfazed by their arrival and obviously accustomed to the presence of police in her home. Mrs. Weir was about thirty, long straight blond hair, very red lipstick. She was pretty in an obvious way, nice figure, but the image couldn't survive the gum chewing or the grating Northern Ireland accent. Her long, bright red fingernails caught the eye as she gestured them to armchairs each.

"My husband's out now," were her first words. "Is there somethin' I can help youse with?"

Sheehan succinctly revealed the purpose of their visit, leaving her in no doubt that her affair with the deceased was not an issue for the police, but might well be an issue for her husband if he were to add two and two together after the detectives interviewed him.

The woman's gum-chewing façade shattered immediately, and she was reduced to shivering, mind-numbing panic. She rocked backwards and forwards on her seat, hands over her face, as she keened, "What am I gonna do? What am I gonna do?"

Sheehan had tried to assure her that no mention of the affair would be made during her husband's interview, but she interrupted him, her face twisted in fear. "He's not stupid. He'll want to know why you're interviewin' him. He doesn't know James. If you mention him, he'll know. Oh, God, he'll kill me."

"Are you sure he has not already found out about the affair? We have him on our list as a possible suspect for James's murder. Maybe he pretended not to know so that he wouldn't be suspected of killing your lover?"

"No, no. He's got a terrible temper. If he knew, he couldn't hide it."

Sheehan was disconcerted at this but tried to hide it. If it was true, Weir might well not be their man.

"Is there anyone you can go to, anywhere you can disappear to?" Sheehan asked.

"Are you serious? I'll never be able to hide from him. He has contacts everywhere, and he owns them all. They're as scared of him as I am. If any of them got sight of me, they would grass me up in a flash."

"You have no relatives at all that you could go to for support?"

She shook her head, desperation evident in her every move. "Just a sister in America. But he'd probably send somebody out to kill the pair of us if I went there."

Stewart tried to comfort the stricken woman. "We can find somewhere to keep you for a while," she offered, "a form of witness protection, until things die down."

"Die down? Die down? You don't know who you're dealin' with. Nothin' ever dies down for him. He never forgets and he never forgives. God …" She gave vent to a fresh bout of anguished tears. "I'm dead." She stared at the detectives with eyes now streaked with dark make up. "I'll disappear, and nobody'll know what happened to me. Oh, Jesus! Oh, Jesus!"

"Go upstairs and pack all you can carry," Sheehan urged. "Get whatever money and jewels you have and come with us to Strandtown Station. We'll protect you."

"He'll find me. He'll find me." She struggled with a small handkerchief that had appeared from nowhere and, emitting a heavy breath, she said, "My only chance is to try and bluff it out. I can just keep denying any affair until he believes me."

Sheehan rose from his seat and handed her his card. "The offer of protection is still open. Here's my number if you change your mind. We'll hold off interviewing him for a day or so until you get time to think about what you might want to do." He looked down at the stricken woman. "I'm sorry, but a day's the best I can do for you."

Now in the car, he said to Stewart, "We're going to have to be very careful when we interview this guy. We don't want that woman's death on our conscience."

"You really believe he'll kill her, sir?"

Sheehan stared through the windscreen, memories flooding back. "No doubt. Some of the atrocities he was involved in during the troubles …" He shook his head. "The guy has no conscience, no empathy, no mercy." His expression hardened. "She thinks she can bluff it out. But she's bound to know he'll beat her to within an inch of her life until she confesses. She has no chance." He thought about this for a while, then said, "It'll cost, and the ACC will go nuts, but organise some surveillance on Mrs. Weir for the next week or so. Get the uniforms to do it in shifts, but tell them to be unobtrusive, ordinary clothes in plain cars. If he tries to disappear her, we'll need to be there to stop him."

TWENTY

1

"From paying myself north of fifty thousand a year, big house, BMW in the garage to … to this." Edward Daly waved a hand dismally at the tiny, sparse sitting room, but his gesture managed to encompass the whole house.

They were sitting with him on hard chairs at a table in the middle of a poorly lit room. Their eyes followed his hand and they took in the worn linoleum on the floor, the peeling wallpaper. He saw their reaction. "All we could get at a moment's notice," he said. "And now being on the dole, I'm dependent on the state to pay the rent."

Allen felt pity for the man but didn't quite know what to say. A line from a Shakespeare play crossed the fringes of his mind. Julius Caesar, was it? 'Oh, what a fall was there!' He chose to be less dramatic in his response, however. "We're sorry to hear of your plight, Mr. Daly, and sorry, too, that we had to question you like this. But …"

"I fully understand," Daly cut in. "If anybody has reason to hate James Fitzpatrick, I have. He didn't give me a chance. But the stress of this thing has beaten me into the ground. I never leave the house. I'm not your killer …" He paused to look directly at them. "… but I can't pretend that I'm sorry he's dead."

The two policemen didn't doubt that what he said was true. They had no idea how Daly might have looked or behaved before the bankruptcy, but they were looking now at a broken man, scrawny, unshaven, hands shaking. It was clear to them that he had neither the physical resources nor the strength of will to have carried out the murder of James Fitzpatrick. Both detectives stood.

McNeill, clearly sympathetic, reached out a hand. "Thank you for b-being so candid, Mr. Daly. I don't think we'll n-need to bother you again."

Daly tried to struggle to his feet. Allen held up a hand. "Don't bother, Mr. Daly. We'll see ourselves out."

The man nodded abstractedly, his eyes already losing focus as he stared abjectly at the middle of the table.

As they walked to their car, McNeill said, "Bloody hell. From a thousand p-pounds a week to about seventy on the dole. How does anyone m-m-make that adjustment?"

"Glad it's not me," Allen said.

McNeill eyed him askance, grinning, "Ah, you'd be all right. You're n-not earning much more than that anyway."

"Very funny," Allen replied. "Get into that car, and we'll go and see what these two brothers have to say for themselves."

2

The Duffner brothers were now working out of a small rented office above a hardware shop on Falls Road. Cheap though the premises were, they had tried to improve their office's appearance with a new, if inexpensive, green carpet, a decent desk, and three or four ordinary chairs with soft seating. The newly painted walls were bare of decoration, however, or any form of framed qualifications. The older brother, Michael, was sitting behind the desk which bore only a telephone and a couple of blue manilla folders. He wore a respectable grey suit which struggled to contain his bulky frame. Jason, slim, unshaven, wearing denim jacket and jeans, was leaning against the wall behind his older brother, eyeing both policemen with undisguised hostility.

Michael, rather more urbane than his younger brother, gestured to the chairs. "Pull up a seat, detectives. How can we help you?"

Allen noticed the cold glint in the man's eyes. *Polished,* he thought, *but not a man to cross.* After they had seated themselves in front of the desk, Allen said, "Your names have come up in a case we're working on …" He held up a hand as Jason bristled aggressively. "It happens all the time. We are obliged to follow these things up. All we need from you is information about your whereabouts last Tuesday evening between ten o'clock and midnight, and we'll be on our way."

"Do we need a lawyer?" Jason asked, belligerently.

Michael silenced him with a look. "No need for that, Jason. The detectives are just doing their job." Addressing the policemen again, he said evenly, "Do you mind if I ask what case you are referring to and what it might have to do with us?"

"We're looking into the suspicious death of James Fitzpatrick last Tuesday. We're talking to anyone he had dealings with."

"Oh, him." Jason's tone was disparaging.

"Ah!" was all Michael said.

"You know him?"

"Of course. He destroyed our business unnecessarily, made us bankrupt, and left us in poverty."

"Unnecessarily?" Allen asked.

"Oh, yes." Michael was speaking now with his anger barely under control. "We owned an offices property worth six million. We had a buyer lined up for one of the penthouse suites, about nine hundred thousand, and a nudge would have closed sales on two of the smaller offices at four hundred thousand each. We owed three million, but we'd have had a couple of million for the bank right there, and we could easily have renegotiated the loan on reasonable terms after that. A month, that's all we needed, but the bastard saw a chance to earn a filthy bonus …"

116

"You knew about that?" Allen asked, surprised.

"Course we did. We weren't without our own contacts."

"Then he called in the loan," Jason rasped, "and then him and the receivers were in cahoots and tried to sell off the best offices to business cronies for around half price. We had to get a court order to stop him doing that."

"He was a vicious, nasty bastard," Michael said, all suavity gone, eyes flashing bitter resentment. "He knew we had the situation under control, but he destroyed us anyway ..." He sucked in a deep breath, unable to finish the sentence.

"That was tough, all right," Allen said, thinking how rashly the two men had revealed motive for the murder. "So, last Tuesday evening?"

Michael, striving for calmness again, began leafing through a diary on his desk. "Tuesday. That was ... ah ... the fourteenth," he said. Then he looked up. "As it happens, we were both here working. We'd landed a couple of new clients, and we were studying their case notes to see how we might best advise them."

"What exactly is it that you d-do here?" McNeill asked.

The older brother raised his eyebrows briefly at the stutter but made no comment. "It's somewhat complicated."

"We've got time," Allen said.

"When Fitzpatrick tried to make us redundant, we fought him every step of the way, in and out of court, meeting with solicitors and barristers, planning defensive strategies, meetings with bank officials, discussions with receivers. It was a long and arduous few months. We lost out in the end, as you know ..."

"No thanks to Fitzpatrick," Jason cut in sourly.

"But we picked up a lot of knowledge about how these things work," Michael went on, ignoring the interruption. "We know what signs to look for in failing businesses, how to negotiate with banks, solicitors, courts, and other agencies, that kind of thing. So we have set up this consultancy firm for people who are threatened with the same experience we had. We either guide them through the process or, sometimes, we can help them to avoid closure and keep their business afloat." He shrugged. "Early days yet, but the trends look promising."

"And you were here working on Tuesday evening?"

"That's right."

"Can anyone confirm that?"

"Well, Jason here …"

"Apart from your brother."

Michael joined his hands in front of him on the desk. He looked completely at ease. "Thing is, detective," he said, "if we'd known we were going to need an alibi for that evening, I would have ensured that people knew we were here." He paused and said in what was meant to be a helpful tone, "Perhaps some people walking by on Tuesday evening saw our light on."

"That would only p-prove the l-light was on," McNeill said. "It wouldn't m-mean that you were here."

"True," Michael nodded, unfazed. "That is, indeed, true."

"Nobody phoned while you were here?"

"No. Hardly surprising, that hour of the night."

Allen riffled through the pages of his notebook. "Do either of you own a car?" he asked.

"I was fortunately able to hold on to mine," Michael said. "Why?"

"Could you tell me the make and colour, please?"

"It's an Audi A6 Saloon, an SE."

"And the colour?"

"Black."

"Thank you," Allen said, noting the information in a small notebook.

"So what time did you stop w-working, and where did you g-go after that?" McNeill asked.

The brothers glanced at each other. "We quit about ten forty-five," Michael offered. "I drove Jason home to his flat. I went in for a coffee and to watch a bit of the recording of Saturday's match."

"Which one?" Allen took up the questioning.

"Man. United."

"Where did you go after that?"

"Home. I still have the house. The bastards couldn't get that. It's in the wife's name."

"What time was that?"

"About midnight. The wife can confirm that. She was in bed, but she was awake."

Allen looked at McNeill. "Anything else, Detective?"

McNeill shook his head. "No, I'm good."

Both policemen stood up. Putting the notebook back into the inside pocket of his jacket, Allen said, "Thank you, gentlemen. If something else occurs to you about how you might confirm your alibi, you can get me at this number." He handed Michael his card, and both detectives shook hands with him. Jason remained resolutely stuck to the wall, his arms rigidly folded.

As they climbed into the car outside, McNeill said, "What do you think?"

"Hard to say," Allen replied. "Can't see Jason having the wit to pull off something like Fitzpatrick's murder. His brother, though, is a different kettle of fish."

"They'd hardly have done it together?"

"Doubt it. Two guys clumping around a crime scene? They would be bound to leave some forensics."

"Jason covering for his b-brother?"

119

"That'd be my guess. That Michael, he's a cold fish. Clever, too. And smart-alecky. Doesn't give a shit that they've no alibi."

"Either they didn't do it or he's c-confident that there's no evidence to attach him t-to it."

"I don't quite know what to make of that. There's no shortage of motive, they're clearly angry as hell, and they can't account for their whereabouts at the time of the murder. And what about that Michael? He's big enough and strong enough to have carried out the killing."

Allen checked his rear and side mirrors and eased out into the traffic on Falls Road. "We'll bring it to the chief and see what he thinks."

TWENTY-ONE

S tewart waved good evening to the officer at the observation window as she walked through the station gate on her way home. She stood uncertainly at the entrance, checking the road left and right, peering into the gathering dusk. The road to her right, with its houses and hedges, seemed empty as far as the bend, as did the road to the left along the redbricked perimeter wall of the station.

As she turned left to walk home, a car pulled quietly out through the gate and stopped beside her. The passenger window came down, and Tom Allen leaned towards her. "Going home, Sergeant? Can I give you a lift anywhere?"

She hesitated for a moment, all sorts of permutations running through her mind. *Is this a pickup? Does he represent safety from the stalker or whatever it is? Am I committing myself to anything if I accept? Maybe it's just what it seems, an innocent offer of a lift.* All the while she was staring at the young detective, unaware of the time passing until she saw growing mystification in his expression. Her mind continued to race. *I need an ally, allies, here.* She stepped forward. "Thank you," she said and climbed into the passenger seat.

Tom still looked puzzled. "Is everything all right? You seem a bit …"

"No, I'm fine. Just wool gathering."

"Oh, wool gathering." He grinned, but it was a short-lived effort.

"I only live round the corner," she said. "Turn right into North Road. That's where I live."

He grinned again, more easily this time. "North Road? Wow! You were lucky I came along. Saved you a hike."

She smiled briefly but he noted a swift return to that same expression she had worn at the gate. She seemed focused, too, on his wing mirror. But already he was turning into her street, and his eyes were needed to watch the road. Denise pointed to a small red-brick house set in from the other larger ones nearby. "That's me."

He stopped at the gate. "All of a minute and a half. How's that for service?" He smiled a goodbye, expecting her to get out of the car immediately. Instead she sat still, staring through the windscreen. Tom was puzzled again. *What's this?* She seemed very uncomfortable, but she was making no attempt to move.

Eventually, she breathed a sigh of sorts and seemed to come to a conclusion. "Tom, thanks for the lift. As you say, it's only a few yards but," she turned towards him, "the last couple of times I walked home in the evening, I had a sense that someone was following me. I didn't see anyone, but the feeling was very strong. I think it might be some of those officers from Lisburn, but that's only a guess."

"Bastards," Tom said. "If you want them sorted ..."

"I don't know if it's even them. But if they're trying to make me feel uneasy, they're succeeding." Suddenly uncharacteristically vulnerable, she added, "I'm a police sergeant, Tom. I shouldn't be jumping at shadows like that."

"Don't be silly, Den ... Sergeant. Stalkers in the dusk, especially unseen ones, would unnerve anybody." They sat for a moment in silence. Then Tom went on, "Is there some way I can help with this?"

She straightened. "No, I'm being silly. I shouldn't have bothered you with it."

"I've told you once already, Sergeant. We're a team here. Any member of the team under threat means the whole team is under threat."

"But what can you do?"

"Maybe I could follow you home on foot tomorrow … uh … Monday evening, y'know, stay well back and see if there's anyone lurking about. I'll not be long grabbing them if there is."

"For some reason, even though I don't hear anything, I think they're in a car."

"Well, either way, I'll find out. If it's a car, we can easily trace the licence plate. We'll know very soon who it is."

"Thanks, Tom. I'm sorry to put you to that bother."

"Look, the sooner we get this sorted, the sooner you can get back to normal. And it's no bother. In fact," he paused, uncertain whether to finish the thought, "I'm happy you trusted me enough to help you with this."

She smiled. "Part of the team, right?"

He smiled back. "Yeah! Enjoy your weekend, Sarge."

The late October evening had already turned quite dark as they sat together in the front of the car, looking like an ordinary couple chatting. A watcher at the corner of the road seethed. His eyes narrowed as he saw Detective Stewart get out of Allen's car and, with a slight wave of her hand, turn into the short drive of her house. Detective Allen's engine coughed and, as he executed a three point turn, the watcher reached for the ignition key and started the powerful but quiet engine of his own car.

Allen slowed as he approached the corner leading back into Dundela Avenue. Suddenly, and without warning, an engine roared, and a large car smashed into the side of the detective's car, hurling him towards the footpath. The assailant's car sped off, but Tom was peripherally aware of two pedestrians walking towards him as his car spun out of control. He had time only to wrench the steering wheel sideways and ram on the footbrake. The pedestrians jumped back as the car managed to swerve past them before crashing into a large hedge that surrounded the corner house. One of the couple, the male, rushed to the driver's door and tried to pull it open. It was badly dented but after some energetic tugging, he managed to get it half-way open. "Are you all right?" he asked urgently.

Tom was too dazed to respond. He was lying sideways, holding his head in his hands. The female pedestrian had joined her companion by this time. "Don't move him. Make sure he's all right first."

Stewart had heard the horrendous crash just as she was closing her front door. She had glanced out and had seen that Tom's car was stuck in a hedge at the corner of the street. She had raced down, and now was pulling the two pedestrians aside as she strove to see how her colleague was doing. "Tom. Tom. Are you all right?"

Tom raised slightly dazed eyes towards her.

"Yeah," he groaned, trying to undo his seatbelt. "Yeah. I'm fine." He tried to straighten up. "What the hell happened?"

"Go easy, Tom. Just sit still for a while until you're sure there's nothing broken." She squeezed in towards him and helped him with the belt, saying, "Did you see who hit you?"

"No ... yeah. He came flyin' outa nowhere, and ... and I saw these two people and had to try to avoid hitting them. Didn't see the other guy at all." He continued to grunt, breathing erratically, as Denise helped him sit upright in his seat. He knew he was badly bruised, and his chest hurt from the force of the seatbelt, but he suspected nothing was broken. He glanced at Stewart and said with a pained grin, "Phone the cops, will ya?"

She gave him an exasperated *tut* and said, "Sit there quietly while I have a quick word with the witnesses." She turned to the couple. "I'm a police officer. Did either of you happen to see the other car?"

The young man, dressed in a duffle coat with the hood up, said, "No. We were just chattin', and suddenly we heard this awful bang. I saw the other guy driving off like a bat outa hell, but he had no lights on, so I didn't get much of a look at him."

"You didn't see the number plate?"

"Sorry, no."

"Any idea of the make of the car?"

Both shook their heads. "It was big," the young girl said. She, too, was wearing a hooded coat.

"I think it was a dark colour," her boyfriend added.

Denise bent back to Tom. "Have you your notebook handy?"

He gestured to the glove compartment. "There's one in there," he gritted, his arms hugging his chest.

"I'm calling an ambulance now," Stewart said. "Just hang on."

She called the ambulance and took down the names and addresses of the two witnesses. "Thank you," she said. "You can go now. If I need to speak to you again, I'll be in touch."

By this time a small crowd had gathered as people left nearby houses to see what was happening. She turned to address them. "I'm a police officer. There's been an accident here but no one has been hurt." She ignored Tom's muffled dissent from the front seat of the car and went on, "Did anyone happen to notice a large dark-coloured car parked here before the accident?"

Neighbour looked at neighbour, but no one could offer any information.

"All right. Thank you. Go on back to your houses, please. An ambulance is on its way."

As the crowd dispersed, she phoned the Police Vehicle Recovery Service as well as the Collision Investigation Unit. No one was going to be driving Tom's car for a while, and forensics would need immediate access to the paint scrapes left by the other car, as well as the tyre tracks left on the road. She put her phone back in her pocket and said to Tom, "How are you feeling now?"

"Pretty sore, but I don't think there are any bones broken. Was that your friends, do you think?"

Stewart was instantly apologetic. "Tom, I'm really sorry for getting you into this." She stared at him, wincing as he winced.

Tom was shaking his head from side to side. "Stop. Stop. This wasn't your fault. The guy who did it is to blame, and God help him when I find out who he is."

"Or who *they* are. I wouldn't put it past those two pigs from Lisburn, Chambers and Wilson. You really made mincemeat out of them the other day. That would have put a big dent in their egos. They'd think nothing of trying to cripple you."

A siren wailed in the distance, ending this speculation. "Here's the ambulance coming now," Denise said. "You go on with them to the hospital and I'll stay here with the car until the Collision and Recovery teams come."

"All right."

"Anyway, I'll need to divert any traffic. We don't want to lose these tyre tracks. Do you have a hi-viz jacket handy?"

In spite of his pain, Allen gave her a quizzical look. "There's one in the boot. Do you think it'll fit you?"

"Funny! I'll wrap it round me … several times."

"You're going to look a bit odd." This with a grin followed by another grunt of pain.

"Doesn't matter. We really need to protect this scene." She looked up. "Here's the ambulance now. I'll call in to the hospital later to see how you're doing."

"You don't need to do that."

She tilted her head towards him. "Team-mates, remember?"

Tom didn't quite know what to make of that, but the ambulance crew were already moving in to check him out.

Stewart explained briefly to the paramedics what had happened while they carefully and efficiently lifted Tom out of the car and on to a stretcher. Stewart gave him a small smile as they carried him past her.

He pulled a face. "I feel like a complete twit lying here."

Her smile widened. "Sounds like you're not dying anyway. I'll see you soon."

TWENTY-TWO

1

When Sheehan and Stewart were ushered into his office the following Monday morning, the CEO of Weir Enterprises was seated behind a massive mahogany desk in an office already plush with armchairs, deep carpet, nouveau art paintings on the walls and, somehow very much in character, a small bar in the corner of the room. He rose as they entered. It was impossible not to notice the expensively tailored suit, the gold cufflinks glinting at the cuffs of the jacket, the sheen of wealth that seemed to gleam on his smooth face. He gestured them into two armchairs and pointed at the bar. "Can I offer you something to drink? Water? Whiskey? Beer? Champagne?"

"No thanks, Mr. Weir," Sheehan said, sitting on one of the armchairs while Sergeant Stewart sat in another close by. "We don't drink on duty."

Mr. Weir's eyebrows rose. "Duty?" he said, his voice sounding surprised. "It's some time now since I had an official visit from the police." He gestured generally at his office. "I presume you are aware that I am fully legitimate now. I don't allow a breath of scandal to touch my present businesses."

Sheehan nodded. "And I'm sure none has," he said. "It's just that we are conducting enquiries into a recent death, a murder actually, and we're contacting people whose names have emerged in the investigations." He separated his joined hands a few inches "For elimination purposes, you understand."

Weir's brows furrowed. He seemed temporarily nonplussed. "I see." He reached into the inside pocket of his jacket, drew out a slim, crocodile skin wallet and made something of show of opening it and extracting two small cards. He handed a card each to Sheehan and Stewart and sat back in his desk chair with what looked like a dismissive smile.

Sheehan didn't look at the card but simply said, "What's this?"

"That's my solicitor's card. You can contact him at that number any time."

Sheehan pursed his lips. "All we need is a moment of your time …"

"And you've just had it," Weir cut in, the veneer of sophistication cracking slightly. He examined his fingernails to calm himself and said, "I have learned a long time ago, officers, that no matter how simple the police's questions are, they always manage to make more out my answers than was ever meant by them." He looked at his watch, a platinum and gold monstrosity. "Now, if you'll excuse me, I have an urgent appointment. Any further questions can be directed to Mr. Brannigan, my solicitor." He rose, went to the door and, holding it open, said, "Have a good day, officers."

The two detectives had little option but to rise and leave. As he was passing Weir on the way out, Sheehan said pleasantly, "Thank you for your time, Mr. Weir. And if we think of anything further to discuss with you, I assume you'll be happy to meet us at Strandtown Police Station?"

Weir smiled thinly. "We'll leave that to Mr. Brannigan, shall we?"

On the way down to the street in the lift, Stewart said to her pensive superior. "Well, one good thing came out of that, sir."

He looked at her.

"If anything happens to Mrs. Weir, it can't be laid on us."

Sheehan stared at the floor numbers whizzing by on the console in front of him. "I'm not so sure. No matter how circumspect we were, our very presence in his office has lifted the lid of a kind of Pandora's box. No knowing what we let out. He'll be ferreting out whatever he can to find out about why we were there. We're a long way from finished with Mr. Weir."

"He seemed anxious not to have anything to do with us."

"That stuff with the cards? That's just a peacock flashing his feathers. He knows he'll have to talk with us eventually, but he wants to cock a snoot at us. That's his new upmarket way of dissing the law that he hates." His expression hardened. "The old 'Bat' is still very much inside that expensive suit."

"What did you make of his reaction when we mentioned the murder?"

"He looked a bit put out, but penny to a pound he was probably wondering which murder we were referring to. He's still got plenty to hide, that guy."

He flicked a switch to indicate that he was preparing to enter the traffic flow and said, "What about Tom Allen? How's he doing now?"

"Just bruises and plenty of pain. The hospital is letting him home this morning."

"You seem very *au fait* with his situation," he said, keeping an eye on the traffic, his expression guileless.

She threw him a glance and was silent for a moment. Then she said, "It's complicated."

"Hah! What isn't?"

Stewart stared ahead. When she had called into the hospital the previous Friday evening and saw Tom Allen covered in bandages and wearing a neck brace, she had experienced again a flush of guilt. Her expression must have shown something of what she felt because Tom had immediately said, "This has nothing to do with you, Sergeant, so don't go blaming yourself."

Geoff McNeill was already in the ward, sitting beside the bed. "Hello, Sergeant. Tom t-told me what happened. You can't b-be responsible for the actions of a nutter."

She had been staring at the bandages wrapped around Tom's torso and around his right shoulder. His right arm was in a sling, making it difficult to pull on a pyjama jacket, so his left shoulder and arm were bare, as well as most of his upper torso, revealing a physique that radiated power and yet was so elegantly sculpted that her mind was filled suddenly with an image of Michelangelo's *David*. Embarrassed, she said quickly, "You've a lot of bandages there. I hope nothing's broken."

"No, just bruises. Well, maybe a couple of broken ribs, but the neck brace is just a precaution. That's coming off." Tom was trying to sound cheerful but the effects of the painkillers he had taken were causing him to slur his words, and he looked ready to drop off.

She touched the edge of the bed. "I'm glad you're all right, but you're obviously tired. I'll go on now."

"Thanks for dropping by," Tom said. "They're letting me out tomorrow, but I have to keep the old ribs bandaged for a few weeks. So no punching, all right?"

God, this guy's irrepressible. She grinned and said, "I'll try to remember but no guarantees." She nodded to McNeill. "Goodnight, then. See you both on Monday, well, depending on what the chief has planned."

Now she heard the chief's voice dragging her back to the present. "Care to tell me what Tom Allen was doing in your street in the first place?"

He'll find out soon enough, she thought, so she told him the story.

2

Weir had stood at the window of his penthouse office, staring down at the two detectives as they crossed the street below towards their car. His eyes blazed as he watched them pull away, and he crossed the office to his desk. He snatched up his phone, dialled, and waited a few moments, tapping his foot impatiently. Eventually a voice crackled at the other end.

"I've just had two pigs in here messin' up my office," Weir snarled. "What do you know about that?"

The caller said something, and Weir snapped, "I don't give two tuppenny shits what you're privy to or not privy to. Do you think I pay you to sit in that station scratching your arse all day? Find the fuck out what those two cops have on me, or think they have on me, pronto!"

He slammed the phone down and threw himself into his chair, his mind racing as he considered the myriad possibilities that might have brought the police to his door.

TWENTY-THREE

W hen Tom Allen entered the Serious Crimes Squad Room for the Monday afternoon debriefing, there were already several members of the team there. All had by now heard of the attempt on his life and were sympathetic. Some offered verbal support as he walked to his desk; others shook his hand. Even McCullough readied himself to deliver a friendly backslap, but McNeill saw it coming and caught the descending arm before it could inflict any damage.

"The guy's c-covered in bruises, Sarge," McNeill said. "I don't think he'd appreciate a whack on the b-back right now."

McCullough raised a couple of sheepish arms, palms facing outwards, and said, "Oh, sorry. Good to see you out and about, Allen."

Sheehan came out of his office and sat near Larkin's whiteboard. "All right, everybody. Time to get this debrief under way." He looked towards Allen. "But first, it's good to see Tom Allen actually walking. It could easily have been a very different story."

Tom grinned and said, "Thanks, Chief." He flicked a glance at Stewart's desk. She caught the look and gave him a brief nod. He smiled back at her and settled into his chair.

"Okay," Sheehan said to the room. "Let's get started. Sergeant McCullough, anything new on the cufflink?"

"We've hit every jeweller in the city and in the entire surrounding district but have come up with nada, zilch." He shrugged. "Nobody recognises it as a type, or part, of any kind of a collection."

"What we keep getting, boss," Simon Miller chipped in, "is that the set was probably custom made for someone who wanted this particular design and colour. We've been told that unless we actually come across the jeweller who made them, we'll probably never know who ordered them."

Sheehan sighed. "That's that, then. Stick it back in evidence. Maybe something'll come up later that will help point the search in some other direction." He looked at his notes. "Any luck with the press cutting or the photograph, Sergeant Stewart?"

"Still searching, sir," Stewart said, sounding apologetic. She brandished a copy of an email. "But I have arranged an appointment tomorrow morning with someone at the Registrar's Office at Queen's University. He's going to let me go through a couple of yearbooks for 2001 and 2002. I'm hoping to find a match for at least one of the faces in the photograph."

"You still think the photograph's important?"

She reddened slightly, uneasy at the minor deception. "I believe that the girl, the photograph, and Fitzpatrick are all linked in some way. I would like to try to find out how."

"Good luck with that. It'll be time consuming. Are you going to look at photographs from all the faculties, or are you able to pin your search down to something specific?"

"No way could I go through them all, sir. I was thinking of finding out which faculty Lynda Bell originally enrolled for, work from there, and hope to catch a break."

"Okay. Call some of the others in if you have to start expanding your search."

"Thanks, sir, but I'll see what I can do on my own for a while."
She paused, then added quickly. "Oh, and sir, I contacted the editor
of *The Dungannon Observer*. He's relatively new, only there about
six years and doesn't remember the Lynda Bell case. But he says
he'll go through the files and see if he can find anything for me. I'm
hoping to borrow a car from the motor pool to go to see him
tomorrow."

"That'll be fine. Do you need anyone to go with you, given that
…?"

"Ah, no, sir," she cut in. "I should be all right. No one knows
I'm going. I also hope to go and see the girl's parents. Don't know
if anything will come of it, but if there is any connection between
her and Fitzpatrick, we would need to find it."

"Sounds like a plan," Sheehan said. He turned his gaze to
McNeill. "Geoff, Tom, how did you two get on with the victim's …
em … victims?"

There were a few grins and one or two puzzled expressions.
McNeill nodded to Allen, tacitly asking him to do the talking.

"The first two we went to, John O'Callaghan and Edward Daly,
are pretty much certainly in the clear, sir. They're broken men,
battered into the ground."

"From easy street, loads of m … money, big cars, to life on the
d … dole. Terrible to see, sir. Daly's a shell. His life's ruined." The
sympathy McNeill had felt for the man still lingered.

"He admitted to feeling no sorrow that Fitzpatrick had been
killed," Allen said, "but said he had nothing to do with it. We
believed him. You could see he had barely the energy to talk, never
mind plan and execute a murder."

"What about the Duffner brothers?" Sheehan prompted.

"Mmm." Allen wasn't sure how to present their findings. "If I
wasn't so sure that 'The Bat' has some serious questions to answer,
I would be inclined to take a hard look at that pair."

"The younger b-brother, Jason, likes to scowl and look hostile.
But he's no threat."

"That's true, sir," Allen agreed, "but the older guy, Michael, is a whole different kettle of fish, a really cold fish. He's the guy in charge. Civilised in the way he speaks, but inside I'd say there's a seriously hard nut capable of anything."

"He was nearly k-kinda laughing at us," McNeill said. "He wasn't the slightest bit worried that he h-had no alibi for last Tuesday night."

"Where did he say he was?" Sheehan asked.

"He said they were both at the office for a while," Allen said, "and then watching football at his brother's flat after that. No confirming witnesses. If the two of them are in it together, that alibi isn't worth a ball of blue. And he clearly knew that, too. But he didn't care."

"Right," Sheehan said. "You know what to do."

"Yes, sir," Allen said. "We'll take a deeper look into their background to see if we can find anything."

"Good," Sheehan said. He spread a couple of sheets of notes on the desk in front of him with the middle finger of his left hand, while trying at the same time to find an easier position on the hard chair he was sitting on. "Sergeant Stewart and I had a chat with Mr. Weir this morning." Everybody looked up expectantly. Allen seemed particularly interested. Sheehan raised an eyebrow at Stewart.

"Wasn't much of a chat," Stewart told the group. "He stonewalled us from the minute we walked in the door."

"Hiding something, d'ye think?" Allen asked, sounding hopeful.

"Don't know. He put on this very lah-di-dah air, offering us drinks. But the second we mentioned murder, he clammed up and handed each of us his lawyer's card. Told us to speak to him and practically pushed us out of the room."

"That sounds very guilty to me," Allen said.

"Probably was," Sheehan agreed. "But we know this guy's record. He has so much to be guilty about that he's probably

136

thinking of half a dozen things we might be seeing him about, and maybe none of them to do with Fitzpatrick's murder."

"Wouldn't count him out yet, sir." Allen muttered.

"Stewart and I also visited Mrs. Weir," Sheehan went on. "Regrettably, it seems that we were right to be concerned for her safety. When we told her that Fitzpatrick was dead and that we wanted to question her husband, she turned forty shades of pale and went into near-total panic. She told us straight out that he would kill her if he ever found out about the affair."

There was silence in the room, followed by a buzz of muttered comments, some in black tones directed at Weir, others expressing concern for the wife.

Simon Miller said, "It's tricky, sir. Where's our jurisdiction on this? I mean, we can't arrest the guy, no matter how big a thug he is, just because we imagine he might murder his wife."

"Yes," Stewart said, "but can we just stand by and wait until we are investigating her murder?"

"If we could get the bastard for Fitzpatrick's murder, that would solve the problem," Allen said.

"He's still a suspect," Sheehan replied, "but, tight-assed as he was when Stewart and I interviewed him, I got the impression that he didn't really understand why we were talking to him. In fact, he didn't even ask us who the victim was. Wasn't interested. Just dived into his wallet and gave us his solicitor's card. And, as well as that," he went on quickly as Allen made to protest, "the wife's absolutely certain that if he'd known about the affair, he couldn't have played dumb. His temper would have gotten the better of him."

"Yeah, well, he's one smart cookie," Allen replied, reluctant to let go of Weir as his main suspect. "He has a hell of a motive, and if he was thinking of bumping Fitzpatrick off, or having him bumped off, he might well have realised the importance of biting his tongue and dealing with the wife at some future date."

"Could there be any connection, or maybe some collusion, between Weir and the Duffner brothers?" Connors asked. "Y'know, a common enemy thing."

Sheehan was silent, pondering that one. "No idea, Declan," he said eventually. "Could you and Oliver maybe look into that?"

Sergeant McCoy's red face deepened a couple of degrees closer to puce as he glared at his partner. This was not how he planned to ease into retirement. But apart from giving Connors a view of his very tight lips, he made no comment.

"Aye, we'll poke around," Connors said. "See what we can find."

"Keep it on the down low," Sheehan warned them. "This guy's ultra-sensitive to anything that smells even remotely of snooping into his business." He looked around. "Anybody else?"

Miller said, "Anything useful come from your visit to the mortuary, sir."

"Not really. Caught the new guy, Jones, on his way out to a meeting. Real snappy dresser. Told us that the victim basically choked in his own blood. Said a lot of confusing stuff about the cut to the throat, but in the end warned us that we can't draw any conclusions from it."

There were a few nodding heads as the team absorbed this, but there was no further comment.

"All right," Sheehan said. "We move on now to the attack on Tom Allen." He turned to Sergeant Larkin. "Bill, you have the floor."

Larkin nodded and began consulting some papers he had in his hand. "I got on to forensics and was able to get a fast forward on this, Tom being one of our own. The report came in only a short while ago, but it's pretty thorough. First off, the collision caused a leak in the perp's car, maybe punctured the fuel hose or the injector return hose. Either way, forensics were able to establish from the leak that it was a diesel car." He looked up and raised a finger. "That's the first thing. The second thing is that they were able to get paint scrapings off Tom's car." He looked at the group over the top of the spectacles he was wearing. "You all know that car paints have their own code and that the colours change slightly each year with each new model. That's why you always have to tell dealers the year of manufacture if you want to buy some touch-up."

"Bill," Sheehan said. "Is there any chance we could have the report finished sometime before midnight, please."

Larkin coughed. "Course, Chief. Well, the paint scrapings were navy blue metallic and by checking the codes, forensics can confirm that the paint came from a Mercedes car, this year's model."

"Which model?" Tom asked.

"Just … just let me get round to that." Larkin held up his finger again. "The third thing is the tyre tracks. These were photographed and forensics were able to establish that they were made by a size 19 x 8.5 and that the tyre is definitely 245/35R19."

"What's that all supposed to mean?" McCullough scoffed.

"It means that it is a very expensive tyre and almost certainly belongs to a Mercedes E class saloon, probably an AMG, and, as I said earlier, diesel. Bloody lovely car to be usin' to bash into somebody else."

"So it's a navy Mercedes E class, cdi, AMG," Allen said. "This year's model would cost a bomb. Can't be too many of them around the Belfast area."

"More than you'd think," Bill replied, "although the navy colour does pare the numbers down."

"You've got a l-list already?" McNeill asked.

"Yes. Forensics are as anxious as we are to catch this guy. As soon as they identified the model, they were onto the DVLA to see who in the Belfast area owns a vehicle of that model and colour." He held up the list. "There are six names here." Then he looked knowingly at the team. "One of them we know."

"Not 'The Bat' Weir?" Allen hazarded.

"No, not him. Our esteemed prosecutor, Robert Turner."

Stewart's insides immediately tensed. *No way. That's impossible.* She shot a glance at Tom Allen. He was staring at Larkin, looking as stunned as she felt.

Sheehan said, "What are you saying, Bill? That we should investigate him just because his name is on that list?" He sounded annoyed.

"No, sir. I'm not saying that. In fact, I can positively say the opposite."

"What does that mean?" Sheehan snapped, growing tired of Larkin's dramatics.

"When we checked out the owners of these models, Turner's name was immediately flagged. He had reported his car stolen three days before the incident, sir. If his car was involved in ramming Tom, Turner wasn't driving it."

Stewart expelled a breath she didn't know she had been holding. How crazy would it have been if Robert had to be investigated by the team? And a little voice sounded in her ear. *What? Do you fancy him now? Don't be silly,* another voice answered. *But he is a friend. He doesn't need to be subjected to that kind of hassle.* Then a thought struck her. If it was Robert's car, it would make sense. It was he who prosecuted Kerley and sent him to prison. Two birds with one stone. Cripple Tom and implicate Robert. She risked another glance at Allen and found him staring at her with both eyebrows raised.

"How does one steal a high-tech car like that?" McCullough asked. "It must have had all sorts of theft-proof gear, would it not?"

"Wouldn't be so hard," Allen chipped in. "I was reading about this the other night. Apparently there's a major flaw in the security of some of Britain's most popular executive cars, including BMWs, Audis and Land Rovers, as well as Mercs. Criminals are using easy-to-buy electronic scanners to steal luxury cars. And they can do it in less than sixty seconds without having to make a scratch on them."

"You're not serious," Connors growled. "How the hell do they get their hands on these scanners in the first place?"

"Good point." Allen said. "Car makers are furious at the failure of law-makers to ban the general sale of these devices. They're being sold legitimately. It's bloody ridiculous."

"God, the modern thief is getting seriously sophisticated. You couldn't be up to them," Simon Miller said, sounding disgusted.

"All right, all right," Sheehan said. "Bill, get a couple of uniforms to look at the cars of the other five owners. Probably a waste of time, but do it anyway. Oh, and find out if Mr. Turner's car has been found. We need to take a look at that as well." He turned to the others. "We don't know what's behind this attack, whether it is related to our current investigation or something completely different. But everybody needs to be vigilant from now on. Any one of us could be next, and this time the victim might not be so lucky."

Allen, who had been hugging his ribs to ease the throbbing, looked up at that. "Aye, really lucky, Chief."

"And we need to have Sergeant Stewart's back as well. This stalker might be a nutter, or some pissed off mates of Kerley's from Lisburn, or somebody completely else."

Stewart had her head down at this point, embarrassed, but also … what? Moved? She could not help but again compare this supportive atmosphere with the gut-wrenching tension, the sniggering harassment, the unveiled contempt that had been her daily and dispiriting lot at her last posting. She raised her head to give her new colleagues a tentative smile, glancing from face to face. Feeling close to tears at the nods and smiles of encouragement that she received in return, she bowed her head again and fought for control. The hard shell that had for so long been her instinctive defence mechanism was beginning to crack.

"Do no harm to have the odd patrol pass by her house from time to time, especially in the evenings," Allen suggested, glancing over at the sergeant's lowered head. Stewart seemed focused on the notes she had in front of her. "Visible presence, y'know? Can't hurt."

"Yes, we could do that. Arrange that with uniform branch, Tom."

"Right, Chief."

TWENTY-FOUR

Stewart, wrapped in a large white bathrobe, was towelling her hair as she emerged from the small bathroom. She couldn't help but think again that, as one of only two women constables in the Lisburn branch, she had endured endless harassment, sexist innuendo, and significant levels of contempt. And how she had hated the horrible nickname that the male officers in the station had used in addressing her. It had started off as 'Stewrat' but soon evolved to 'Rat stew'. She shuddered her disgust.

But here in Belfast, under Jim Sheehan's watch, she was treated by the team as … almost as a younger sister to be safeguarded and protected. The contrast was so overwhelming that tears, and not for the first time, started into her eyes. Even this evening, Geoff McNeill, who was to give the injured Tom Allen a lift home, insisted on seeing that she was safely ensconced in her house before going back for Tom.

As she reached for the hairdryer, the phone rang. She lifted it unthinkingly, still wrapped in thoughts about how good her life had become.

"Hello?"

"Have you told anyone?" It was the robotic voice of her mystery informer.

Her pause rendered the caller less than pleased. The electronic voice seemed to acquire some force. "Have you told anyone?"

"No, I haven't," she said firmly, gripping the phone more tightly.

"Have you been to Dungannon yet?"

"No," she replied. "Why do you ask?"

"Take the broken cufflink with you and check out the jewellers there."

"How do you know about …?" She stopped talking when she heard the click of the caller hanging up.

She replaced her own phone, her mind racing. So the cufflink might be relevant after all. But how did the caller know and, indeed, how much more does he know? Were the caller and the killer one and the same? If so, why was he attempting to guide her to a solution to the case? Surely he couldn't possibly be seeking capture? Or was he just someone who was possessed of facts that had enabled him to deduce who the killer is? But again, why not just report the killer? Why use her, or more accurately, why lead her along in little steps? And how did he seem to know so much about her? She shivered involuntarily and shivered again as another thought struck her. Was there any connection between the caller and the shadowy personage who had been following her home? *No. No. That has to be Chambers and Wilson. And using Robert's car, the bastards.* She reached again for the hairdryer. "What was that you were saying about how good your life had become?" she muttered aloud, but at the same time determining not to let herself fall victim to fear. *God, we're going to throw the book at them when we catch them.* She stopped at the thought. *We?* She grinned. *Yes, we. We're part of a team now.*

TWENTY-FIVE

1

S tewart hopped on to the bus that would take her back to the Strandtown station. As she settled herself on her seat, she rubbed her eyes and blinked a few times. It was only noon, but three hours staring at a computer screen takes its toll. The young man in the Registry Office at Queen's University had been pleasant, even if his preferred mode of communication was Geek. Initially, when she asked to see some student records from 2001, she had been regaled with a series of regulations about disclosure of student data. But when she showed him her badge, he remembered, and was able to quote verbatim that "… there are times when the university is under a legal requirement to provide data on request to law enforcement agencies where legally required to do so and where crime detection or prevention can be aided by the release of data."

She was bombarded then by details of student registration via the Registration Wizard, various means of storing and retrieving data, the different levels of data and who has access to it, and that the kind of information she was looking for was termed 'transcripts'. Stewart's patience was wearing thin at this point, and by dint of soft persuasion, a smile or two, and asking pointed questions about where she could carry out her search, she finally found herself ensconced in a corner of the library with one of the university's laptops, and digital access to student records for 2001, not before, however, being subjected to one further lecture on the usefulness of 'cloud' in data retrieval.

The young man had not heard about the Lynda Bell episode, but he had been able to speak on the phone to an older colleague, the Head of Student Registration and Services, who remembered the girl and was able to advise Stewart that she should look initially through the records for students of the Faculty of Arts.

With the photograph she had found on Fitzpatrick's laptop on the table beside her for comparison, she trawled through student record after record. Her chief interest was centred on the photograph of each student which was handily located on the top right-hand corner of each application form. After two relatively fruitless hours, she had not seen any photographs that resembled the faces of the three young men on the laptop photograph. She took a break, searched for the nearest ladies' toilets, and washed her face and eyes in cold water.

Refreshed, she returned to her task, and about half an hour later she came across a photograph of one of the young men, Peter Shaw. There was no doubting that he was one of the youths in the laptop photograph. She noted his name and his home address, hoping to check later with his parents for his current whereabouts.

Another half hour passed, bringing her to the end of this particular series of transcripts without any further hits. She couldn't face another set of transcripts, but figured that the information she now had on one of the three young men would offer her enough material to garner other leads.

2

Although she had never been to Dungannon before, Stewart found it a direct drive via the M1 from Belfast. Direct, perhaps, but not as peaceful as it might have been because of the scratchy windscreen wiper that the insistent October mizzle forced her to use most of the way there. But the distance wasn't interminable. Scarcely an hour after she had left the Strandtown station, where she had barely taken time to grab a sandwich in the canteen and collect the cufflink from evidence storage, she arrived on the outskirts of the town. She knew little about its geography, but she was aware that the town, like many others in the province, had suffered severely during 'the troubles'. Almost fifty people had been killed in and around Dungannon in the conflict, and there had been many bombings there, one of the deadliest of which was a loyalist car bomb attack on the Hillcrest Bar in March 1976. Four Catholic civilians were killed in that explosion. The peace process, however, had made the town safer, but new simmering animosities ensured that the town still had problems.

As she eased her way carefully along the A29 into the town, keeping an eye on her sat nav, Stewart hoped that she could carry out her enquiries without incident. She had heard that in the previous ten years or so, the number of immigrants in Dungannon had increased tenfold, by far and away the largest increase of any town in the North. Most of the new inhabitants had come to the town to work in the local food processing plants. This influx has led to a string of attacks on immigrants in the area, some racially motivated, others involving clashes between rival groups of immigrants. Stewart breathed a silent prayer that she would be in and out, her work done, before any of the local disaffected youth, usually unemployed, decided it was time for another 'demonstration'.

She found her way to *The Observer Newspapers* building, an oddly shaped edifice that looked like a couple of large hangars attached to a private house. But inside were the normal rooms and offices one would expect to find, and a friendly receptionist directed her to the editor's office.

The editor was a courteous man who stepped out from behind his desk to shake her hand in welcome and introduce himself as Gregory Nugent, before directing her to a chair in front of him. He was much younger than she had expected, scarcely forty, but he had the harassed look of someone who is constantly searching for documents and papers and never finding what he wanted. He did, however, have a small sheet on his desk which he handed to the policewoman.

"I spent some time checking the archives," he told her, "but there was very little information about this unfortunate young lady other than what you had already told me. I did find a record of the funeral and the parents' address, but there were no other stories."

He spread his hands in apology. "Sorry about that. I had hoped for something better. Perhaps your best bet is to visit the parents. Obviously they would be of more help to you than I can be."

Stewart stood and shook his hand again. "Thanks anyway, Gregory, and thanks for taking the trouble to do this search."

"Not a problem," he smiled. Harassed he might have been, but he was not immune to the charms of the young policewoman.

"I'll take your advice," Stewart said, "and drive round to the parents' house."

The editor managed to leap out from behind his desk and get to the office door before her, holding it open for her as she left. She smiled at him once more and headed down the stairs towards the exit.

3

The Bell house was one of a number of semi-detached houses in Wellbrook Avenue. It was situated in a pleasant area, with plenty of space and green grass between the road and the row of houses. Stewart knocked on the door and waited. A woman, maybe in her late fifties, answered the knock. Stewart introduced herself and sought for a diplomatic way to explain why she was there. The woman almost immediately exhibited signs of stress, placing her hand on her breast and looking upset.

Stewart said immediately, "Perhaps we should go into the house and sit down."

"Yes, yes," Mrs. Bell said, still looking anxious as she led the way into a sitting room just off the hall. "Forgive me. Would you like a cup of tea? I'll just get my husband."

"Tea will be fine, thank you," Stewart said. "Please take your time."

While Mrs. Bell was making the tea, her husband came into the sitting room and greeted the policewoman. Sixtyish, balding, with a green woollen cardigan stretched somewhat on a substantial paunch, he shook hands and said, as he sat in a chair near Stewart, "I'm Raymond Bell. You wanted to talk about our daughter?" He seemed more mystified than upset.

"Yes, Mr. Bell," Stewart replied. "I'm so sorry to bring the tragedy up again after all these years, but your daughter's name has come up in connection with a case we are working on in Belfast. If you could tell me something about any friends your daughter might have had at university, it might be a great help to us."

Mr. Bell looked even more mystified. "I don't see how ..."

"It's just that we discovered a newspaper article referring to Lynda's death on someone's laptop. We are just simply trying to establish connections." She smiled, hoping she looked disarming. "You know what police work is like. Dozens and dozens of tiny avenues have to be explored, many of them leading nowhere, but they can't be ignored. I'm afraid it is my job to go down this one." Seeing the sadness that suddenly filled the man's face, she added hastily, "And I deeply regret having to disturb you like this."

At that point, Mrs. Bell came into the room with a small tray bearing three cups of tea and a plate of biscuits. Raymond got up and pulled a mahogany occasional table into the centre of the room where all three could have access to it. Mrs. Bell handed Stewart a cup of tea and sat down on the sofa.

Her husband helped himself to a cup and a biscuit and sitting back, said to his wife, "The detective wants to know about Lynda's friends when she was at university. Do you remember anything about them?"

The woman shook her head, looking vague. "It was a long time ago," she said. "And Lynda never really said much about them anyway."

"She did talk about one girl," Raymond said, clearly trying to remember. "Someone she knocked around with ... oh, what was her name?"

"Oh, yes," his wife said. "It was … em … Geraldine? No, not that. It was … oh, do you remember the girl who introduced herself to us at the funeral?"

Raymond's face was blank, but suddenly his expression cleared. "Oh, yes. Lovely girl. Couldn't stop crying."

"That's the one. What was her name?"

Raymond was lost in thought for a moment. Then he said, "I don't remember her surname, but I'm pretty sure her first name was Jacqueline."

"That's right," Mrs. Bell agreed positively. "That's what it was." She looked at Stewart regretfully. "I'm afraid I don't remember her surname either."

"Don't worry," Stewart said. "The first name is a great help." She paused and said, "I don't suppose you would know if Lynda had a boyfriend."

The couple looked at each other, nodding. "Oh, she had. She had," Mrs. Bell said, sounding almost exasperated. "But Lynda was such a quiet one. Would never talk to us about stuff like that."

"Can you tell me anything about him?"

"Very little, I'm afraid. We wouldn't have known about him at all if it had not been for …" She smiled sadly at the memory, and tears came to her eyes.

Stewart looked questioningly at Raymond.

"She had come home for a weekend break," he explained, "and she was going back to college. She seemed happy and excited about going back. Her mother here was telling her to wrap up well and keep warm." He looked at his wife. "I think you said something about there being all sorts of viruses and germs about."

Mrs. Bell nodded agreement. "Yes, and she sorta laughed and said that it wouldn't matter if she caught anything, that she had her own personal doctor. I asked her what she meant, and she said that he wasn't really a doctor but a medical student. Then she laughed and went out. I never heard any more about him."

149

Stewart wrote something in her notebook, then said, keeping her tone neutral, "Do the names Peter Shaw or James Fitzpatrick mean anything to you?"

Both shook their heads. Raymond suddenly seemed less certain. "Did I see that name Fitzpatrick in the paper about something recently?" he said.

Stewart skirted the question. "I was just asking in connection with your daughter's time at college. No need to concern yourselves about it." Then she looked earnestly at both parents. "I am so sorry to have to ask this, but do you know what caused Lynda's depression?"

Both shook their heads, looking distressed. Raymond said, with a hint of lingering anger, "Lynda always kept herself to herself even about normal things. Something like this, eating away at her, she shoulda told us or told somebody. But she never did. She just let it eat away at her, staying up there in her room, never coming out, wouldn't eat, losing weight, no interest in anything ..." His face relived the toll of those days. He swallowed and went to a dresser at the far wall of the room. He returned with a framed photograph and handed it to Stewart. "That's the way she used to be." His voice was a mixture of sadness and pride. He glanced a little more closely at Stewart. "You know, she was not unlike yourself, the same shape of face, blond hair ..."

Stewart studied the photograph. The guileless, innocent face of a nineteen year old student looked back at her. Stewart could see why Raymond mentioned a similarity in their looks. To her eyes the resemblance was faint, but it was there, although the hairstyle of twelve years ago was very different from her own shortish bob.

Stewart looked again into the happy, optimistic eyes, and her stomach clenched. *First rule: don't get emotionally involved.* But what had happened to this poor girl was beyond endurance. *How the poor parents must have suffered.* Struggling to keep the tears from her eyes, she said, "She was beautiful." Then, on impulse, she added. "I don't suppose you have a photograph of her that I could borrow for a while?"

150

Mrs. Bell said, "Yes, there are plenty in the album. I'll get you one." She left the room. Raymond nodded, sniffed, and took the photograph from her to put it back on its shelf. By the time Mrs. Bell returned with a coloured photograph of Lynda, which she handed to the young detective, both parents were showing signs of considerable distress. Stewart, although wanting to press for more information, decided it would be too cruel to push any further. "I'm so sorry to have brought all this up again, but please believe me, I had no choice." Then by way of distraction, she reached into her handbag and took out the evidence bag. She showed them the cufflink. "Do either of you recognise this?"

Both looked mystified. "No, we've never seen it," Mrs. Bell said.

Raymond said, "There's a couple of good jewellers in town who might be able to help you with that."

Stewart opened her notebook.

Raymond said, "You could try McCall's in Irish Street or …"

"And there's McQueen's in Scotch Street," his wife added. "They're both very well established."

Stewart noted the names and rose from her seat. "Thank you so much. You have been very helpful. And I really am sorry to have brought back such sad memories."

Raymond rose, too, leading her to the door. "I wouldn't worry too much about that," he said kindly. "The memories are never very far away."

"Goodbye, Mrs. Bell," Stewart said from the door," and thanks for the tea." She wasn't sure if the woman heard her. She was staring out through the window with a lost look on her face. "Bye, Mr. Bell," she said to Raymond, shaking hands with him at the front door. "If anything comes from my enquiries that I think you should know, I'll be sure to come and tell you."

He had tears in his eyes. "I would really appreciate that," he said. "We know something happened to her at college, but she would never talk about it. It would be nice to have some closure around it."

"I hope I'll be able to find out something for you. Thanks again."

Stewart's lips were tightly pressed as she walked back to her car. Whatever mild empathy she had earlier felt for the unknown girl in the newspaper clipping was now a raging vortex. She pitied the parents. She grieved for the girl, now a real person and not just a name. She raged at whatever circumstances had led to so tragic a disintegration. *No way was she going to leave this situation unresolved.* She would find the perpetrators of whatever evil act had broken Lynda's spirit, and she would bring them to justice. Or had justice already been inflicted upon one of them? Again she wondered what might be the connection between James Fitzpatrick and Lynda. *Nothing beneficial,* she wagered, given what they have already learned about the banker. Her mind played with the word. Banker? Wanker. *How much more apt,* she thought grimly.

4

Scotch Street is built on a steep incline. Stewart noted as she walked up the hill that the street, like many streets in Northern Ireland during what politicians tended to refer to as the 'economic downturn', had its share of thriving shops neighbour to other premises that were boarded up with For Sale or To Let signs on them. McQueen's had a small frontage but looked prosperous. Stewart paused a moment to regain normal breathing before entering the shop. A young, well-dressed lady at the counter, responding to Stewart's polite request, went to find the manager.

She returned quickly with a formally dressed, silver-haired man in tow. He smiled tentatively, rubbing his hands in front of him. "Good afternoon, officer. How can I help you?"

Stewart glanced at a customer who had just entered the shop. "Is there somewhere we could speak privately?"

"Of course. Come into my office."

He led her to a room at the back of the shop, part office, part workshop. At one end there was a long table with various bits and pieces of watches and jewellery, obviously waiting for repair. He offered her a chair near another table which served as a desk. Sitting down, he said, clearly a little uneasy at the presence of police on his premises. "So what seems to be the problem, officer?"

"Nothing to worry you, sir," she assured him. "I'm just trying to trace a piece of jewellery." She took the plastic evidence bag from her handbag and set it on the table. The manager relaxed visibly. He lifted the bag. "Do you mind if I take this out for a closer look?"

"Please," Stewart said.

Somewhat oddly, he removed his rimless glasses and set them on the table while he studied the cufflink. He noticed the young detective's quizzical look. "I'm short sighted," he smiled. "When I have to look closely at something, I can see it much better without my glasses."

He studied the cufflink for a few minutes, his eyebrows down.

"You recognise it, sir?"

"I do. This is my work. But it was some years ago. I'm trying to remember." He studied the object again. "I think I made these for a young woman. It was definitely some time ago."

"Twelve years?"

He looked up. "Yes, could be as far back as that." His brows were down again then awareness dawned. "Oh, dear. I remember now. I made this as part of a pair for a young lady who wanted them as a present for her boyfriend. Poor girl. She … uh … she died shortly after that. She lived here in Dungannon. Lynda Bell. I know her parents. Ah, dear. That was a sad time."

"Yes, I have been speaking to her parents about it," Stewart said. "I don't suppose you remember the name of the boyfriend?"

"Nnno. I don't believe she told me his name." For a moment something seemed to click. Stewart almost leaned forward, anxious to hear what he had remembered. "But I remember that she mentioned that he liked to dress well. She said there was a particular suit he sometimes wore that she wanted this special colour of cufflinks for."

"Would you know if the boyfriend was local?"

The jeweller stared through her for a few seconds, straining his memory banks. "I ... don't think so. I think she met him at university." He shook his head sadly. "Ah, dear. That was a really tragic case. She was a lovely girl." He put the cufflink back into the evidence bag and handed it back to Stewart. "I'm sorry I couldn't have been of more help."

"No. It's fine. You've helped a lot. Every little piece of information is useful." She stood up and offered him her hand. "Thank you very much. I'll see myself out."

5

Tired though she was, Stewart rushed back to Queen's University. The young geek smiled his pleasure at her reappearance and was happy to listen as she explained what she needed. Thankfully, this time she was not going to have to trawl through the transcripts. In fact, she was not going to have to do anything. He, instead, would employ his considerable technical expertise to access the names and addresses she wanted.

She listened, with what she hoped was a rapt expression, as he talked non-stop gibberish while his fingers flew over his computer's keyboard. Her brain was turning to soft mush by the time the young man, smiling broadly, handed her a printout of the results of the search he had just conducted. Lassitude had almost overcome her, but she satisfied herself that a haul of the names and home addresses of thirteen Jacquelines made the mental fatigue a small price to pay. She thanked the young man profusely for his kindness, earning another short lecture, a massive beam, and a plea that she would come back again soon.

TWENTY-SIX

'The Bat' Weir glanced at the screen on his mobile phone. He recognised the caller's name. "Well?" he said brusquely.

"The big flap is about the murder of James Fitzpatrick. He's a banker."

"I know who he is. Why are they looking at me?"

The caller hesitated, fearing an eruption. "Something about your wife and Fitzpatrick …"

"How the hell do they know about that?"

"It's what they do. Ferret stuff out."

Weir was silent for a minute, his brain tumbling. "Are they looking at anybody else?"

"Yeah. Two brothers on the Falls Road. The Duffners."

"I know them. Fitzpatrick railroaded them into bankruptcy." His brain started whirring again. More to himself than to his caller, he muttered, "Wonder if there's some way of deflecting the filth away from me and towards them?"

"Can't help you there."

"You can, and you will," Weir snapped. "That's what you get paid for."

"But what do you expect me to do?"

"A word in somebody's ear, a false trail."

"I'll need help if the lead is to be convincing."

Weir pondered that. Then he said, "Just put one of them at the scene at the time of the murder, uh, the bigger one, he's a tough nut. He'll make a good suspect."

"How am I going to do that?"

"Get a witness who saw him there, y'fuckin' eejit. Somebody who lives in the area that we have somethin' on. And make sure he's reliable … respectable. Somebody the cops'll believe."

"But what if nobody saw him?"

"For crying out loud, y'stupid gabshite."

"Oh, right," the caller replied, finally understanding "You want me to …?" But he was speaking into the ether. Weir had already terminated the call.

TWENTY-SEVEN

It was after five o'clock in the evening. It had been a long day, and Stewart was close to exhaustion, but she had come back to the Serious Crimes Room to organise her notes and to prepare some items for the whiteboard. As she entered the room she noticed Tom Allen at his desk, talking on the phone and taking notes. She also saw, with some surprise, Robert Turner standing at the whiteboard with the chief. Turner saw her enter, gave her a wide smile, and waved her over to the board.

Shrugging out of her raincoat and dropping her bag on her desk, she went over to the two men. Sheehan gave her a polite nod.

"The chief inspector's been bringing me up to speed," Turner said cheerfully, "but I understand that you have been carrying out some important investigative follow-up today?"

Stewart glanced at Sheehan who, with a slight inclination of his head, indicated that she should go ahead and make her report. "I'll just get my notebook," she said, leaving the two men waiting while she went back to her desk to retrieve her bag. By this point Tom Allen had hung up his phone and was an attentive listener. As she searched in her bag, Stewart felt the need to break the silence. "Any word on your car yet?" she asked.

Turner shook his head. "Nothing yet. Could be on the continent by this time, for all I know. But at least the insurance company has given me a courtesy car, so I am still able to get about."

"Anything useful come from your research?" Sheehan prompted.

"I think so, sir, although I haven't had time to process it all." She hesitated. "If I could just put it in perspective for Mr. Turner?"

"Robert, Denise. Robert."

She gave him a quick smile and said, "We seem to have three fairly strong lines of enquiry in this case. Detective Allen," she gestured at Tom, "is strongly of the opinion that Ronnie Weir is our main suspect. But he is also looking at two brothers who have a strong motive and no alibi. They are viable suspects as well. I am not in a position to eliminate either of those lines, but I am following a series of leads that are building up a picture for me and starting to pull some of the evidence we have into some sort of sense."

She had both men's interest now.

"Sense?" Sheehan said.

"Well, sir, I'd be the first to admit it is all highly speculative but …"

"Maybe you could be a little more specific, and we might be able to work with you on this," Sheehan said. He hated abstractions, preferring facts that he could twist and shape.

"Yessir. You know that I was trying to find some link between the newspaper clipping about Lynda Bell and the photograph of the three young men found on Fitzpatrick's laptop. I spent three hours at Queen's this morning searching through student transcripts from 2001. We know that Fitzpatrick was one of the young men in the photograph. I was able to identify a second one. His name is Peter Shaw. I haven't had time to follow up on him yet because, as I told you, sir, I had to go to Dungannon to see the girl's parents."

"You seem to be straying a bit from the main investigation," Turner said. "Why would you chase after this girl's story?"

"Well, I can't help but feel, given that Fitzpatrick kept the photo and the cutting on his laptop all this time, they have to be of some significance." She pinned a copy of Shaw's transcript on the board.

"Maybe so," Turner said, ever the inquisitor, "but even if there is a connection between them, what would that have to do with the murder?"

Stewart reached into her bag again and posted the coloured glossy of Lynda Bell. Both men stared at the photograph.

"Is that her?" Sheehan asked.

"Yessir."

"Beautiful girl. Have you found out what happened to her?"

Stewart tried to clarify events in her mind before speaking. Then she said, "Hers is a tragic story, sir, but many of the details are missing. Something happened to her at university, but no one knows what it was. The girl simply dropped out, went home. Basically she locked herself in her room, went into a deep depression, probably anorexia as well, and finally committed suicide."

"Whoa!" Turner breathed, staring at the photograph. "What a torrid end for such a lovely creature." He turned to Stewart. "But I still don't see what the connection is between her," he pointed to the photograph of Fitzpatrick and his two friends, "and these three young men. Or, even if there was a connection, how would it relate to the murder of Fitzpatrick?"

Stewart looked at her boss whose expression seemed to say that he was with Turner on this one. "Well, this is where the speculation comes in. I know it's off the wall, but please bear with me. Supposing that these three boys in the photograph had something to do with what caused Lynda to drop out ..." She paused and, reaching again into her bag, took out the evidence bag with the cufflink in it and pinned that on the board.

Sheehan's eyebrows went up. "What are you doing with that?"

"Just a spur of the moment notion I had, sir. Thought I'd take it to Dungannon with me to show it to the parents."

"Did they recognise it?" Sheehan was seriously interested now.

"No, but they sent me to a jeweller who did." Stewart dropped this bombshell in a quiet voice, knowing no dramatics were needed.

"Oh, ho!" Sheehan grinned. "That's going to put McCullough's nose right out of joint. So, what's the story with the cufflink?"

By this time Tom Allen had joined the group and was a fascinated, if silent, listener.

"Lynda ordered the pair of cufflinks as a present for a boyfriend she had at the time. Unfortunately, she never spoke to her parents about him, so I have no details on him. She had a friend called Jacqueline who might be able to help, but she won't be easy to find. I went back to Queen's as soon as I returned from Dungannon and have got thirteen possibles but God knows where they are now after twelve or so years."

"So what exactly is your theory, Sergeant?" Allen asked.

Turner nodded. "I was about to ask the same thing."

"Well, like I say, it's a bit off the wall at this point. I've no evidence as such. But suppose these three young men did something to cause Lynda's disintegration. Mad guess, maybe some form of sexual molestation. And the boyfriend, after twelve years of heartbreak, has snapped and is now out for revenge ..." She let that hang in the air.

Three pairs of eyes stared at her.

Sheehan nodded, measured in his response. "It's plausible. But why would he wait twelve years to start seeking revenge?" he asked, and added with a slight grin, "Or does he think revenge is a dish best served cold?"

Tense though she was feeling, Stewart could not but return his smile. "The trouble with speculation, sir, or, if you like, building a fancy story around a few facts, is that there will be dozens of unanswered questions. That's one of them, sir."

"I suppose I'll get the same response if I ask why the watch was stopped at eleven-o-five?"

"It's serious guesswork now, sir. Maybe what happened to Lynda happened at eleven oh five, and the killer wants the victims to remember the hurt in the worst possible way."

Sheehan smiled widely. "You are not without imagination, Sergeant." His smile faded. "But I have to admit, what you're saying is strangely logical."

"Just an off-the-cuff answer, sir. It's all I can think of."

"Off-the-cuff ?" Sheehan said, with raised eyebrows. He let it go when there was no response. "Did you get anything at all on the boyfriend?"

"Very little, sir. According to Lynda's mother, he was a medical student. The jeweller also told me that the boyfriend was someone who liked to wear nice suits, hence the cufflinks. They were a special order for a particular suit the boyfriend wore. Other than that, I have nothing."

Sheehan's brain was now buzzing. "Did he lose the cufflink at the crime scene, do you think, or did he leave it there deliberately?"

Stewart half-chuckled. "I don't have a crystal ball, sir. But if we assume the boyfriend is the murderer, might he have left the cufflink there as some sort of symbol, maybe a memento to Lynda's memory, or maybe a reminder of what Fitzpatrick had done?"

"Taking a risk it might be traced, isn't he?" Sheehan said.

"Yes, but maybe he thought it would never be traced back to him. All we have now is guesswork. Neither the jeweller nor the parents know anything about him, and even if we ever found him, he could deny all knowledge of the cufflinks. There's nothing to link him to them."

Tom grinned. "Nice pun, Sergeant." He ignored her mystified look and went on, "You did great work today, but are you not building this fairly elaborate story around the fact that a photo and a newspaper cutting happened to be on the same computer? Bit of a stretch, isn't it?"

"I agree absolutely." Stewart was not offended by this. She had already been over this ground several times on her drive back to the station. "We need more facts, more connections. I need to find Peter Shaw and this Jacqueline girl. I need to find the third man in the photograph. We need to know what, if anything, they can tell us. And, of course, they may know nothing, which means that the whole house of cards will come tumbling down around me. I'll start hunting for them tomorrow."

Turner was still grinning broadly. "My money's on you, Denise." Then he inclined his head to one side. "And don't forget our celebration dinner when you've put this criminal behind bars."

Stewart blushed. "The team'll do that, Robert." Edging back towards her desk, she went on, "I need to organise my notes for the next debrief before I go home."

Sheehan stood aside to let her pass. "Good work, Sergeant. Right or wrong, you've certainly given us something to think about."

"Thank you, sir."

"Nice work, Denise," Turner said after her. "Look forward to hearing how you get on with the next part of your investigation." He turned to Sheehan, and they went into his office, conversing about these new revelations.

Tom went to his own desk and tidied a few papers into one of the drawers. He went over to Stewart and said, "Need me to walk you home, Sergeant? It's dark now and the stalker or stalkers might still be hanging about."

Her mind filled with the events of the day, Stewart had given no thought to the menacing presence that had been pursuing her. "God, Tom, I'd forgotten about that. Yes, please. I'd appreciate the company. That avenue is pretty isolated. Just give me a minute to tidy up here."

TWENTY-EIGHT

T he rain had stopped but a sharp wind was gusting when Stewart and Allen emerged from the station gate. Although it was more or less dark, Stewart could not refrain from checking the street right and left. She saw nothing untoward, however. Both pulled up the collars of their raincoats and, hands in pockets, turned left. Stewart set a brisk pace, as much to combat the cold as to get home quickly.

Allen winced as he struggled to keep up. "Easy there, Sergeant," he grunted. "You've got the walkin' wounded with you here."

"Oh, sorry," Stewart said, slowing down. "Are you still in pain?"

"Nah! Just a bit stiff."

Stewart grinned at him. "How are you going to manage if somebody attacks us?"

"Well, I'm hoping my size will be a deterrent." He walked backwards for a moment, checking the street behind them. No one was following them. He turned back to her with a grin. "And anyway, you're here."

"Oh! Does that mean I have to walk you back to the station after you've walked me to my house?"

"Oh, God," he chuckled. "We could be goin' back and forward all night." He picked up the pace a bit. "I'm starting to loosen up now. Come on, let's get you home."

They walked in companionable silence for a couple of minutes. Then Allen said, "Do you really believe we're looking for a vengeful boyfriend in the Fitzpatrick killing?"

"I've no proof, but when the parents showed me Lynda's photograph this afternoon, I found myself wanting to tear the head off whoever caused her all that suffering. And it struck me that if I felt like that, what must her boyfriend have felt like."

"Yeah, I see what you mean. All a bit tenuous, though."

"I know. There's hardly a single fact in the story. Just my imagination running riot. I wish now that I had taken time to think things through before spouting that all off in front of Turner and the chief."

"I think he fancies you."

"Who? The chief?"

"Nooo! Turner."

"Don't be silly," she said, but she said it without much conviction. Every time she was in his company, he was all teeth and compliments. "And even if he does," she added, "I don't fancy him."

"You kiddin'? Handsome guy like that? Loads of money, famous." He gave her a sideways look. "And connected. That on its own should be worth something to an ambitious young detective."

"You mean female detective, don't you?" she snapped, slightly irritated. *Sexism is so ingrained, even in the nicest of men.*

Tom was caught slightly on the hop. He'd forgotten about her defensive shell. He stopped, caught her arm, and turned her towards him. "I did not mean that at all. Don't get me confused with those other guys." He released her arm and started walking, saying over his shoulder as she caught up to him, "To be honest, I'd try for a wee relationship with Turner myself if I thought he'd give me a leg up."

She raised her eyes skywards and shook her head in exasperation. But the moment had passed. She knew she'd been unfair to him. Trying for light-hearted, she asked, "Do your friends know?"

"Huh? Know what?"

She waggled her eyebrows at him. "That you're … uh … you know …?"

"Hey! Leave it out. I was only kidding."

"Hmmm! I think I'm going to have to keep an eye on you." They had arrived at her gate. "Well, this is me. Thank you for seeing me home."

Tom clicked his heels and bowed slightly. "Always a pleasure, ma'am."

Engrossed in their banter, neither noticed the car, all lights off, which had eased silently into the corner of North Road some fifty yards beyond the pair. The driver was peering into the darkness, focused on the two young detectives. Through their narrow slits, his eyes gleamed hatred.

As Tom turned to leave, Stewart hesitated, unsure of what courtesy might demand at this point. On impulse, she said, "Would you like a cup of coffee?"

His face was unreadable but Tom stared at her for a few seconds before saying neutrally, "That would have been nice, but Geoff's calling for me at the station. He's probably there now."

"Okay! Some other time, perhaps."

"Definitely. Goodnight, Sergeant.

"Goodnight, Tom."

TWENTY-NINE

Sheehan was stretched out in an armchair in front of the television. He was leaning awkwardly to one side, but he seemed focused on the screen. Margaret knew him better than that.

"Your hip acting up again?"

"A bit, aye. I'll rub something on it later."

"Do you want me to switch the television off?"

"What?"

"You've been staring at that screen for the last fifteen minutes, but you have no idea what's going on there, have you?"

He grinned. "Just work. Lot to think about."

She turned off the television and sat back in her chair. "So what's going on?"

"Stewart arrived in this evening with some interesting findings. Took her only one afternoon to find the jeweller who made the cufflink. McCullough and Miller have been all over the shop with it for several days and got nowhere."

Margaret smiled. "Well, you know how it is, Jim. If you need anything done right, give it to a woman."

"Aye right! But she's bright. I'll give you that. She believes Fitzpatrick's killer is the vengeful boyfriend of the young woman in the clipping, Lynda Bell."

"Wow! How did she arrive at that? Does that mean that Weir's off the hook?"

He ran through Stewart's theory and said, "She has hardly a fact to work on, but her conclusions make a kind of insane sense. I mean, her story brings the cufflink, the clipping, the photograph from Fitzpatrick's laptop, the girl's suicide, everything, into a coherent whole. Turner's all over it."

"He was there?"

"Yes. He's taking a great interest in this case. He's looking forward to prosecuting the killer when we find him."

"You're sure it's the case he's interested in?"

He looked at her. "Yeah, why?"

She shrugged. "It seems to me that every time you mention his name, Sergeant Stewart's in the picture, too."

He sat back in the armchair and folded his arms, a quizzical expression on his face as he stared at her. "You are sharp, my wife. I will have to be careful if I ever find the need to hide anything from you."

She raised her eyebrows. "Oh? And what would you need to hide from me?"

"Nothing, darling. Absolutely nothing. I'm an open book."

She smiled. "I know. So, what about Turner and Stewart?"

"It's strange that you should latch on to that. Now that you mention it, he's all charm and smiles when she's around, full of compliments. And he's always praising her to me, too, as if he was pushing at me to be aware of how clever she is. She's only just been promoted, but he jokingly said something the other day about her being on a fast track. I don't know what to make of that."

"How is she around him?"

"Embarrassed most of the time, I think. He's a seriously confident guy, but he's a bit over the top. Seems to feel he can say what he likes. She tends to duck out when he starts. Goes back to her desk, that sort of thing."

"Ah! So there might still be a wee chance for Tom Allen?"

He rose from his chair. "Will you gimme a break from all this office romance stuff? I'm trying to work on a case here." He held out a hand. "C'mon. Let's go to bed."

She, too, rose and took his hand. "Best offer I've had all day."

THIRTY

Ronnie Weir drove his Bentley up the long drive to the front door of his red bricked mansion. Ignoring the garage and leaving the car parked on the wide expanse in front of the house, he let himself in through the elaborately wrought front door. Once inside, he found his wife watching television in their home cinema.

She looked up as he entered. "Hi, Ronnie," she smiled.

He looked at her somewhat strangely and gestured to the television. "Do you like this?" he asked.

Puzzled, she asked, "This programme?"

"No. This fifty-six inch, widescreen, with all the latest in Dolby surround sound."

She wasn't sure why he was asking her this, but she said, "Yeah, it's great."

He nodded, the same strange expression on his face. "Okay! Come with me now."

He led her to their magnificent lounge, a symphony in white—two expensive white leather sofas and matching armchairs, heavy white pile carpet, off-white brocade drapes on the windows, designed in complicated folds, a magnificent mirror with a heavy gold frame on the wall above an ornate white marble fireplace. They had had the room redesigned over two years ago, yet he said to her now, "Well, what do you think?"

Growing increasingly uneasy but striving not to show it, she said, "I think it's gorgeous."

"Uh huh! Only the very few are fortunate enough to live in this kind of luxury."

She strove for some enthusiasm. "Yeah, I'm really lucky, Ronnie. I love our beautiful home."

He just looked at her, the same strange stare, and said again, "Follow me now."

He led her down along the blue and gold carpeted hallway, down past the elaborate staircase that led to the upper floor, and into the kitchen. Here again were all the signs of opulence. A dark brown ceiling, inlaid with several small, strategically placed, halogen lights, looked down on a kitchen straight out of *House and Home*. Cleverly designed cupboards, shining wall tiles, mostly in different shades of oyster shell, Italian tiles on the floor, all exuded wealth. Weir waved an arm sideways, as if showing the room to a visitor. "Most women would kill for a kitchen like this."

The game, whatever it was, was making Mrs. Weir distinctly nervous. Not sure what was expected from her, she said, "Yes, it's all beautiful, Ronnie. The whole house. I love it."

He came close to her, his lips pursed, shaking his head slowly from side to side. "And yet, it's not enough for you."

"Wh ...what?"

His arm lashed out and the loud smack to her face was as shocking in its suddenness as it was in its brutality. Her head snapped back, tears springing to her eyes, her cheek already reddening from the force of the blow.

"Ronnie ..."

"Don't Ronnie me, you bitch." He buried his right fist in her abdomen, and when she involuntarily bent double from the force of the blow, he whacked his knee into her face and slammed his other fist into the side of her head, knocking her back against the kitchen wall. She bounced sideways, blood flowing profusely from her nose. She had now turned her back to her husband, gasping for breath and clinging to the wall for support.

"It just wasn't e-fucking-nough for you, was it?" he gritted, breathing heavily now.

He hammered two further vicious blows into her back, and she began to slide to the floor in agonising pain. He seized her arm roughly, meaning to drag her towards him, but because her body was falling awkwardly away from him, and he had seized her with such vehemence, a bone in her arm snapped with a loud crack.

"Fuckin' bitch," he snarled. "You did that on purpose."

Mewling piteously, she tried to crawl away from him, but he seized her by the hair and, pulling her head back, delivered a murderous blow to the side of her face. Her head smashed against the wall, leaving an immediate splash of blood on the tiles and spatter on the floor. Weir stepped back, wanting no trace of blood on his shoes or his clothes but, carefully selecting a dry spot, he continued to kick his now unconscious wife in a paroxysm of fury as she lay defenceless on the floor.

All veneer of sophistication fell away as his accent and language reverted to his days as a brutal UDA enforcer. "Any fuckin' nosy cops pokin' around, you tell them that it was a couple of thieves what broke into the house and done this to you, you filthy slag." Out of breath, he stepped away from the prone body of his wife on the kitchen floor and spat, "If you need a bloody ambulance, phone for it yourself."

Straightening his suit jacket and tie, he left the kitchen and went back out to his car.

Two policemen, parked some forty yards away, watched him leave. One took out a notebook and noted the date and time of departure, *Tuesday, 21st October, ten twenty pm.* The one in the driver's seat said, "He didn't stay long."

"No, but at least she's still in there," his companion replied. "So we stay." He sighed. "Another long bloody night by the looks of it." And adjusting his seat backwards, he began to stretch out.

"Hey! Don't you be going to sleep."

"Just making myself comfortable."

Conversation then became desultory, interspersed with long silences. Sometime over an hour later, headlights swept the street, and Weir's Bentley returned, idling in front of the black, electric gates as they slowly opened. Although the arched gates were tall and the pillars to which they were attached were close to eight feet high, the wall leading from them on either side was barely five foot in height. Thus the watching officers were able to keep sight of the car as it drove up the drive, past the many shrubs and small bushes that bordered the immaculate lawns. The officer in the passenger seat again noted the time. *Eleven thirty-five.* Putting his notebook away, he said, bored, "I'd say that's the end of the excitement for the night."

His companion was nodding acquiescence when they heard the sound of a siren in the distance. He cocked his head, listening. "More like an ambulance than one of ours," he guessed.

Even as he spoke, the electric gates to the Weir residence began to open again, and an ambulance came barrelling up the street towards the house. Both policemen sat bolt upright, wide awake now.

"What the f…?" the driver said.

The ambulance turned into the Weir gate and hurtled up the drive. Two paramedics jumped from the cabin, ran to the back of the ambulance, and pulled out a wheeled stretcher and a rug.

By this time, Weir was standing at the open front door. "This way," he was shouting urgently. "Down to the kitchen." The paramedics chased after him, and the watching policemen saw them return a few moments later carrying a supine figure on the stretcher.

"What the hell do you think's happened?" the policeman in the passenger seat asked, neck craning as the figure was loaded into the ambulance.

"Could she have fallen or had a heart attack or something?"

"Aye! Or maybe the bastard's beaten the shit out of her."

The driver stared through the windscreen as the ambulance began turning to leave the drive. "What the bloody hell are we supposed to do now?" he asked, tense with shock.

"There's nothing we can do. Maybe follow the ambulance. But we can't break our cover," his companion answered, anxiety dripping from the words. "We'll just have to report it in."

They hunkered down in their seats as the ambulance sped past them, anxious not to be seen in the wash of the vehicle's lights.

THIRTY-ONE

Stewart was scarcely an hour in bed when the phone rang. Groggy, but still victim to unease at the late call, she lifted the receiver. "Hello?"

"CDI Sheehan here, Sergeant. Just got a report that Mrs. Weir has been admitted to the Royal Victoria A and E Department. Apparently she's been badly beaten. I'm going over there now to see what I can find out. Want to come along?"

"Definitely, sir."

"I'll pick you up in ten minutes."

Stewart was ready and waiting when Sheehan arrived. She climbed quickly into the passenger seat, and they sped off.

"What happened?" she asked immediately.

"I don't know much more than I've already told you. The two policemen assigned to watch the Weir house saw someone being carted off in an ambulance and reported it in. I just got the message a few minutes before I phoned you. When I checked with A and E, all I was told was that a lady had arrived in, very severely beaten."

"Do the officers know anything else?"

"Just Weir's movements, which were a bit odd. He got home about half nine and left the house again about a quarter past ten. He

174

came home again about half-eleven, and about seven or eight minutes later the ambulance came for Mrs. Weir."

Stewart reflected on the timings. After a moment, she asked, "Could he have beaten her up during those seven or eight minutes?"

"No, that was how long the ambulance took to arrive. He'd have had to phone them as soon as he got into the house. Whatever happened to her, happened before he got home at half eleven."

"No, I mean, could he have deliberately called the ambulance and then beat his wife while he was waiting for it to arrive knowing that she'd need it by the time he was finished with her?"

Sheehan looked at her. Something tugged at his mind. He didn't know what it was. He recognised the feeling. It was one of those moments, moments he had experienced in the past, when his subconscious would somehow tell him that he was possessed of significant information that he had not yet processed. Something important. He was convinced it had been triggered by what Stewart had just said, but he was sure it had nothing to do with the ambulance. He struggled to grasp it, but it was just fog. He turned his face to Stewart, brow furrowed. "What did you say?"

Stewart noted his odd expression and repeated tentatively, "I just wondered if maybe he had called the ambulance first and then beat up his wife while he was waiting for it."

Again that frisson of … something. He shook his head. *Whatever it was, he wasn't going to figure it out now.* They had reached the Royal Victoria A and E Department. He parked at the end of an ambulance bay, pulling a Police at Work sticker from under the seat and placing it on the dash as he got out of the car.

"We'll hear what the paramedics have to say before we start speculating," he said.

They walked into the crowded reception area, showed their badges to the nurse behind the desk, and asked to speak to whoever was in charge. A couple of minutes later a harassed lady doctor, wearing a sweater and jeans but with a stethoscope hanging around her neck, met them in the waiting room and invited them into an examination room at the other side of the door.

"Good evening, officers. I have very little time as you will doubtless have deduced. How can I help you?"

"A Mrs. Ronnie Weir has just been admitted ..." Sheehan began.

Her face assumed a mixture of disgust and disbelief as the detective was speaking. "God, yes," she said. "We've been trying to make her stable."

"Any chance we could speak to her for a few seconds?"

The doctor's head was shaking almost before Sheehan had spoken. "Absolutely no way. She's heavily sedated, severely concussed, and will be unconscious for at least the rest of the day."

"Do you know what happened?"

The doctor shrugged slightly. "The two paramedics who brought her in said that the husband told them he had been out of the house for an hour or so and found her like that when he got home. He said that she had regained consciousness long enough to tell him that burglars had broken into the house while he was out and had attacked her because she had tried to stop them carrying out a robbery."

Stewart was moving restlessly, struggling to retain a professional impassivity. "Was she badly hurt?" she asked.

The doctor's expressive face provided the answer even before she spoke. "I've never seen anything like it." Her disgust was evident. "The animals who did this must have been out of their minds on drink and drugs."

Stewart's control slipped. She looked distraught. "How bad?"

The doctor exhaled a heavy breath. "Broken arm, broken ribs, smashed nose, severe head wound, dislocated jaw, damage to kidneys and spleen ..." She raised her hands, almost registering helplessness. "Absolute mindless brutality." She looked at her watch and began backing out of the room. "Look, I'm sorry. I have to go. There are patients waiting in several of these examination rooms."

"Thank you, Doctor," Sheehan said. He handed the woman his card and added, "Can you please let me know if she regains consciousness?"

The doctor took the card, but said, "It's hardly likely she'll do so on my watch. She'll be in a ward by then, I'm sure."

The two detectives went back to their car and, as she was pulling on her seatbelt, Stewart exploded. "Burglars, my ass," she fumed. "The bastard did it himself."

Sheehan raised a hand to silence her as he spoke into his mobile phone. "Bill, get on to Robbery, will you, and ask them to check out an incident that happened at Ronnie Weir's house tonight around eleven o clock."

Stewart heard faint chirping as Larkin responded.

"Yes, extreme urgency. And tell them to copy their report to me as well, ASAP." Larkin was saying something else when Sheehan interrupted him. "And get on to the two beat cops who were watching the house. I want to know everything they saw down to the last detail."

Sheehan switched off the phone and started the car.

Stewart was still incensed. "Does he really believe that after a beating like that, she'll support his stupid story?"

"You know as well as I do how it is with battered wives. Some don't have the courage to report the abuse. But violence of this level …" He steered out of the ambulance bay into the hospital avenue. "She might well decide that she's not going back."

"If we could get a chance to speak to her when she regains consciousness," Stewart said, "we might be able to convince her to shop the bastard."

Sheehan glanced at her. "You're a bit wound up there, Sergeant."

She breathed heavily for some seconds. "Sorry, sir, but I have the awful feeling that if we hadn't interviewed Weir, this might not have happened."

177

"Don't put that on yourself, Stewart," Sheehan said sharply. "We do our job. Stuff like this is down to the perps. It would be great if we could prevent crime," he was shaking his head, tight-lipped, "but all we generally get to do is to enter the scene after the crimes are committed and try to sweep up the pieces. That's how it is. That's how it'll always be. So keep your emotions under control, or you won't last a year in the job."

Stewart absorbed this for a few minutes. "You're right, sir. Sorry. But we can still try to help her, y'know, extensive safety planning, arrange restraining and non-molestation orders for her, get legal support in bringing court proceedings. And if she has no money of her own, there were positive changes introduced last year to eligibility for legal aid for victims facing risks of catastrophic harm. There are even opportunities in special cases to go into witness protection."

"And you know all this because …?"

"Some of my duties last year in Lisburn involved a couple of battered women cases." Then she added, "But nothing like what we've heard about tonight. Holy God! An assault like that? That's grievous bodily harm with intent, sir. We can charge him with that. And it's definitely custodial, sir, if we can get a guilty verdict."

"Perhaps, but not us. It's not our bailiwick, Stewart. Remember, we're Serious Crimes. Wait and see what Robbery finds out. The Domestic Abuse Unit may have to be called in, too." He rubbed a hand across his jaw and mused, "But I'd sure love to have a crack at him in an interview room." He drove in contemplative silence. "Yes, maybe we should bring him in as a suspect in the Fitzpatrick case and see what we can squeeze out of him."

"I'd like to sit in on that, sir."

Sheehan emitted a dry chuckle. "We'll see." He noted they were nearing North Road. Relenting somewhat, he said, "We'll try to get a wee chat with Mrs. Weir in the morning. Depending on what she says, we'll see where we can go from there." He glanced at the dashboard clock as they turned into her street. "Nearly two o'clock. Get some sleep, Sergeant, or you'll be fit for nothing tomorrow."

"Thanks, sir," she said as she climbed out of the car. "I will. Goodnight, sir."

Sheehan grunted. "Aye! Good morning, Sergeant."

THIRTY-TWO

S tewart was finishing a somewhat bleary-eyed breakfast when the phone rang. She lifted the receiver gingerly and said, "Hello?"

"Stewart. DCI Sheehan. How soon can you be ready?"

"You can come right away, sir."

"Right. I'll pick you up in about fifteen. We've found Peter Shaw."

"Peter Shaw? Oh, Peter Shaw. Sorry, sir, my mind was on Mrs. Weir. That's great. How did we find him?"

"Not so great, Sergeant. I'll fill you in when I get there."

Sheehan arrived in less than ten minutes but Stewart was waiting for him. As she climbed into the car, she said, "What's going on, sir?"

"Shaw's been murdered," Sheehan said tersely as he drove off.

Stewart was stunned. She had fully intended to initiate a search for him that same day. "My God! What happened?"

"No details yet. But we'll find out soon enough."

"Middle of the night, Tuesday. Same as last time. Anything significant in that?"

"No idea. Maybe your finding the name rushed the killer into silencing him before he could talk to us."

"How would he have known I found the name?"

"True. But if he did know, what does that say to us?"

"Doesn't bear thinking about. Where are we going, sir?"

"He lives ... lived ... in Parkgate Drive."

"Good grief! I don't believe it. Here we were getting ready to initiate a nation-wide search for him, and he's practically living on my doorstep."

Sheehan allowed himself a grim smile. "Police work. If I was American, I'd say that it can throw some really strange curve balls at you."

They were travelling at some speed along Mersey Street, and Stewart said, "Oddly enough, I was looking at houses here a couple of months ago, so I know the area. Parkgate Drive is the second turn on the right ... if you'd care to slow down a bit, sir."

Once into the street, they saw an ambulance and some police vehicles parked outside a modest, redbricked terrace house. The medical examiner's car was there as well. *Dick complains a lot,* Sheehan thought, *but nobody ever beats him to a crime scene.* A couple of scene-of-crime officers encased head to toe in white coveralls and carrying various items of equipment were just making their way through the front door.

Sheehan parked as close to the scene as he could and, after squeezing themselves into white protective suits that Sheehan had produced from the boot of his car, the two detectives followed the SOCOs into the house. The building was far from huge, but the lounge, which was the focus of their attention, was reasonably spacious. The furnishings were sparse and functional, consisting of no more than a small sofa and a couple of matching armchairs, a television in the corner, and some mats on a wooden floor. Also on the floor was the dead body of Peter Shaw, lying in a large pool of blood. He was flanked by doctors Campbell and Jones who, too, were enveloped in protective clothing.

Stewart felt sick as she looked at the young man on the floor, at the huge gash on his neck, at the head that lolled sideways, at the hands tied behind his back. The hair was thinning and the face was somewhat fuller, but he was the laughing youth from the laptop photograph. Whatever he had done, he surely didn't deserve this.

Campbell glanced up as the two detectives entered. "Ah, Jim. I was expecting you."

"You should've been a detective," Sheehan grunted. He looked down at the body. "So, what do we have?" Campbell was raising a hand in preparation to offer his usual detailed response when Sheehan raised his own hand, palm out. "Just the bare bones, Dick. We'll get the lecture later."

Campbell sniffed. "Hummph. Okay, what you have here is a replica of James Fitzpatrick's murder." He said no more.

Sheehan looked at him, "Well?"

Campbell said, "You wanted the bare bones. You got the bare bones."

Jones and Stewart glanced at each other. Neither of the two of them quite knew what to make of this interplay.

Sheehan emitted a resigned sigh. "Okay, Dick, I apologise. Give us the lecture."

Campbell stared at the detective, raised his chin, and assumed a professorial expression. Sheehan's eyes twinkled briefly. "Andrew," Campbell said to his assistant, "perhaps you could expound?"

Jones stepped forward a pace, pointed to the body and, in that surprisingly deep rumble said, "You can see the trauma to the nether regions. The penis was surgically removed … uh … perhaps not with surgical skill but competently enough, and forced into the victim's mouth."

"Post-mortem, I hope?" Sheehan said.

Jones said solemnly, "This time I believe so, yes. I'll be more certain after we examine the body." He bent to point at two burn marks on the back of the corpse's neck. "The victim was tasered like the last one, as you can see here, so I would have to assume he wasn't able to put up much of a fight."

"There looks to be more blood from the throat this time," Sheehan said.

"Yes," Doctor Campbell cut in, unable to restrain himself any longer. "The cut to the throat is different, a wider, more determined slash than the last time. The spatter indicates that the carotid artery was cut."

"The killer knew what he was doing?"

"Maybe. Or maybe he's beginning to get the hang of it."

Stewart felt her stomach lurch. She was almost overwhelmed with nausea and here were these two men, chatting casually, seemingly oblivious to the tragedy of the death.

Sheehan caught her eye and noted the expression on her face. He knew what she was thinking. "Coping mechanisms, Stewart. You, too, will eventually find your own way to deal with scenes like this."

Doctor Campbell was nodding agreement. He put a hand on Jones' shoulder and said, "I've only just made a similar point to my young friend here."

"So, basically the cut to the throat did it, and the other stuff is more or less window dressing?" Sheehan asked.

"We'll know for sure after the post-mortem," Campbell said, peeling off his rubber gloves, "but I'd guess you've pretty much called it."

"And the time of death?"

Campbell gave him a smug look. "Five past eleven last night."

"You checked the watch?" Sheehan said.

"Uh huh. Just like the other one. Winder pulled out and watch stopped at eleven-o-five." He gave the detective a sideways glance. "And this murder, like the last, was also on a Tuesday."

"So what do you think that means?" Sheehan asked him.

182

The doctor stepped back, his expression scathing. "You're asking me? You, the detective, are asking that of me, the medical examiner?"

"All right. All right. I was just being rhetorical. I knew you wouldn't have a clue."

"Hummph!" the doctor grunted, but he was grinning. He glanced at the body again. "Are you happy for us to take the deceased away now?"

"Yeah, go ahead."

Campbell turned to Jones. "Andrew, get the paramedics in here with their stretcher. We'll head on now."

Sheehan said, "We'll call in and see you in a couple of days."

Campbell grinned. "I would expect nothing less. Have a good day, Jim." He smiled at Stewart. "Nice to see you again, Sergeant."

The detectives stood back as the medics left, nodding their goodbyes. Sheehan said to Stewart, "Call in the officer on the front door. See what he knows."

Stewart was back in a minute with the beat officer in tow. "Sir, this is Officer Blake."

Sheehan nodded a greeting. "What can you tell us?"

The officer produced a small notebook and read from it. Stewart pulled out her own notebook and wrote as the officer talked. "The victim's name is Peter Shaw. He is divorced. He teaches in a local high school and shares the rent of this house with another colleague from the school, a Mr. Neil Corr. It was Mr. Corr who found the body. He had been out all night …" The officer looked up from his notebook. "He did not say where he was, but I would suspect he was with a girlfriend." He turned to his notes again. "He says he was coming home to get cleaned up and collect his briefcase for school. He found Mr. Shaw lying like that on the floor when he came in."

"What time was that?"

"Sometime around seven thirty this morning, sir."

"Where is he now?"

"He's down in the kitchen with my colleague, sir, drinking hot tea. For the shock, you know."

"Thanks, Blake," Sheehan said. "You can resume your duties on the door."

When the policeman had left, Sheehan said to Stewart, "Well? What do you think?"

"Same killer. Has to be the same motivation."

"You're still thinking revenge?"

"It's at least an option."

"That it is, Sergeant. Wish we had more evidence. But Weir is still in the frame, too. Don't forget he was out of his house at the time this murder was being committed."

"Could be coincidence, sir. We need motive. I can understand that he might have had a problem with Fitzpatrick, but Shaw's only a schoolteacher. It's not very likely their paths could have crossed."

Sheehan was pursing his lips and shaking his head. "You're making assumptions, Sergeant, to protect your theory. We haven't even started investigating Shaw's killing. Remember I told you to garner facts and evidence. If you focus too closely on a fairly exclusive solution, you might dismiss as irrelevant something that could later be found to be very important."

Stewart didn't argue. The chief was right. She didn't have any real evidence. Nonetheless, this second murder looked like it could fit like a glove into the scenario she had earlier outlined to Turner and Sheehan. She would consider all the evidence gathered by the team, but she was not yet ready to relinquish her belief that Fitzpatrick and Shaw had been killed by Lynda Bell's vengeful boyfriend.

Sheehan left her to her reflections and walked over to a couple of forensic officers who were dusting the room for fingerprints. They were officers he didn't recognise. "Find anything unusual in your search?" he asked.

One said, "Depends what you mean by unusual, sir. Basically the place is as clean as a whistle, but there was something under the sofa."

"A cufflink?"

The man looked startled. He held out a gloved hand, palm upwards. Part of a brown cufflink with gold marbling was sitting in the middle of it. He was grinning lopsidedly. "The word is that you're good, sir, but this is weird."

"Just inspired guesswork, son," Sheehan said straight-faced, throwing Stewart a sideways glance. Her eyes were glued to the cufflink. "Bag it, please, and give it to Sergeant Larkin."

"Sergeant Larkin?"

"Exhibits Officer. Balding guy with round glasses. He's bound to be about here somewhere."

"Oh, yes, sir. He's up searching the bedrooms."

"Thank you, Officer."

Stewart said, "Sir …"

He stopped her with a raised finger. "I know. We'll talk about it later. Let's go down to the kitchen and speak to Mr. Corr."

THIRTY-THREE

T he compact kitchen was probably twice as long as it was wide, but Stewart was impressed by the space-saving design, even if the cupboard units were a somewhat garish lime green. A slim, dark-haired man in his late twenties, jeans, grey sweater, open-necked shirt, sat at a small table in the middle of the floor, accompanied by a uniformed police officer. He was very pale, clearly still in shock, and when he looked up at the newcomers, his listless expression registered little.

The officer stood smartly to attention when Sheehan and Stewart entered. Sheehan said, "Thank you, officer. We'd like a few words with Mr. Corr now, if you wouldn't mind."

"Of course, sir," the officer replied, heading for the door. "I'll just wait outside."

Sheehan sat in the chair that the officer had just vacated while Stewart stood back, notebook at the ready. "I'm sorry we have to talk to you in such tragic circumstances," Sheehan said. "Do you think you're up to answering a few questions?"

Corr moved the empty mug in front of him to one side and said, "I suppose now's as good a time as any."

"You weren't at home when the … incident occurred?"

"No. I spent the night with my girlfriend. Just got in around half seven and found …" He swallowed and fell silent.

"Okay. Please give your girlfriend's name and address to the sergeant before we leave." He gestured vaguely to the kitchen. "How did you come to be living here with Mr. Shaw?"

"Peter got divorced a while back. He put a notice in the staffroom asking if anyone would like to share the rent of a small house with him. I think he's paying alimony and wanted to economise. It so happened that I needed digs at the time and the location suited me. So I spoke to him about it, and we agreed to share."

"Were you close? Would you know if he had any enemies?"

"No, we were friendly enough but not best friends. Just house mates. I didn't hear anything about enemies."

"How did his behaviour seem recently? Did he appear to have anything on his mind, something bothering him, perhaps?"

"Noooo, not really. He did receive a phone call a few nights ago that seemed to affect him. He kinda turned in on himself for a while, but it didn't last more than a day or so."

"Do you know what the call was about?"

"No. He didn't say."

"His ex-wife will need to be informed. Do you know where she lives?"

"Sorry, he didn't talk much about her. I wouldn't really know where to start looking for her."

"Did he say anything at all about her?"

Corr shook his head. "Not much. Oh yes, we were having a few drinks one night, and he did say that the divorce was acrimonious."

"Nothing else?"

"Just that he didn't get on with her father … a controlling kind of a guy. Probably him who put the dent in their marriage."

"Did he say anything about him?"

Corr's eyebrows went down as he searched his memory. "Just that he was a big-shot property developer. I think he said his name was Duffin. No, not that ... em ... Duffner. That was it. Duffner."

Sheehan's expression remained neutral but he did shoot a glance at Stewart. Her eyebrows were high as she stared back at him. "Did he say why he didn't get on with his father-in-law?"

"Not really. It might have been something to do with the fact that he seemed to be butting too much into his daughter's life. Peter hated that."

"Did Duffner try to contact Shaw at any time recently?"

"Don't think so. If he did, Peter didn't mention it."

Sheehan handed the man his card. "Thank you for your help. If you think about anything else, something untoward that might have occurred in the past while, please give me a call at either of those numbers."

Corr took a wallet out of his hip pocket and put the card into it. "Okay, I will. But I don't really imagine there'll be anything."

Stewart asked for and noted Corr's girlfriend's address as Sheehan rose to leave. He offered Corr his hand. "Thanks again. I'll make sure our officers give you all the help you need right now."

The two detectives left the kitchen, leaving the young man sitting at the table in pretty much the same state as they found him. Sheehan said to the policeman who was waiting outside the kitchen door, "Keep an eye on him. He'll need support."

"We'll keep him right, sir," the officer replied.

Out of earshot of the officer, Stewart said, "What was that you were saying about curve balls, sir?"

Sheehan shrugged. "The thing about coincidences, Stewart, is that sometimes that's all they are. Coincidences." He gave her a sideways glance. "So how does this new information fit into your scenario about a vengeful boyfriend?"

"It doesn't, sir. It just confuses me."

Sheehan emitted a dry chuckle. "Join the club."

They met Sergeant Larkin in the hall on their way out. "Find much, Bill?" Sheehan asked.

Larkin shook his head. "Very little. You know about the cufflink, of course. We'll take his briefcase and laptop to the station and go through them." He looked at Stewart. "Unless Sergeant Stewart wants the laptop?"

"No, you go ahead, Bill," Stewart said. "Maybe I'll have a look at it later if you don't find anything."

When they had settled in the car *en route* to the station, Stewart said, "Sir, there's something I need to tell you. I was sworn to silence, but I think you should know." She then told him about her mystery informant and the leads he had been giving her.

"We all tend to work on the QT with our informants, but you were right to tell me about this one. He seems to know an awful lot about the case."

"That's what I was thinking, sir."

"Any idea why he is targeting you?"

"Not a clue, sir. I've racked my brains but can come up with nothing."

"And you're sure he isn't one of your old informants or anyone you know."

"Not an old informant, sir. That's for sure. But he may know me. He seems to have some access into what I have been working on, however he's getting it."

Sheehan tooted his horn impatiently at the driver in front, an elderly lady who seemed reluctant to attempt the right turn into Connsbrook Avenue. Stung, she took off, risking life and limb in an effort to join the traffic flow on the far side of the road. Sheehan pulled across smoothly behind her. "Do you think he knows who the killer is?"

"Don't know, sir. I think he might suspect he knows. I mean, it was his prompting that led me to the ... the vengeful suitor theory."

Sheehan grinned. "Good name for a book." Then serious again, "We could use the name of the third youth in the photograph. On today's evidence, he's probably the killer's next target." He paused to negotiate the turn into Hollywood Road. "If your informant phones again, try to get him to tell you the third fellow's name. He'll need protection."

"He tends to hang up awful quick, sir, but I'll do what I can. I think I'll go back to Queen's anyway and look through some more student transcripts. We might find him that way." She hesitated, then added, "I was wondering, sir, if we could keep the informant's existence between ourselves for now. For whatever reason, he was really insistent that I tell no one. I have a feeling he might well be privy to information from the station. If he discovers that I have told somebody about him, he might well clam up."

"Huh? You think there's a plant at the station?"

"No idea, sir. He just seems to know so much about what's going on. Where's he getting his information?"

"Okay. We'll keep it between ourselves for the moment." He drove for a while, lost in thought. "Still don't see what he's getting out of it. If he resents what the young men did, the killer is clearly sorting that out for him. If he himself is the killer, why on earth give you information that might lead to his apprehension? And, again, why you? Is he trying to make you look good or what? Or is he trying to lead you up the garden path? One of your old friends from Lisburn, maybe, setting you up for some sort of a fall?"

Stewart was shaking her head. "Any or all of the above, sir. I just have no clue."

Sheehan saluted the duty officer at the observation window as he drove though the station gate. As he parked the car, he said, "So, Duffner's not out of the picture. Weir was wandering around without an alibi when Shaw was murdered. And your vengeful suitor, whoever he is, cannot be discounted either." He shook his head. "We're not going to solve this now. Small steps, Stewart.

Small steps. And one step at a time. Before you go to Queen's, I'd like you to get a car and go to the hospital and talk to Mrs. Weir. Try to get her to tell you if it was Weir who beat her. That'll give us what we need to bring the bastard in for questioning. And we'll have plenty to question him about, the Fitzpatrick killing, the assault, probably about Shaw, too."

"Right, sir. I'll just go in for a quick coffee before I go."

THIRTY-FOUR

1

When Sheehan and Stewart entered the Serious Crimes Room later that morning, Tom Allen was sitting at his desk, just replacing the phone. He seemed excited. On seeing them, he rushed over, holding his ribs with his left arm and pointing backwards towards his phone with the thumb of his right hand. "Sir, we've just had a call from a witness in the Fitzpatrick case."

"Took their time," Sheehan said. "Are you sure it's genuine?"

"He says he had not seen the media appeals. Happened to be talking to a friend who mentioned them and that set him thinking."

"Uh huh! So what did he see?"

"He saw a heavyset man coming out of Fitzpatrick's house around eleven thirty on the night of the murder. His description fits Michael Duffner, sir."

Both Sheehan and Stewart tensed immediately. Duffner again.

Allen noted their reaction. He stared from one to the other. "What?"

Sheehan said, "We've just come from the Shaw crime scene."

"So?"

192

"Shaw was divorced. His ex-wife is Michael Duffner's daughter."

"Holy shit!" Conflicting emotions crossed Allen's face. "What the hell does this all mean? How does this affect Weir?"

"Don't know. Just another weird fact in a case full of weird facts." He grinned at the unintended pun. Weir-d fact. God! He shook the pun from his head. "How reliable do you think your witness is?"

"He's just one of the neighbours. No reason to think he's a nutter."

"Did he see the suspect's face?"

"Says he did, sir. The suspect walked under a street lamp before getting into his car."

"Did he describe the car?"

"Dark coloured Audi, sir."

Sheehan's expression showed some uncertainty. "Very convenient at this juncture. What do you think, Stewart?"

"Depends on the witness. He'll have to be thoroughly checked out. If he's genuine, everything's back up in the air again."

"Do a wee background check and go and see him," Sheehan instructed Allen. "Take Geoff with you." He looked around. "Where is he?"

"Teacher/Parent morning. Took an hour off to go to the school with his wife. He'll be in shortly."

"Okay! The two of you set up a photo array when you get there and see if this witness picks Duffner out. If he does, get him and Duffner in for an identity parade."

"On it," Allen said, turning away.

"And Tom," Sheehan cautioned, "a fair photo line-up, right? Similar types, okay? Don't be bringing five skinny blond guys and one of Duffner."

Tom grinned, looking at Stewart. "This isn't Lisburn, sir. It'll all be above board."

Sheehan went into his office, and Stewart went to the small table beside the sink to make herself a cup of coffee. Allen was already at his desk Googling his witness. "I'm making coffee," she called to him. "Do you want some?"

He looked up. "Yes, please." As she waited for the kettle to boil, he asked, "So how did your visit to the crime scene go?"

"You've got the highlights. Divorced guy. Shared a terrace house with a colleague. Colleague found him this morning. Same MO as Fitzpatrick."

"Duffner's son-in-law, huh?"

"Yes. Saw you holding your ribs. You okay?"

"Yeah, I'm fine. Jumped up from the desk too quick." He gave her a direct look. "Thanks for asking."

She spooned some coffee grains into two mugs and poured boiling water over them. Handing Tom a cup, she said, "Weir was out of his house for a couple of hours last night at the time of the second murder. No alibi yet."

"Jesus! Is all this getting strange or what?"

"You know Weir's wife was badly beaten last night?"

"Yes, I heard."

"We think Weir himself did it. I'm going over to the hospital now to talk to her. If she fingers her husband, we're pulling him in."

"God, I'd love to get in on that interview."

She smiled. "Stand in line." She stepped forward and looked over his shoulder. "Any luck Googling your witness?"

Tom pointed to the screen. "Bernard Sloan, retired civil servant. Exemplary record. No priors, no nothing. Made it to Deputy Principal. Nothing earth-shaking there."

Stewart nodded. "Seems genuine. Good luck with the photo line-up. Keep me appraised." She drained her cup and stepped away. "Well, I'm off to the hospital. I'll let you know what happens."

"Okay. 'Bye."

She gave him a small wave as she left. "See you later."

2

Allen watched her leave, a small smile lighting his face. It was still there when he began printing out the information on Sloan. He grabbed the sheets from the printer, slipped on his jacket, and headed to evidence to get some photographs. He had made light of the chief's comment about the array, but he was very aware that a photo line-up should not be conducted in such a way as to highlight the suspect so that the witness is inevitably led to an identification. It had happened before. An over-zealous officer, pushing for a conviction, makes his photo line-up unduly suggestive. Any hint of this and a competent defence lawyer can easily ensure that the affirmative identification is excluded from the subsequent prosecution. Allen was not about to make that mistake.

McNeill was in the squad room when Allen returned. Allen grabbed his overcoat from the rack at the wall and said, "Right, Geoff. Let's go."

"Go? Where?"

"Piney Way."

"Ohhh, posh! Glad I put my suit on this morning. What's t-taking us there? Whoa, that's where Fitzpatrick lived. We revisiting the s-scene of the crime?"

"No. I'll explain in the car. Come on. Don't hang about."

Sloan's house was a somewhat less elaborate affair than the Fitzpatrick residence. It was a smallish bungalow, carport to one side, short driveway, and built with the red brick so prevalent in these areas. The two detectives parked on the road outside the house and went to the door. Their ring was answered by a man in his early seventies, round shouldered, strands of hair stuck to a balding head, rimless spectacles perched on the end of his nose, and a newspaper in one hand.

Allen showed him his warrant card. "Detective Allen," he said. "This is my partner, Detective McNeill. We spoke earlier on the phone."

Sloan stepped back and opened the door wider. "Of course. Please come in."

He led them across a small hall into an airy lounge with a large bay window. He pointed to a sofa and armchairs. "Please, sit down." His movements were a little quick, somewhat nervous. "My wife and daughter are in town shopping. Can I get you a cup of tea, coffee?"

Both detectives declined and sat on the sofa. Sloan sat in an armchair. "How can I help you, officers?"

"Just following up on your phone call," Allen said.

Sloan had already set the newspaper on a little occasional table handily situated between the sofa and the armchairs and was now sitting back with his hands clasped on his lap. Allen noted that the fingers were almost white from the tension of the man's grip. "Of course," he said. "That's to be expected."

"Can you remind us about what you saw, please?" Allen prompted him.

The man unclasped his hands and pushed himself back up in his armchair. His face was calm, but his movements continued to exude tension and nerves. McNeill, observing this, wondered if the unease was the normal reaction of the average citizen unaccustomed to dealing with the police, or something else. But what would the man need to be worried about?

"Well, as I told you on the phone," Sloan said, "I only just got to hear last night that the police were looking for witnesses to anything unusual outside James Fitzpatrick's house last Tuesday night. I'm still not sure if what I saw has any meaning, but I was coming home from bridge and I saw a man leaving Fitzpatrick's house around eleven thirty."

"And you saw him clearly?"

"Yes, there's a lamp post near the gate." Sloan's head was nodding up and down, almost excessively punctuating his evidence. "I saw him as he walked under it."

"Did you recognise him?"

"No, I'd never seen him before." The man was squeezing his hands again. "That's what brought my eyes to him."

"Would you recognise him again?"

"I think so."

Allen opened the small portfolio case he was carrying. He gestured to the occasional table. "Do you mind if I spread a few photographs here?"

Sloan was out of his chair with surprising alacrity. He lifted the newspaper and a couple of magazines from the table and dropped them on the floor at the side of his armchair. "Please, feel free."

Allen spread six colour photographs on the table, all around eight or nine inches square. "Do you recognise any of these men?" he asked Sloan.

Sloan leaned forward in his chair, peering at the photographs. From the outset, his eyes kept flicking to the photograph of Duffner, but he seemed to want to take his time, to study all of the photos. After a few moments he pointed to Duffner's photo. "I'm pretty sure that's the man I saw."

"Pretty sure?" Allen asked. "How sure is that? You might have to argue about this with an aggressive defence barrister."

Sloan's lips tightened. Again McNeill sensed anxiety, but the man's response was positive. "I am sure that this is the man I saw."

Allen gathered up the photographs and began to put them back into the portfolio. "That's excellent, Mr. Sloan. Thank you for that." He pulled the zip on the case to close it and added, "Do you think you might be able to come to Strandtown Police station and pick this person out of an identity parade?"

Sloan seemed unable to hide some distress at this request.

"You'll be perfectly safe," Allen assured him. "You'll be viewing the parade from behind a one-way window. No one will see you."

Almost as if he was acting against his own wishes, and clearly uncomfortable, Sloan said tentatively, "Well, all right. If you think it will help."

"It would be a great help," Allen said enthusiastically. "Thank you so much. We'll contact you when we're ready, probably in the next day or so. Will that be convenient for you?"

"I'm retired now," Sloan replied. "Pretty much any time will suit me."

"Great." Allen rose and offered the man his hand. "This is really good of you."

Sloan shrugged self-deprecatingly. "Well, you know, my duty as a citizen and all that."

McNeill, too, shook the man's hand as they left and said, "Thank you, sir."

Back in the car, McNeill said, "Well, what do you think?"

Allen was gleeful. "I think we have the bastard dead to rights."

"No, I'm t-talking about Sloan."

Allen eyed him. "What about Sloan?"

"The man was crappin' himself. Do you not think that was a b-bit odd?"

Allen's eyebrows came down for a moment. Then his face cleared. "Nah! People are always nervous around cops. You've seen that oftener than I have."

McNeill nodded as they drove away from the house. "I suppose you're right."

THIRTY-FIVE

S tewart parked the unmarked police car in the hospital car park, and made her way to reception. There she learned that Mrs. Weir had been taken to the Female Surgical ward, and her condition was described as stable. She found her way to the ward by following the many signs in the corridors, eventually speaking to the nurse in charge and asking if she could see Mrs. Weir for a few moments. The nurse demurred until she saw Stewart's warrant card. Without further argument, she led the detective into the ward and down to the patient's bed.

Mrs. Weir was a sorry sight. Her right arm was in a sling; her face, neck, and chest were covered in bandages; a saline drip on a stand was attached to the wrist of her good arm. Also attached to the hand of her good arm was the hand of her husband who was sitting by the side of the bed, exuding sympathy for his poor wife's condition. Stewart was taken aback when she saw him, but it was too late to retreat.

She stepped closer to the bed and said, "Good morning, Mr. Weir. Just following up on the assault on your wife."

The man, urbane as ever, said, "Good of you to take an interest. I need those two scoundrels found and prosecuted to the fullest extent of the law."

Stewart looked at the woman. Her eyes were moving erratically like those of an animal in distress. "I wonder if you might be able to answer one or two questions, Mrs. Weir?" Stewart asked.

The woman's eyes turned to her husband, and she said something unintelligible through clenched teeth.

"I'm afraid my wife will find it difficult to communicate with you this morning," Weir said. "She has metal plates in her jaws, and some wires and stitches. She won't be saying much for a day or two."

Stewart said carefully, "I'm sorry to hear that. Perhaps she could nod her response to direct questions?"

Mrs. Weir seemed frightened, but her husband held his hands apart in an expansive gesture. "We could try that," he agreed.

"Did you see who attacked you, Mrs. Weir?"

The woman nodded calmly enough, but her eyes remained frightened and restless.

"Can you describe your attacker or attackers?"

Again the woman looked troubled and hissed something through her clenched teeth.

Her husband was happy to act as interpreter. "Masks," he said. "She says that they were wearing masks."

"Did they come into the house from the front?"

The woman shook her head.

"They came in through the back?"

An affirmative nod, but again her anxious eyes flashed back and forth between the sergeant and her husband.

"You were in the kitchen when they broke in?"

Another nod.

"And you tried to stop them?"

A nod.

"How? Did you physically attack them?"

A shake of the head and another hissed addendum. Weir, who was listening carefully to his wife's attempt at speech, again interpreted. "She just screamed, and they attacked her to keep her quiet." He stood up. "Look, Sergeant, I've already reported all of this to your colleagues. My wife is in no fit state to answer any more of your questions. Shouldn't you be out looking for the miscreants who did this?"

"Of course, sir." She turned to the patient. "I'm sorry to find you in this state, Mrs. Weir. I hope you get well soon." And with a nod to Weir, she left the ward.

Stewart was still furious when she reached the car park. *He has intimidated her into silence.* She climbed into the car and hammered the heel of her hand against the steering wheel. *Smug bastard. Wants the **miscreants** caught.* She stepped out of the car again, only half sure of her intentions. A brisk wind was blowing, and dark clouds were beginning to roll in from the west, filling the sky. Rain for sure. Even with the thought, she felt the first drops on her hand, but she continued to survey the car park. She'd heard Weir drove a Bentley. *Can't be too many of them parked here. Shouldn't be too hard to spot.* Huddled against the increasing rain, she turned almost full circle before she caught sight of it, parked quite close to the hospital end. *Might have known. Too important to walk.*

She scurried back into her car again, brushing the raindrops from her coat. *Calm down,* she admonished herself. *You can't think in this state. So what are you going to do? Do? I'm going to sit here. I'll sit here until midnight, if I have to. He's bound to come out sooner or later, and then I'll go back in and have another chat with Mrs. Weir.* Her brain ticked over, waiting for its next thought. She tried to visualise the conversation with the abused woman, wondering how she might convince her to report her husband and speak against him in court. She rejected a number of possible opening gambits and then sighed in frustration. *Shit! I'll wing it.*

The rain was becoming heavy now, splashing hard against the windscreen and rendering visibility minimal. She sat back in her seat and switched on the radio, anticipating a long wait. In that she was wrong. Weir was already out of the hospital and was hurrying towards his car. Because of the rain, she had almost missed him. He had been hidden beneath a large blue and white golf umbrella which, fortunately, had caught her eye because it was the only movement in the park. She sat still, almost holding her breath, as she watched him get into the car, drive around the car park and out through the exit.

Once he had disappeared from the hospital avenue, she jumped out of her car, oblivious of the rain, and hurried back to the building. She spoke again to the same charge nurse, explaining what she intended to do and asked her to witness the conversation. The nurse wasn't happy, but when Stewart reminded her of the horrific beating the patient's husband had inflicted upon her, the nurse agreed to help. As they walked to the bed, she asked the nurse for the woman's Christian name.

"Sarah, but she calls herself Sally."

When she saw them approaching her bed, Mrs. Weir began to hyperventilate, and her eyes rolled violently in her head. Her fear was palpable. She seemed almost to be attempting to retreat into the bed. The nurse attended to her for a few minutes, cajoling her into quiescence and then stood aside while the detective sat in the visitor's chair.

Stewart took the woman's hand in hers and said, "I want you to listen to me, Sally. No nodding, no shaking. Just listen, okay?"

The woman's breathing remained irregular, but her wild eye movements had calmed down.

"I know you're frightened. I know your husband forced you to agree that two robbers beat you. Now, the question is, do you really think you can go back to live with him, a man that violent? You must know that the least wee thing will set him off again, and he might kill you the next time."

The woman was shaking her head, trying to pull her hand loose, but Stewart held tight.

"Look at me, Sally. Look at me, please. I have been involved with this kind of thing before. Believe me, you do not have the option of going back. It's the worst move you could make. Let me help you. I will put two strong policemen on guard at the ward door. No one will get in. Your husband will be arrested, and I will personally ensure that you are taken into protective custody when you leave the hospital. We'll give you a new identity and arrange for you to go into a witness protection programme or, if you like, you can use that identity to go and live with your sister in America. No one will know that you're Sally Weir. She'll be dead and gone."

The woman was looking at her now, her eyes fixed, her breathing less frenzied. She hissed something. Stewart leaned forward and asked her to repeat it slowly. "He hash friendsh," the woman said.

"Doesn't matter. Most of them are probably lowlife. We have years of experience in spiriting away abused wives."

"He'll fin' me." The woman was becoming frantic again.

"Look, he'll be in prison. He can do very little from there. And he'll be there for a long time. What he did to you carries a heavy sentence."

Mrs. Weir looked at the nurse who was nodding her head. "Men like this don't change, Sally. Please listen to the detective."

Stewart rubbed the woman's arm again. "Sally, it's straightforward. You don't have to do a thing. Just leave everything to me. I will make one hundred per cent sure that that animal will never get near you again. All I want you to do is nod when I ask you this question, all right?"

The woman was still frightened but gave a tiny nod of assent.

Stewart glanced at the nurse and then said slowly, "Sally, was it your husband who assaulted you? Nod if it was."

Sally's eyes showed terror again. She knew the nod would have a monumental impact on the rest of her life. *If this policewoman had got it wrong, she was a dead woman, but God only knew what horrific torture would be inflicted upon her before that.* Her breathing became agitated again.

Stewart squeezed her hand. "Sally, please. Be sensible. Let me help you. I ask again, was it your husband who beat you?"

Sally waited a beat longer, then nodded slowly, tears rolling down her cheeks. *God, what was going to happen now?* She watched the detective write something in her notebook and ask the nurse to sign it. The detective turned to her again and took her hand once more. Sally's eyes were huge and filled with fear as she looked at the detective whose face reflected sympathy and determination.

"Just lie there, Sally," the detective said. "You've done the right thing. Don't worry any more. Leave everything to me."

Stewart left the ward and made for the hospital exit. The rain was over now, and the sun was shining again. The blacktop road, the buildings, the hundreds of cars in the car park, glistened in the bright sunlight, pristine after the downpour.

Just outside the hospital door, she made a phone call. "Chief, Stewart here. I might have gone a wee bit over the top, sir, but as a matter of urgency, could you please arrange for two constables to stand on duty outside the Female Surgical ward in the Royal Victoria. No one is to be allowed to visit Sally Weir. I will explain when I see you."

There was a moment's silence on the line. Then Sheehan said, "Okay!"

"And, Chief, could you also issue a warrant for the immediate arrest of Ronnie Weir?"

Again, Sheehan took a few seconds to assimilate this. Then he said, "What's the charge?"

"Inflicting grievous bodily harm with intent."

"You're sure we can make it stick?"

"Mrs. Weir has talked, sir."

Another moment of silence and then, "All right. It'll be done. Get back here as quickly as you can and fill me in."

"Be there within the half hour, sir."

As she was putting her mobile phone back in her handbag, Stewart again felt that prickle behind her eyes. That her new boss should repose so much unquestioning trust in her brought her to the brink of tears. Her admiration and respect for him as leader and as a man soared.

THIRTY-SIX

R onnie Weir sat at his desk studying some pages of accounts. Whatever was written there was clearly disturbing him. He was flicking back and forth back to pages he had seen earlier, seemingly attempting to match some of the figures there with those on the later pages. His expression continued to grow darker as the reconciliation he was seeking continued to elude him. The phone on his desk rang. He snatched it up and snarled, "What?"

Accustomed to his brusqueness, his receptionist's voice remained level as she said, "There are two gentlemen from the PSNI to see you, sir."

Weir continued to stare at the papers, but now he wasn't seeing them. "Tell them I'm busy. Get them to make an appointment for next week."

After a moment's pause, his receptionist said, "They say it's urgent, sir."

"I can't see them now. It'll have to be tomorrow. Tell..."

Whatever else he intended to add was interrupted as he heard his secretary exclaim loudly, "Sirs, excuse me, sirs, you can't ..."

At that point, two men entered the office. One was young, at least six and a half feet tall and built like a rugby player. The other was much older, ruddy faced, and paunchy.

Weir opted for bluster. "How dare you barge into my office like this? The Assistant Commissioner will hear about this. You'll have to leave. I'm too busy to see anyone now."

"Sir," the larger man said, "it is our obligation to inform you that we are here to arrest you for the crime of grievous bodily harm with intent." He took a small card from his pocket and began to read from it. "You do not have to say anything. However, it might harm your defence ..."

Weir threw out an arm and tried to bat the card out of Connor's hand. "This is nonsense. Get out of here, the two of you. I will call my solicitor, and you can speak to him."

Connors gazed at the man, his expression placid. "Detective McCoy," he said, his eyes still on Weir, "how would you constitute the action you have just witnessed?"

McCoy's expression was equally innocuous. "I'd have to say it was tantamount to resisting arrest, Detective Connors."

"Uh huh. And what are our legal obligations in respect of resistance, Detective McCoy?"

"I'm afraid we are obliged to use reasonable force to effect the arrest, Detective Connors."

Weir was seething, seething because of the utter lack of respect inherent in the detectives' mockery, and seething because he was suddenly convinced that the bitch had grassed him to the cops in spite of his threats. *Pain? She thinks she's felt pain? She has no idea about pain, the slag, but, by Christ, she soon will.*

Connors stepped forward holding out a pair of handcuffs. "Could you stretch out your wrists for me, sir, please?"

Weir stepped back, attempting to keep the desk between him and the detective. Connors paused, pursed his lips, placed the handcuffs on the desk, and stepped around it to confront the suspect. Weir pulled himself to his full height and tried to stare down the detective. His defiance lasted barely a second, brought to a sudden end by the pile-driving blow from Connor's huge fist into his solar plexus. The air left Weir's lungs in a rush as he whipped forward, bent double.

206

Connor's face remained impassive. Retrieving the handcuffs from the desk, he said, "Might I have your wrists now, sir, please?"

"You bastards," Weir gasped. "You'll pay for this. I'll have your jobs ..."

"Yes, yes, you'll have our guts for garters," Connors said, affecting weariness. "We've heard it all before. Your wrists, sir, please ..." He paused. "Or, you may wish to resist further. I would appreciate that, sir. I have to admit that I quite enjoy using reasonable force."

"Very mannerly, Detective Connors. You are a credit to the PSNI," McCoy said.

"Thank you, Detective McCoy. My mother always brought me up to be polite, regardless of the circumstances."

"And she did a wonderful job, Detective Connors. She'd be very proud of you."

Connors held out the handcuffs. "And now, Mr. Weir, your wrists, please."

Weir, almost apoplectic, was spitting fury, his expression murderous. The carefully constructed veneer of sophistication was now shattered. In its place was the slit-eyed, venomous persona who used to be 'The Bat'. Raging inwardly, frustrated beyond endurance, but powerless for now, he straightened himself and held forward his wrists for the cuffs. "I know your names," he snarled. "I know your faces."

He continued to glare at them while his brain broiled with visions of the tortures he was going to visit upon these two nonentities. *How dare they disrespect him like this? They'll learn, the wee shites. They've no idea who they're dealing with. He would get his chance; he always did. By Christ, he'd batter them until every bone in their bodies was broken. He would torture them until they couldn't stop screaming in agony. And when they'd suffered every humiliation and every excruciating pain known to man, he was going to rip the fuckin' heads from both of their bodies and play football with the damn things. We'll see how polite they are then. Bastards!*

Connors fastened the suspect's wrists behind his back and, taking him by an elbow, led him from the office. Weir growled at the shocked secretary who was sitting upright behind her desk, the fingers of both hands over her mouth. "Keep the office ticking over. I'll only be a couple of hours."

THIRTY-SEVEN

"So what kind of trouble have you landed me in, Sergeant?" Sheehan's half-grin removed any sting there might have been in his words.

They were sitting in Sheehan's office, the chief behind his desk. Stewart's mind was churning. There was so much to be done and so little time. "Sir, Weir was at the hospital when I got there, and it was clear that his wife had been intimidated into silence." She explained in terse terms how she had acquired the confirmation that Weir was the assailant and listed some of the promises she had made.

"Ouch!" Sheehan said. "We're going to have to do some fast manoeuvring. What kind of condition is she in? Is she fit to leave the hospital?"

"She's not great, sir. You heard what the A and E doctor said. But we might be able to extract her quietly in a couple of days."

Sheehan emitted a weary chuckle. "Extract? MI5 are we now?" He rubbed his forehead with his fingers. "It's going to be seriously tight. Connors and McCoy are bringing Weir in now, but I don't know how long we'll be able to hold him." He sat back and stared at his sergeant. "His lawyer will be screaming to have him brought before the magistrate immediately, and no doubt he'll be able to argue bail. But it will take a while to set up a court hearing. I'll have to let the Domestic Violence Unit in on the arrest but I think I can keep him in custody for thirty-six hours since he was arrested by warrant and the charge is serious."

"Sir, you have the entitlement to extend that if there is danger of physical harm to another person."

"I know. I know." Sheehan said, beginning to feel pressured. "God, I'm glad to see that your time studying for your sergeant's stripes wasn't entirely wasted. Yes, I do have the authority to squeeze another thirty-six hours out of it, and maybe a further twenty-four, if we can hold up the court proceedings. But everybody's so into human rights these days." He fiddled reflectively with his wedding ring as he pondered the matter. "There is always the issue of Fitzpatrick's murder, of course. We still have to question Weir about that. Might be some capital there. But it's all a bit iffy. His solicitor will definitely be fighting for the earliest court appearance."

"We might be able to convince the magistrate to keep him on remand until the trial," Stewart suggested.

"Maybe, but he's no doubt got a slick barrister in the wings. Best guess, I think maybe you might be able to count on only two days, three at the most. What do you need to do?"

"We'll have to find somewhere to hide Mrs. Weir, a safe house. I'm sure Weir's tentacles reach everywhere. Then she, or maybe I, will have to go to her house while Weir's on remand and gather up whatever belongings she can take away with her, some clothes, whatever jewellery she has, money if there is any, that kind of thing."

"Does she have a bank account?"

"Don't know. I'd be surprised if she did. I can't see that controlling bastard giving her that kind of autonomy."

Sheehan's half-grin reappeared. "Autonomy? Aye!"

Stewart's expression remained serious as a thought occurred to her. "She might have a credit card. I don't know what daily limit there would be on it, but she can withdraw the full limit each day during the time Weir's banged up. That'll give her a few pounds to work with." She paused and seemed uncertain about whether to proceed.

"What is it, Stewart?"

"I was wondering, sir, if we could keep this information to a very limited circle. I learned in Lisburn how easily information can get …"

"Our team's tight, Stewart," Sheehan interrupted her. "I trust them completely."

"I know, sir. But it's a big station. And there are more than just cops working here. I was thinking more about keeping the info within the team. If a sliver of what we're trying to do reaches the wrong ears …"

"I get it. Loose tongues sink ships and all that. Okay, we'll keep it need-to-know," Sheehan agreed. "What about your other investigations? Any closer to finding the boyfriend?"

"Not yet. I've contacted seven of the Jacquelines. Some were hard to track down, so it's a bit time consuming and a bit fruitless so far. None of these seven knew Lynda Bell, but I'll get on to the others as soon as I can."

"Fair enough. Let that sit for a while. I suppose right now Sally Weir's a priority. Stick with her for the time being. Go and see what you can arrange while we deal with the line-up and interviews. That'll give you a few hours to lay some groundwork. What are you proposing to do about her?"

"Well, she's going to have to appear in court to testify against Weir, so we'll have to figure out some way to keep her in protective custody until the hearing."

"With police protection round the clock?"

Stewart shrugged slightly. "I suppose so."

Sheehan groaned. "This at a time when the policing budget is being severely cut."

"The witness is 'intimidated', sir, 'in fear', and 'under threat of serious harm.' These are all handbook terms, sir. We can't ignore them."

"I know. I know. But we can't deal with that ourselves. We're going to have to inform the Prosecutor's Office. They'll need to be involved in ensuring that the witness's fear is allayed and that she is given the requisite protection. "

"She's also going to need all sorts of documents to support her new identity, passport, credit cards in the new name, a bank account in the new name …"

"Oh, Christ!"

"Yes, sir. And she'll also need a fake birth certificate, driving licence …"

Sheehan hissed in a frustrated breath. "Will you quit! Look, you can't be wasting your time on all of that stuff. We need you back on the Fitzpatrick-Shaw case. Liaise with the Witness Care Unit. Get them working on it. You can keep an eye on what they're doing, but I want you back looking for that boyfriend."

"I'll get on to them right away, sir."

"Talk to the Prosecutor's Office as well. Tell them I sent you. What are your plans for Mrs. Weir after the court hearing?"

"Once the new identity is established and all the papers in order, we'll whisk her off to her sister in America. Maybe lay a false rumour that she's hiding out in the south of Ireland, something to distract Weir's henchmen. Even from prison, he'll be running things."

Sheehan emitted a tired breath. "The Assistant Chief Commissioner's gonna love this."

THIRTY-EIGHT

1

Connors and McCoy led Weir into one of Strandtown's interrogation rooms. It was the usual sparse, featureless space found in police stations the world over – wooden table, some hard chairs, a narrow window covered with a Venetian blind, the slats of which were now raised to allow observation of the room. There was a recording device at one end of the table, a telephone on the wall, and a wall camera mounted high in one corner. Connors chose to lean casually against the door while McCoy directed Weir to one of the chairs.

"Sit down, please," McCoy said.

Weir continued to stand, glowering at the detective. Connors stood out from the door and moved slightly. Weir sat down.

"Now, sir," McCoy said, "we'll have to leave you on your own for a wee while. I hope that's all right with you?"

Weir glowered at him.

"You have a right to be informed of the charges against you in writing as soon as possible, but it's going to take time for us to get the paperwork sorted."

"I want my solicitor," Weir snarled.

"Yes, sir," McCoy said, "we'll arrange to have someone bring you a phone so that you can call him."

"And take these bloody cuffs off."

"All in good time, sir. We have to talk to the chief inspector."

The two detectives left and Weir sat fuming on the hard chair, staring wildly around as if contemplating escape. His foul temper was in no way assuaged when he learned, having had to wait almost half an hour before a constable came in with a phone, that his solicitor was in court and was unlikely to be available for at least two further hours.

Detective McCoy returned about twenty minutes later with a couple of sheets of paper and a small, plastic bottle of water.

"How much longer are you going to keep me waiting here?" Weir snapped at him.

"Well, you've requested a solicitor, sir. We're not allowed to question you until he is present." He unlocked the cuffs from Weir's wrists and added, "Here's some water for you. Try to make yourself comfortable until he comes, sir." He pointed at the sheets on the table. "You might also wish to study the charge sheet while you're waiting, although I'm afraid there's some information missing regarding your first court appearance and your bail conditions, if any. We'll wait for the chief inspector to sort these things out."

"So I'm expected to just sit here for the next couple of hours?" Weir sneered.

"Well, we could take you down to one of the cells if you'd like, sir."

"Go to hell."

It was all McCoy could do to maintain the façade of politeness he and Connors had adopted, knowing how much it annoyed the suspect. His face did turn a shade more ruddy, but he simply said, "We'll let you know when your solicitor arrives, sir," and left the room.

For Weir the wait seemed interminable. He drank some of the water and drifted back from time to time to the charge sheets. They were copies of standard proformas, most of the spaces left blank.

The direct charge, however, was filled in, and his rage boiled every time he looked at it. 'Grievous bodily harm with intent'.

The bitch is dead. The bitch is dead. The bitch is dead. The words hammered in his head like train wheels clacking on metal tracks. As time passed, however, he realised that he needed to clear his head and calm himself. He did not want to make any slips when the chief inspector came to question him.

2

While Weir was fulminating in the interrogation room, Mr. Sloan was standing in a smallish antechamber which had a large two-way mirror on one wall. Through the mirror he could see six large men standing in an identification line, each holding a number, and all respectably dressed in suits and ties. Three of them were policemen, although Sloan did not know that, and one of them was Michael Duffner. DCI Sheehan and Sergeant Stewart were squeezed into the small room with Sloan, as was another lady, dark-haired, attractive, about forty years old.

"The process is simple, Mr. Sloan," Sheehan explained. "All you have to do is …"

"Careful, Chief Inspector," the dark-haired lady said. "I trust you are going to say nothing that might jeopardise my client's best interests."

"Wouldn't dream of it, Ms. Thornton," Sheehan said. He turned to Sloan. "All you have to do is to tell us if the man you saw outside James Fitzpatrick's house at eleven thirty on the night of Tuesday the fourteenth of October is standing in that line-up."

Sloan gazed somewhat myopically through the window, adjusted his rimless glasses, and stared again. "They are all very similar in build and appearance," he said, sounding distinctly nervous.

"That's deliberate," Sheehan said. "The suspect is entitled to an identification process that ensures his rights. You have to be able to pick him out of that kind of grouping. If you feel that you can't be sure, please say so. Your evidence must be strong enough to stand up in court."

"What he means," Ms. Thornton added, "is that if you are in the least bit unsure as to whether you can make an identification or not, then you are obliged not to identify anyone."

"Thank you, Ms. Thornton," Sheehan said. "I think our witness has the picture." He placed himself between the solicitor and Sloan. "No need to be nervous, Mr. Sloan. No one but us knows you're here. Take your time. If you're sure you can identify the man you saw, please point him out and say his number."

The faint light in the antechamber shone dully on Sloan's bald pate as he studied the men in the line-up. His eyes ranged back and forth but Sheehan, who was watching him closely, experienced some surprise, becoming aware that Sloan was not actually focusing on anyone, that he did not seem to be subjecting the men before him to any kind of serious scrutiny.

Sheehan did not have time to pursue the thought, however, because Sloan abruptly said, "It's the third man from the right, number four."

Somewhat taken aback at the suddenness of the identification, Sheehan said, "Are you sure?"

"Yes. It's definitely number four."

"Okay! Sergeant Stewart will give you a form to sign when we go back to the office, and then you're free to go."

Ms. Thornton was already leaving the room at this point. "We'll need your signature, too, Ms. Thornton," Sheehan called to her.

"I've done this before, Chief Inspector," she replied icily.

Sheehan nodded and then said to Stewart, "Could you make sure that Mr. Duffner is safely ensconced somewhere until we can get time to speak to him."

THIRTY-NINE

W hen he learned that it would be a couple of hours before Weir's solicitor was due to arrive, Sheehan decided to interview Duffner first. He sent for Detective Allen, and the two of them entered the interrogation room together.

The man was seated, but his body language exuded tension and stress in equal measure. He had not yet been informed as to why he was being detained, and when the detectives entered the room, he rose furiously from his seat, shouting, "Why am I being held here? Where's my solicitor?"

Sheehan gestured to the chair the man had just vacated and said calmly, "Please be seated, sir."

"I'm entitled to a solicitor," Duffner railed, continuing to stand.

"Please be seated, sir," Sheehan said again. "Your solicitor is on her way."

Even as he spoke, there was a knock on the door, and Ms. Thornton entered, taking the chair beside Duffner. Duffner sat down, finding it difficult to balance his bulk on the smallish chair. "What the hell's all this about?" he said to her.

She held up a restraining hand. "Let's hear what the policemen have to say."

Sheehan switched on the recording machine. "Interview with Mister Michael Duffner, Wednesday, twenty-second of October, at," he checked his watch, "three twenty-five, p.m. The interview is being conducted by Chief Inspector Sheehan and Detective Allen. Also present is the defendant's solicitor, Ms. Patricia Thornton." He sat back and said, "Mister Duffner, you have just been picked out of a line-up by a witness who claims he saw you outside the residence of James Fitzpatrick at eleven thirty on the night of the fourteenth of October."

Duffner's face expressed initial puzzlement, followed by some moments of intense concentration as he tried to work out the implication of the date and time. Suddenly he understood and, clearly shocked, he shouted, "That was the night Fitzpatrick was killed. Are you trying to say that I was at the house at the time of the murder?"

"We're not trying to say anything, sir. We are informing you that we have a witness who claims to have seen you outside the house very shortly after the time of death."

Duffner was hyperventilating, apparently thunderstruck. "Absolutely no way can he have seen me. I wasn't there." The man could hardly speak. Whether it was because of the revelation he had been observed at the crime scene, or because he believed the witness was lying, wasn't clear, but he was shaken beyond measure. "I wasn't there, I'm telling you. Your witness is lying or he is mistaken." All anger was replaced by a tone of desperation. It was as if he knew he would not be believed, despite the fact that he was telling the truth.

Allen glanced at Sheehan. Both of them had expected a denial, but this air of defeat, this lack of bluster from a man so strong, was not at all what they had expected. Sheehan continued to stare at the suspect, sensing Allen's uncertainty and experiencing it himself.

"There is a very distinct possibility that your witness is mistaken, Chief Inspector," Ms. Thornton said. "He was pulling his glasses on and off trying to see, yet he was only a few feet away from the line-up which was brightly lit. How much more difficult would it have been for him to see, ah, whoever it was he saw, late at night from a moving car? I'd say you'd have to take this witness's testimony with a very large pinch of salt."

"I don't know who your witness saw," Duffner added, this time with a great deal more vehemence, "but I can absolutely swear it wasn't me."

"So, where do you say you were at that time?" Sheehan asked.

"I told your colleague here," he nodded towards Allen, "that I was working at my office with my brother at that time, and watched football at his apartment after that. That's where I was."

Ms. Thornton rose from her seat. "Chief Inspector, you have nothing. If you charge my client on the basis of this identification, you'll be laughed out of court. We're leaving now."

"Sit down, Ms. Thornton, please. We're not finished." He turned to Duffner. "Do you know a Mr. Peter Shaw?"

Duffner stared at him, wondering what was coming next. "Yes," he said. "He used to be my son-in-law."

"I understand that the relationship between the two of you was less than cordial?"

"Don't answer that, Michael," Ms. Thornton interrupted. "Where are you going with this, Chief Inspector?"

"All in good time, Ms. Thornton. Mister Duffner, where were you last night between the hours of ten thirty and midnight?"

"I was watching a football match on the television at my brother's apartment."

"Oh? The same alibi you had for James Fitzpatrick's murder."

Ms. Thornton said, "Surely you don't expect my client to respond to incomprehensible innuendo? Where are you going with this?"

"Your client had a strong motive for wanting revenge on James Fitzpatrick. Fitzpatrick is now dead, and a witness places your client at the scene. Your client had a reportedly stormy relationship with his ex-son-in-law, Peter Shaw, and now he, too, has been found murdered. Your client's name keeps cropping up, Ms. Thornton, and his alibis are less than convincing. That's where we're going with this." He turned to the suspect. "Care to comment, Mister Duffner?"

Duffner was looking distinctly uneasy now, but he said forcefully, "I can't help it if you don't believe my alibis. They're the truth, and they're all I've got. I didn't get on well with Shaw, but he's been divorced from my daughter for some time and I have had no dealings with him since. Why would I want to murder him now?"

Sheehan stared at him. The man's voice had more than a ring of truth, and his comments made sense. He felt even less confident about the situation when Duffner added with some force, "And I definitely wasn't at Fitzpatrick's place last Tuesday night. You'd need to have another word with that witness of yours."

Ms. Thornton stood up again. "You're fishing, Chief Inspector. Unless you are prepared to charge my client, and I would hope you wouldn't be that foolish, we're leaving now."

"Our investigation into Shaw's death has only just begun, Ms. Thornton, so we're still gathering evidence." He turned to the suspect. "You are advised to keep yourself available for questioning, Mister Duffner. Please don't leave town until such time as you are informed that you are no longer a person of interest in this case." He spoke into the machine, "Interview ends at three forty-one, p.m."

Sheehan waited for the two to leave before saying to Allen, "You were unusually quiet, Tom."

"Something about him, Chief. He seemed to be telling the truth. Different from when me and McNeill talked to them. Nowhere near as cocky but …"

"Aye! I had the same feeling. How sure are you about Sloan?"

"Not sure at all now. We're going to have to have another chat with him, that's for sure."

"What would be the point in him lying, *if* he was lying?"

"Unless he was compelled …?"

"Check him out. One or two things I noticed about his attitude at the line–up … I'm not happy about him at all."

"On it, Chief."

FORTY

Mr. Sloan was having a cup of tea with his wife in their kitchen when the doorbell rang. When Sloan answered the door, he recognised the same two detectives who had interviewed him at his home a day or two before. Suddenly nervous, he said, with a hint of quaver in his voice, "Good evening, detectives. I have just come from the station. Is there a problem?"

"Just a couple of follow-up questions, sir," Allen said, neutrally. "Do you mind if we come in?"

He led the two policemen into the front room and shouted down the hall to his wife, "It's more questions from the police station about the identification, Martha. I'll talk to them in the parlour."

The two detectives sat on the couch while Mr. Sloan sat sideways on to them in an armchair. He seemed unable to sit still, his hands and fingers in constant movement. It was clear to the two detectives that the man was extremely nervous. "So, what is the problem?" he asked, unable to wait for the policemen to speak.

"I wonder if we could just go over your evidence again, sir," Allen said. "We need to straighten out one or two small anomalies."

"Anomalies?" The man looked suddenly agitated, but tried gamely to hide it.

"Yes. You were driving home from bridge, sir?"

"That's right."

"At eleven-thirty at night?"

"Yes."

"Do you usually come home that late?"

Mr. Sloan was strangling his fingers, but he managed to sound calm. "No. We had a prize night that evening, and we played a couple of extra rubbers. I would normally have been home an hour earlier."

"I see. It's just that I phoned one of your bridge members a while ago and he said that he left the club just after ten."

Mr. Sloan may have been many things, but he was no actor. He almost had apoplexy when Allen said this, but he recovered quickly and said, "Yes ... some of the members were out of the running for prizes and went home early."

Allen nodded. "I see. Okay. When you saw the suspect under the lamp post, what was he doing?"

"Doing?"

"Yes. Was he just standing there, lighting a cigarette, walking past, what?"

"He was walking."

"Of course. He'd be trying to get away from the crime scene, so he was hardly going to hang about."

"I would imagine so."

"So, he was moving fairly fast then?"

Sloan stalled, aware of the implications of the question but lost for an answer.

Allen pressed. "Sir?"

"Moderately fast."

"And you were driving your car?"

"Yes."

"Moderately fast?"

"Well within the speed limit."

"So, we have a man walking moderately fast along the street late at night, ostensibly fleeing a crime scene, head probably hunched into his shoulders to avoid recognition. You are driving along a relatively dark street, you suddenly happen on this man, and you swear that you were able to see him clearly enough to pick him out of a line-up a week later. Does that about sum it up?"

"I saw him under a lamp post."

Allen's tone hardened. "And he obligingly hung about to give you time to study his face so that you could recognise him at some point in the future?"

Sloan's hands were white with tension as they clenched each other. His face, pale at the best of times, was almost ashen. "I saw him clearly." His voice was barely a croak.

Allen leaned forward on his seat, and McNeill made a great show of taking out his notebook and thumbing it open. "Sir," Allen said, his expression grim, "are you aware of the penalties for making a false statement to the police during a murder enquiry? It's called perverting the course of justice and carries a prison sentence. Prison at your age, sir, with all those murderers and psychos half out of control. Is that what you want?"

Sloan was now shaking like a leaf. "Why are you telling me this?" The quaver in his voice was very pronounced now.

Allen pushed harder, convinced the man was about to break. "Because we know you are lying to us, sir, and it would take only minimal investigation to prove it." Allen stood up and looked down at the now terrified man. It was abundantly clear that the man had, in fact, falsely accused Duffner. "We'll give you one chance to retract your statement, sir, but it'll have to be now. If you persist in lying, you will definitely go to prison."

Sloan bent forward, his face in his hands. "Oh God! Oh God!" he moaned. "They made me do it."

"Who made you do it?"

Sloan looked up at Allen, his face a sudden mask of venom. "That bunch of loyalist fuckers that work for Ronnie Weir," he hissed. Then he put his face in his hands again and moaned once more, "Oh God! Oh God!"

Allen glanced at McNeill whose face expressed the same mystification he himself was experiencing. He sat down again. "You'd better explain from the start, sir."

Sloan sat back, with the air of a man who has lost everything. He began to speak, almost in a monologue, as if the words had been churning around in his mind for a long time. "It's simple. I'm a married man, as you know. Twenty years ago I was a senior civil servant attached to the Police Federation. I ... I ... got involved with a young man. Uh, we had a short but lurid affair. I had never done anything like that before. It was over quickly, and I thought that was the end of it. Then I began to get these ... these explicit photographs through the mail. No letters, no demands, just the photographs." Sloan stared desperately at the policemen, seeming to seek understanding. "I was terrified of exposure. Then one day I got a phone call asking for some information about PSNI movements that I was privy to. Obviously I refused but then the person said, 'Do you want to see those photographs all over the local press?' They had me after that. I was their mole. I learned through time that it was Weir who was running me. Nothing ever came out. I suppose I was lucky, and the calls ceased years ago, after I retired ... until a few days ago." Sloan lifted his eyes, his face haggard. "My wife never knew anything about this. They asked me to phone Strandtown Station to volunteer information ... well, you know the rest."

"You were feeding information to loyalists about the police du ... during the troubles?" McNeill asked, unable to keep the contempt out of his voice.

"Only during the tail end of them, and during the aftermath of the Good Friday Agreement." Sloan's voice lacked any inflection now. He had lived with the guilt of this for so long that any comment he might make about it would be bereft of emotion, autonomic.

Allen wasn't quite sure how to deal with this bombshell. There was far more here than a simple false statement. Despite the blackmail, the man was guilty of a serious betrayal of trust. In his position it had to be something akin to treason. "Sir, you're going to have to come back to the station with us. Get yourself a coat, and let your wife know it'll be days rather than hours before this is resolved."

Sloan dragged himself from his chair, head low, broken in spirit. After he had left the room, McNeill said, "Holy shit!"

Allen could only shake his head as he dialled Sheehan on his mobile phone. "Sir, have you questioned Weir yet?"

"Not yet, no. Still waiting for his brief."

"There's something you need to know."

FORTY-ONE

W hile her determination to bring closure to Lynda Bell's case remained undiminished, Stewart knew that she had only the smallest of windows within which to work in order to bring some form of security into the life of Sally Weir. For that reason, all her current energies were being expended in helping the abused woman. After her conversation with her boss, she had gone straight back to the hospital where she spent some time comforting the woman, assuring her that her safety was paramount and that she would be given all the protection she needed.

Sally's jaw was still bound with wires and clips as well as covered with a bandage, so talking continued to be difficult for her. After some time of patient listening and questioning, however, Stewart learned enough about where Sally kept her jewels, her private money and credit cards, her clothes and hand bags to feel that she could go to the house on her behalf and gather up what she would need.

Stewart was now prowling, at least that's what she felt she was doing, around the Weir mansion late that same Wednesday afternoon, and despite the fact that she knew the house to be empty, she was practically walking on tiptoe, scarcely daring to breathe. Aware of her tension, she admonished herself. *You're a cop in a crime scene. Calm yourself.* But it wasn't exactly a crime scene, and she was here to remove goods and valuables. How would a magistrate view that? *Well, I have Mrs. Weir's permission.* Have you permission from the owner of the house? She shook her head angrily. *Will you quit, for God's sake.*

Her first errand was to pack a couple of suitcases and retrieve a handbag from a top shelf in one of the wardrobes in Sally's bedroom, hidden in a folded duvet. Stewart found the handbag easily and checked to see if the contents were as Mrs. Weir had described. They were. It contained a substantial amount of cash, squeezed into a number of tight rolls, each held together with an elastic band. There were some items of jewellery, too, as well as a couple of credit cards in Sally's name. *The lady's not as slow as she might like to pretend,* Stewart thought. And the husband clearly had no idea that this money had been hidden there. Obviously Weir had not credited his wife with sufficient intelligence, or 'street smarts', to plan for a possible disintegration of their marriage.

There were a couple of decent-sized suitcases on a top shelf in one of the wardrobes, and Stewart hastily packed whatever she could find in the way of clothes that she considered most useful for the next phase of Mrs. Weir's life. She hauled these downstairs, together with a raincoat and a warm overcoat which she carried over her shoulder. Despite the fact that she knew Weir was being detained at the station, she was practically running, feeling an ever-present sense of haste as she rushed out to her borrowed car to offload the stuff she was carrying.

She looked around the grounds outside and across the gate to the road. Thank heavens that grey mizzle was still hanging around. No one was observing her, not even a neighbour. She expelled a long breath and ran back into the house. One more errand. It had taken time to understand the story Mrs. Weir had told her as she vainly tried to move her jaws in order to pronounce words, but Stewart finally learned what the woman wanted. It was a story that might have been ludicrous had the situation not been so dire.

Mrs. Weir had been shopping in one of the Belfast Christmas markets a year or two before and had come across a dish shaped like a hen. The lid was, in fact, pretty much a sculpted hen's upper body, replete with painted brown feathers, red coxcomb and large yellow beak. Sally thought it had been cute, a 'dinky' dish in which to serve roast chicken. Her husband, however, had considered it to be cheap and tawdry, not something to be seen in his elegant kitchen, and commanded her to get rid of it. Reluctant to do so, she tucked it into a top corner in one of the kitchen cupboards and more or less forgot about it until one day she was spring cleaning and rediscovered it in its hiding place. The dish was covered with a patina of dust, and as she was washing it in a basin of soapy water, it occurred to her that her husband had never touched it. He probably did not even know that it had been in the cupboard.

That was when she thought the chicken dish would be a safe place to start putting together a nest egg of cash. When Mrs. Weir said this, she made some strange noises and began to shake. It took Stewart a few minutes to realise that Sally was giggling. "Nesht egg, geddit?" she had explained.

Sally had made it clear she was under no illusions that it was her personality that was allowing her to retain her place in the Weir mansion. She was there because of her looks alone, and she lived constantly in fear that her husband, a man with a cruel streak a mile wide, might one day tire of her and throw her out. Should that happen, she vowed that she would not leave empty handed. Fortunately Weir was generous with 'shopping' money and often threw her a couple of hundred pounds to go out 'shopping' while he held 'meetings' in his home. There were times too, after episodes in his life that she never learned anything about, when he would return home in expansive mood and toss her even more generous sums. She spent some of this, mostly on cheap items, to create the impression that she was using the money, but in fact she was saving most of it.

The chicken was now filled almost to overflowing with twenty pound notes, wrapped, like those in the handbag, in small tight rolls. Stewart grabbed it from its shelf and, holding the hen lid on the dish as tightly as she could, almost fled from the house.

FORTY-TWO

Weir's solicitor, Mr. Arthur Brannigan, entered the station in a rush. He was a short man, portly, bald, but with a fringe of black hair running past his ears and around the back of his neck. He was somewhat flustered, demanding from the desk sergeant an immediate meeting with his client. Sergeant Rushe, large, red-faced, slow moving, had seen it all before. And he served the solicitor with the same lugubrious witticism that he had served to many before him. "My name might be Rushe, sir, but let's just take our time. Wouldn't want to do anything rash now, would we? I'll just phone the chief inspector, so I will."

While the sergeant was on the phone, Brannigan fidgeted and paced, constantly checking his watch, clearly anticipating a stormy greeting from his short-fused client. The sergeant replaced the phone and said staidly, "The chief inspector will be with you shortly, sir, so he will. We are just waiting for one of the detectives who will be joining you in the interrogation room, so we are." He pointed to a hard bench against the wall. "If you'd care to sit, sir. He won't be long, so he won't."

In the event, it was a civilian secretary who came to lead Mr. Brannigan to the interrogation room, where he found Chief Inspector Sheehan and Detective Allen waiting for him outside the door. When the policemen led the solicitor into the room, Weir was immediately on his feet.

"What the hell took you so long, Brannigan? Get me out of here. Now!"

Mr. Brannigan raised a pacifying hand. "Please be calm, Mr. Weir. We'll have you out of here in a few minutes." He turned to the chief inspector and attempting to look brisk and efficient, he said, "We're leaving now, Chief Inspector, unless you are intending to charge my client with a crime that has some basis in truth."

"Please sit down," Sheehan said calmly, as he switched on the recorder and stated the date, time, and the persons present at the interview. Then he said to the solicitor, "While we haven't interviewed your client just yet, I can assure you that he will not be going anywhere in the immediate future." He pushed a couple of pages towards the solicitor. "You may wish to take a few minutes to read the charge sheet."

Mr. Brannigan snapped up the papers with one hand and studied them quickly, his face darkening as he read. "Why is Serious Crimes involving itself in matters essentially the province of the Domestic Abuse Unit?"

"Because it is only one of a number of issues we need to talk to your client about. And Serious Crimes will definitely be involved with the others."

"Do you have any witnesses to this preposterous allegation?"

"Mrs. Weir herself has confirmed the assault in the presence of one of our detectives and a senior hospital nurse." He turned to the suspect. "Do you have anything you wish to say, Mr. Weir?"

"She's lying in her teeth," Weir snarled. "I don't know why she's changed her story, unless maybe she's trying to get at me. I've already explained to your officers what happened. She was beaten by two thugs attempting to rob my home."

"And what time was that, sir?"

"Some time around eleven o'clock in the evening."

Sheehan changed tack. "Is there access to the back of your house, sir, by a way other than via the front gate?"

Thrown off guard, Weir stared at him for a few minutes, trying to fathom the implications of the question. At length he said, "No. To get to the back you have to go in through the front gate. There's a large hedge all round the back of the property."

"So, the two thugs you refer to, however clandestine their movements, would have to have gone through the front gate?"

Weir looked distinctly uneasy, unclear as to why these questions were being asked, but fearing a trap. He strove, however, to remain aggressive. "Obviously."

Sheehan turned to Mr. Brannigan. "For your information, sir, we have two witnesses who had sight of the front gate of the Weir residence from early evening and, not only can they confirm the comings and goings of Mr. Weir, they can also confirm that, until the ambulance arrived, no one else entered or left the premises."

"What! You were having my place watched?" Weir exploded.

Sheehan ignored the outburst and, before Mr. Brannigan could comment, he tossed Weir the hand grenade he'd been holding back. "Why did you blackmail Mr. Sloan into making a false claim about having witnessed Mister Michael Duffner outside the Fitzpatrick residence on the night of Tuesday, the fourteenth of October?"

Mr. Brannigan was outraged. "Don't answer that, Ronald. Chief Inspector, you know better than that. What evidence do you have for this ridiculous accusation?"

"Mr. Sloan's own word. He saw the error of his ways and confessed to making the false statement. He's currently in custody and states that he was forced into making the false witness statement by Mr. Weir and some of his colleagues."

Weir had gone white, but his solicitor said, "This is nonsense. We categorically deny the accusation. You have only the word of a nonentity against a man of Mr. Weir's standing."

Sheehan changed tack again. "Mr. Weir, would you please tell us where you were on the night of the fourteenth of October between the hours of ten thirty and midnight?"

"I … I … would need time to think." Weir appeared on edge. "When was that exactly?"

"It's the same night you were asked about when two of our detectives visited you?"

"Oh, that night! I was at home, with my wife."

Sheehan studied him steadily. The man was lying, but he played along.

"She'll confirm that?"

"Don't see why not … Oh, sorry. I did go out to the office for some papers. I was gone for about half an hour or so."

"Oh? What time was that?"

"Shortly after eleven, I think."

"Working late, weren't you?"

"I often do, and I needed those papers in order to finish what I was doing."

Sheehan noted the shifting eyes, the lowered head. More lies. "Did anyone see you at the office?"

"I don't think so."

"Where did you go between ten thirty and eleven thirty on the night of the twenty-first of October? In case you can't remember when that was, it was the night you brutalised your wife."

"Inspector!" Brannigan almost howled.

"Answer the question, please, Mr. Weir."

"I was at my office. Same errand. Papers I needed that I hadn't brought home with me."

"Did you by any chance take a detour via Parkgate Drive?"

"Don't answer that, Ronald," Brannigan intervened. "Where is this leading, Chief Inspector?"

Sheehan ignored him and continued addressing Weir. "It is clear that we will need to question you further about your comings and goings on the nights of the fourteenth of October and the twenty-first of October. Your explanations are singularly unconvincing." He stood up. "In the meantime, Mr. Weir, you are now officially charged with the crime of grievous bodily assault with intent. You have already been read your rights."

Mr. Brannigan was quickly on his feet, too. "We can answer all your charges and fully intend to do so," he said haughtily. "Right now, we demand conditional police bail."

Sheehan shook his head. "Denied."

"Denied?" Brannigan looked shocked, while Weir looked ready to erupt. "On what grounds?"

"You know the law, sir. Your client has no alibis for two murders, and he is connected in all sorts of ways to one of them. We can hold him for a minimum of twenty-four hours for that alone. But he has, in fact, been charged with grievous bodily harm. This is a serious accusation and, should we release him, there is every likelihood that we would be putting his wife in imminent danger. I have all the rights I need to detain him in custody."

"Do something, Brannigan," Weir growled. "Don't let this nobody bamboozle you."

Brannigan tried to soothe him. "We'll push for a court hearing at the soonest opportunity ..."

Weir rose from his seat, anger tearing at him. "Push for a court hearing? You mean I have to be detained in the cells?"

"Only for a day or so. I'll have a magistrate's hearing set up as soon as I can."

Allen spoke for the first time, almost *sotto voce* but with quiet conviction. "And much good that'll do you. No magistrate will grant you bail with your record and the charge that's already hanging over you." He rose and produced a pair of handcuffs as if by magic. He held them out towards Weir and said, with rather less courtesy than that exercised by Connors and McCoy earlier in the day, "You may settle yourself for a lengthy stay, boyo!"

Weir turned to his lawyer, almost in desperation. "Brannigan …"

Brannigan was mopping sweat from his brow with a large, coloured handkerchief. As he put it back in his pocket, he said, "Just for a day or two, Ronald. Just for a couple of days."

Sheehan ended the interview, recording the time before switching off the machine. Not normally a vindictive man, he couldn't resist calling to Allen who was leading the furious prisoner to the door, "Oh, Detective Allen, when you get a minute, could you please notify Mister Duffner that he is no longer a person of interest in these cases."

FORTY-THREE

tewart had offloaded Sally Weir's belongings into her own home. It was her intention to take care of them until Sally was ensconced in a safe house during her wait for Weir's trial. She returned the borrowed car to the police compound and went back to the incident room to check her messages before going home. The room was empty, except for Tom Allen who was tidying his desk in preparation to leave.

Tom smiled. "You've missed an exciting afternoon, Sergeant."

Stewart grinned back. "Believe me, I've had all the excitement this afternoon that I could handle." She switched on her laptop and checked her emails. Nothing urgent. Some spam. She'd clean it up tomorrow. Powering off the machine, she said, "You heading home now?"

"Yes, and I've got my car back. Anybody giving you a lift home?"

"No, nothing arranged."

"Okay! I'll take you. Sounds like we've got stories to swop."

Just after six o'clock on a wintry October evening, it was full dark when they drove out of the station. Some scurrying leaves were being blown around the road, but there was no other sign of movement. A few minutes brought them to Stewart's house and, although she had looked over her shoulder and out through the back window a couple of times, nothing appeared to be following them.

"Here we are," Tom said, parking at the pavement in front of Stewart's house. "Make sure you lock all the doors and windows."

"Don't worry. That's always my first check." As she climbed out of the car, she hesitated for a moment, and then said, "Would you like a cup of coffee or a bite to eat?"

Tom strove for a neutral tone, although the invite had caused his heart to flutter wildly. "Yes, sure, I'd like that."

As she led him in through the hall and into the lounge, Tom looked admiringly around. "This is nice," he said. Then he pointed to a corner of the room where there was a thirty-two inch television set, a large marble fireplace, an occasional table, and a full bookcase. "See that area over there?"

She nodded, half grinning. "Yes, I've seen it before."

"Well, you could put my whole apartment in there. So this is really great. You're very lucky."

"Hah! You should try paying the mortgage." She pointed to a maroon leather sofa that had its back to a wall. "Sit."

He sat. "Good job I've been to canine school."

"Ha, ha," she said. "Could you just hang on there until I get out of this work gear? I'll only be a minute."

"Sure. Take your time."

While she was out, he studied the room a little more closely and envied her. The walls were a vague pastel cerise colour that offset the furniture. There were a couple of modern paintings on the walls, prints. They didn't make much sense to him, but the colours matched the room. This was such a step up from his own place, and the overall impression was one of spaciousness. *I'll have to get a house,* he was thinking, when she reappeared. She had changed into a lavender lambswool v-neck sweater and a pair of figure-hugging jeans which sported the obligatory tear above the left knee. Her short blond hair had been given a fast once over with a hairbrush but she had not attempted to adjust her makeup.

236

When Tom saw her, his eyes widened. This shapely creature was generally hidden beneath sensible work clothes, and his breath caught as he stared, awed.

Stewart noted his expression. "What?"

"Don't be gettin' all prickly on me, Sarge, but you look gorgeous."

She gave him an arch look. "What? In these old jeans?"

"God, Sarge, don't get me started on the jeans, puh-leese."

She sat in the armchair opposite him and said, smiling, "How's about we dump the 'sarge' when we're off duty like this? It's Denise, okay?"

"That'd be nise … uh … nice, Denise." He couldn't stop staring. "Forgive me, Sergeant … Denise … but you just look fabulous. How come there's no boyfriend? Surely they must be knocking your door down in droves?"

She didn't immediately reply but stared instead into the empty fireplace. Her playful smile disappeared and was replaced by something sad, something wistful.

Tom saw the change in her and was immediately contrite. "Uh … sorry, Denise. I hadn't realised. I'm trampling all over your personal life. Please forget I asked."

"No, it's all right, Tom. Normally I can deal with it, but it hits like a brick out of the blue sometimes. It's worse when it's unexpected."

"Bad breakup?"

"Yes. I loved him. Then I discovered he was two-timing me. Well, actually, four-timing me. I dumped him fast and feel at times like I hate him. But in spite of that, the old feelings can sometimes …"

"Tell me about it," Tom said. "I was engaged when I was dumped. And when I tried to visit or phone to talk about it, she placed a restraining order on me."

"Oh, my God, that must have been tough."

"Well, it was at the time. Took an age to get over it. But it's been a couple of years. I'm fine now." He gave her a lopsided grin, "Sorta."

She sat back on the chair and curled her legs beneath her. He noted that she was wearing what looked like little black ballet shoes. "So, have you someone now?" she asked, trying for casual, but an odd inflection in her voice gave the question a somewhat artificial tone.

"No. I've had a few relationships since, but they tend to dry up pretty quickly. I don't know why. What about you?"

"Nobody since. I just live for my job now. But I'm surprised you're flying solo." Then she added with a grin, "I mean, there's bound to be someone out there, somewhere, who might think you're passably good-looking."

"Gee, thanks. Yes, I've met some lovely girls, but after we get past the getting-to-know-each-other stage, it all seems to crumble. And I think the fault is mine, whatever I'm doing."

Denise smiled ruefully. "Couple of oddballs, huh?"

"No … no … it wasn't that," Tom said, his expression deadpan. "They're perfectly normal. I think the relationships just fizzled out."

"What are you talking about now?" Denise said, her eyebrows scrunched.

Tom couldn't restrain a chuckle. "Nothing. Nothing. It's okay."

Then realisation dawned. Trying not to grin, she said, "God forgive you, Tom Allen. That's very cheeky."

"Just a little whimsy to brighten an otherwise …" He stopped himself, suddenly aware he was heading for trouble.

Denise gave him a sharp look. "An otherwise what?" she said, attempting to sound severe. "An otherwise dull and boring conversation?"

Tom threw himself back on the sofa and stared at the ceiling with clenched teeth. "No … no … aarrgh! I wasn't going to say that at all. I was going to say to brighten a … em … series of ponderous comments by myself in the middle of what is an otherwise witty and intelligent conversation."

She laughed. "God, you're incorrigible. I'm going to make the coffee."

Tom was grinning as he watched her sashay into the kitchen, convinced that the wiggle of her pert bottom might have been less pronounced had he not been sitting on the sofa observing her.

She poked her head back in through the door. "Would you like some pizza? I got one in yesterday. There's plenty for two."

"Sure, that'd be great."

"Okay. I'll just heat up the oven. It'll take a little while."

She came back in and sat down. "You were in on the Weir interview today?"

"Aye! God, the bastard was lying through his teeth the whole way through it."

"Still sticking to his story about the two thugs?"

"Yes, but we've the two cops who were watching his house to prove that there were no burglars. He's dead in the water with that one. It's the Sloan thing that we don't get."

"What do you mean?"

"Oh, yes. You missed that. Geoff and I re-interviewed Sloan about his testimony. Load of lies. He had been blackmailed by Weir into fingering Duffner. Wasn't a word of truth in it."

"You're kiddin'. So Duffner's off the hook?"

"Yes, a red herring. But what was Weir playing at? Was he at the scene himself and tried to throw us off the scent by using Sloan and Duffner? If so, why? We couldn't get anything out of him at the interview except his bogus alibis."

"You think he's the killer?"

239

"Who knows? But he was definitely lying about where he was at the time of the killings. If he wasn't there, where the hell was he?"

"There's still those bits of cufflinks. Had he anything to do with them? What does this do to my boyfriend theory?"

Tom shrugged. "It's all still up in the air. Different bits fit into different places and other bits don't seem to fit in anywhere. We'll see what the team has to say at the debrief tomorrow afternoon."

A sharp, shrieking sound came from the kitchen. "That's the timer," Denise said. "I'll put the pizza on. Should be ready in about fifteen minutes. Do you want tea or coffee?"

"Whatever you're having will do."

She was back again in a couple of minutes.

Tom said, "What about Mrs. Weir? What's the story there?"

She told him about the events of the day and, as they talked, he became conscious of the aroma of peppers, cheese, and pepperoni filling the room. Hunger gnawed at him. "Wow! That smells delicious," he said.

"It's just about ready. C'mon. We'll eat in the kitchen."

The kitchen, like the rest of the house was neat and compact, red fitted cupboards, white Italian marble tiles on the floor, and beige patterned tiles on the walls. Tom liked it.

As they ate, they spoke of things inconsequential for a while until Tom said, "I'm the first to admit that issues of gender discrimination have tended to pass me by. I have rarely given the matter any thought, and I suppose I am trampling all over women's equality rights all day without even knowing I'm doing it. But in all seriousness, how bad were things in Lisburn?"

She gave him a long look, then said, "Your equality instincts are fine. That's because you're innately fair." Her eyes became blank as she focused on a spot on the table. "But there was nothing fair about those, forgive the language, bastards in Lisburn."

"It was bad, huh?"

"If only you knew. At first it was just small things, snide stuff, ignorant remarks about women that I was meant to overhear. There were all sorts of insults if I didn't have the coffee ready before," She made quote marks in the air. "… 'the men' arrived. And if any chores or messages had to be done, the more menial the better, it was always, 'Send the woman.'"

"Ignorant bastards," Tom said.

She looked up at him. "It got worse, a lot worse. Kerley's crowd had absolutely no respect for women of any kind, no surprise considering the sideline he was running. The insults became more ribald, more vocal. Sometimes they would pretend not to see me and bump into me, knocking me to the ground. They were always exaggeratedly apologetic when they did that, but they'd be laughing before they'd be a couple of steps away. Thank God there were a few decent cops there who didn't like what Kerley's crowd were doing, and they tried to protect me as best they could. But they could only do so much." She paused as she remembered something else and said, "Promise me you won't tell anyone else what I'm about to say."

He held two hands up. "Absolutely. I swear."

"With a name like Stewart, I was always going to have trouble. It wasn't long before I was being called Stewrat and that quickly became Ratstew. I hated that, absolutely hated it. And they knew it and quite openly called me these names to my face." Her face began to show some distress. "And they never left my locker alone. They were always breaking into it, messing it up, even stealing things. One morning I opened it and found a filthy dish in it with a dead rat on it. I could hear the giggles and guffaws outside the locker room …" She stared at him, near to tears as the memories stung. "Uh … I don't want to talk about this anymore."

Tom's emotions were all over the place, sympathy for what she had endured, disgust at what these men had done, anger at the gross disrespect she had been subjected to and, oddly, an almost overpowering regret that he had not been there to protect her. He could scarcely speak. "Bastards," he growled. "Bloody bastards. Thank God you got your own back." His eyes were cold as he added, "Wonder how much giggling and guffawing is going on in Kerley's cell right now?"

She gave him a wan smile. "Yes, there's that."

She got up to clear the plates and cutlery into the sink. Tom rose, too. "I'm sorry I brought that all up," he said, "but you must know it's all behind you. You'll never experience shit like that at Strandtown."

"I know," she said, leaning on the sink and staring down into it. "I know." Then she turned to Tom and added, "And I'm so grateful to have ended up there."

They stood in the kitchen, quite close to each other, looking into each other's eyes. Both knew that they had now arrived at a landmark of sorts in their relationship but neither was prepared to acknowledge it yet. Tom certainly knew that he was not about to be invited back to the lounge to watch television. "Thanks for the lovely meal, Denise. I really enjoyed it. Sorry about that Lisburn stuff. We'll never bring that up again." He made a show of looking at his watch. "Goodness, I've taken up a lot of your evening. I'll drift on now." He turned and headed for the hall but stopped to say, "All windows and doors securely locked, right?"

She nodded, smiling, and followed him to the door. She stood on the step, arms folded across her chest, as he went out of the gate and around the car to the driver's door. She was still smiling when there was the sudden roar of a powerful engine and a screech of tyres. A dark automobile, with no lights on, careered from the far side of the road and hurtled towards Tom.

"Tom!" she shrieked.

But Tom had heard the clamour and had managed to leap on to the bonnet of his car as the charging four-by-four ploughed violently into his front wing. There a thunderous crash, followed by a harsh metallic crunching and scraping, as the attacking vehicle screeched down along the side of Tom's car before speeding off. The force of the collision knocked Tom off the bonnet and he landed heavily on the footpath. Denise was there almost as soon as he hit the ground, calling anxiously, "Tom! Tom! Are you all right?"

Tom tried to move, feeling heavy, awkward, and in pain. "Christ!" he groaned. "That's terrible."

"What?" Denise cried, her alarm doubling "What's terrible?"

"It's only out of the workshop. They'll go nuts when I bring it back."

"That's not one bit funny, Tom Allen," Denise chided him. "Never mind your car. Are you all right?"

He tried to sit up, alternately gasping and holding his breath. "Bloody ribs. Hurt my elbow and my knee. But I'm all right … I think. Did you get the make of the car or the number?"

"No. Too dark. Big four by four, but they all look pretty much the same. And the lights were off. Couldn't see the plates. Sorry."

Some neighbours had heard the crash and were now on the street, trying to learn what had happened. One man noticed Denise struggling with Tom and came over to see if he could help. Denise thanked him but told him they could manage. He retreated back to his house but, like a number of others, continued to stand at his front door, watching.

Tom pulled himself into a sitting position and leaned with his back against the passenger door, still wheezing. "Who the hell is doing this? Is it me or you they're after?"

Denise began to help him up. "You can't sit there. Come on back into the house and let me have a look at those bruises."

When he got to his feet, Tom hung on to the car and staggered round to the driver side. The wing was badly mangled and crushed in over the front wheel. The driver door, too, was heavily dented, and bashed so far in that Tom was unable to open it. "Dammit. I won't be driving this home tonight." He turned to Denise who was pulling at him, trying to lead him back into the house. "Will you call Collision Investigation, please, and Vehicle Recovery as well?"

"Yes, yes. Let's get you inside and sitting down first."

Back on the maroon sofa, Tom removed his jacket while Denise made the calls. He had some deep grazing along his left arm as a result of the fall and similar scratches on his left knee. They were quite raw but there was little blood.

Denise came over to have a look. "They don't appear to be life threatening," she said, "I'll put some antiseptic cream and a couple of large plasters on them. You'll be all right in a day or two."

Tom lay back on the sofa, the adrenaline leaving him. He felt suddenly weary. He breathed a heavy sigh and said, "That's twice … and I was lucky twice. Will it be third time lucky for our unknown assailant, I wonder?"

"Don't talk like that," Denise said, almost crossly. "But we know now that you have to take extra precautions."

"It's like 'the troubles' all over again. Is it your friends in Lisburn, do you think? Why the hell do they keep targeting me?"

"I don't know. Whoever it is must be insane. They're taking terrible risks. They could quite easily have been caught tonight or run into somebody else when they were trying to escape."

Tom thought about that. "Yeah! There's more than a hint of craziness in the guy's … or the guys' … behaviours. Y'think Chambers and what's-his-name took umbrage to my shooing them unceremoniously off the premises the other day?"

"Chambers and Wilson?" She shook her head. "Dunno. That'd be a pretty drastic reaction, even for them."

"Maybe they're out to get you for what happened to Kerley, and are mad at me for being around as protection."

She didn't answer right away, sitting in tight-lipped silence. Eventually she said, "They're a bad pair, there's no doubt about that, but I don't know whether something like this would be their style."

"Well, we're going to find out," Tom said resolutely. "I'm going to tail them from the Lisburn station for the next couple of evenings to see where they go. I'll sort it with the chief." His eyes blazed. "And God help them if they go anywhere near you."

They locked eyes, but she didn't speak. Then Tom said, "I'll just phone Geoff and get him to take me home. Uh … will you deal with the two units when they come?"

"Don't worry about that. Are you sure you don't want me to call an ambulance? You might have broken a couple of ribs again."

"Nah! They're still quite tightly bandaged. They just got a bit of a shock, that's all. They feel okay."

He took out his mobile phone and called Geoff. When he explained what had happened, Denise could just about hear furious squawking at the other end of the line. Tom hung up and grinned. "He thinks I'm trying to get myself killed."

"Can you blame him?"

"He'll be here in a few minutes."

She rose and headed for the kitchen. "I'll make a wee quick cuppa tea."

"Thanks." He leaned his head back on the couch and exhaled a long breath. Despite the agitation he had just experienced, he felt ready for sleep. Almost mumbling, he said, "Like I said earlier, an exciting day."

FORTY-FOUR

1

Despite the loss of sleep, Stewart was out of bed and dressed when the chief inspector phoned the following morning to say that he would be picking her up in ten minutes. As she gathered up her bag and overcoat, she wondered how Tom was doing and whether he did, in fact, have Geoff drive him to A&E to get checked out. She toyed with the idea of phoning him to see how he was. *No. Wouldn't have time. Boss'll be here in a minute. What's this? Excuses for copping out of what is simply the right thing to do? Why wouldn't you phone? He's a colleague. He was injured at your very door, probably because he was helping you, and you're iffy about checking up on him? No, I'm not. I'll be quite happy to check later.*

She looked out through the window and saw Sheehan's car pull into the far end of her street. *There y'are. I knew I wouldn't have had time.* A quick check to make sure that all the windows were closed and she went to the front door to meet him.

"Good morning, sir," she said, as she climbed into the front seat. "I suppose you heard about Detective Allen."

Sheehan's face expressed concern. "No, I didn't. Hope it isn't bad news?"

"Not really, but …"

She told him what had happened the night before and Sheehan lapsed into one of the long silences that she was gradually becoming accustomed to. She figured that he was processing the new information and trying to fit it into some sort of template that only he could see at this stage in the investigation. She had heard enough stories about him and the way his mind worked to know that this was not a time for conversation.

Just as they were driving up to the hospital mortuary, Sheehan muttered, eyebrows down, "I'm not so sure that these events are as isolated as they appear to be. There's some sort of connection to our case. I know it, but I'm damned if I can see it."

With that cryptic remark, he got out of the car and went into the morgue. Both Doctor Campbell and Doctor Jones were already there. Jones was standing at a small table, a large organ, probably a liver, held somewhat aloft in his right hand while he adjusted a small weighing machine with the other. Campbell was bent over the metal autopsy table, finishing the torso stitching to the body of Peter Shaw.

Campbell turned as they entered and greeted them with his customary beam. "Ah, Jim. Sergeant Stewart. What can I do for you this bright Thursday morning?"

Sheehan's cursory nod was a great deal less effusive than the doctor's beam, but Campbell took no offence. Jim was just being Jim. "Morning, Dick. What have you got for us that's interesting?"

Campbell spread his arms and said grandly, "Everything we have here is interesting, Jim, even fascinating. You know that."

"Hummph! Anything new on the Shaw case?"

"You've already got the basic report. What more do you want from me?"

Sheehan said, deadpan, "Some fibres, some blood spatter that doesn't belong to the victim, some skin from under the victim's fingernails, and, oh yes, I'd like some unexplained DNA, please."

Campbell laughed aloud. "Good man, Jim. You've got this mortuary humour thing down pat, haven't you?"

Sheehan's expression remained unchanged. "I wasn't being funny, Dick. What have you got?"

Dick grinned again. "Nothing from your wish list, that's for sure. We did check the inside of the body bag, sometimes something minute can fall off the body, but no luck, I'm afraid. Same with the plastic bags on the hands. Nothing. Your killer was careful, and clever; educated even, I would think."

"What do you mean?"

"Well, Jones and I were looking again at the cut to the throat. He said that you were asking a lot of questions about that."

"It was you who started me."

"Oh? Okay. Basically what we now think is that the perp was bright enough to check out where to do both cuts, maybe in a medical book, maybe online. He made the cuts in more or less the right places but, even if he had the theory down pat, he didn't seem to have the practice he needed to do the cutting with real surgical efficiency."

"Amateurish?"

"Definitely."

"I'll ask you the same question I asked Doctor Jones last time we were here. Is there any chance the cuts were made by someone who knew what he was doing but botched them enough to make them look like the work of an amateur?"

Campbell stared down at the body on the table, musing on this. He was shaking his head slightly but with some hesitation. "Only you could look for this kind of devious twist, Jim." He bent closer to peer at the throat, now sewn to post-autopsy tidiness. "I can't say that what you're suggesting is impossible, but why on earth would the killer want to go to such lengths?"

Sheehan shrugged. "This sort of thing is always done to deflect or to hide something." He stared hard at Campbell. "Maybe the killer is a medical examiner and he doesn't want the investigators to know that he is skilled in surgical cutting."

Campbell grinned weakly. "Knock it off, Jim. What motive would I have?"

The corners of Sheehan's lips twitched. "Well, that still has to be determined."

Campbell blew out his cheeks and looked at Stewart. "Sergeant, do you intend to spend any length of time working with this man?"

Stewart grinned. "That's up to him."

"Well, take my advice and seek a transfer soon. He'll have your brain tied up in knots before the year is out."

Sheehan said, "Thanks, Dick. We'll head out now. If something else occurs to you, give me a ring. I'll see what I can do to get you off the list of suspects when I get back to the office."

"Get outa here. I told you the killer was clever. You're not going to find any evidence to convict me."

Sheehan said, grinning openly now, "So long, Dick. Good day, Dr. Jones."

Jones, who had been standing, seemingly transfixed, with a liver in his hand during the exchange about the cuts, nodded an acknowledgement and placed the liver back on the weighing scales.

2

When Stewart arrived at the incident room after lunch, most of the team were already at their places and the room was buzzing with muted conversations. She was surprised to see Tom Allen there, sitting at his desk and talking over his shoulder to Geoff McNeill. He looked fine. He spotted her about the same time she saw him and he gave her a thumbs up and a friendly smile. She glanced at the chief's table as she went to her own desk to power up her laptop and noted Robert Turner was there, too. He was chatting with the chief and had not noticed her come in. She experienced a sudden frisson of ... of what? Stress? Pressure? Every time she saw him, despite his good looks and obvious liking for her, she experienced something negative, a wish that he was somewhere else. *God, he'd just love to know that.* Yet he was always pleasant to her. Maybe he just came on too strong. It was almost as if he were constantly trying to push her in a direction she didn't want to go. *Tom doesn't push,* a little voice in her head said. She dismissed the thought and sat down. By the time she had checked her emails, the rest of the team had arrived. Bill Larkin was standing by the whiteboard as usual, marker in hand, waiting expectantly for the day's revelations.

Sheehan gave a cough of sorts and said, "Okay, everybody, let's get started." He waited for silence, and then said, "Once again we welcome Crown Prosecutor Turner to our debriefing, and thank you, sir, for your interest." Turner gave the team his version of a friendly smile. Most considered it patronising. Sheehan went on, with a somewhat perplexed grin on his face, "It seems that we now tend to open our debriefs with congratulations to Detective Allen for cheating death in order to attend our sessions." He was met by one or two answering grins but, for the most part, the team's expressions were grim, and one or two were furious. One voice near the back, not particularly *sotto voce*, was heard to mutter, "No way the bastard's going to get away with that."

Sheehan addressed Tom, one eyebrow raised, "Two debriefs, two attempts on your life. I hope there is no causal connection here. I trust you are none the worse for your experiences of last evening, Detective Allen?"

"Right as rain, Chief. Couple of extra bruises, maybe, but right as rain," Tom replied, with an answering grin.

Sheehan's face hardened. "Joking aside, Tom. You could have been killed … twice. What's going on?"

"Dunno, Chief. I still think it's Sergeant Stewart's stalker, but for some reason, he, or they, sure seem to have it in for me."

Sheehan glanced at Denise. "Stewart?"

"We're at a loss, sir. Detective Allen has half a notion that some of Inspector Kerley's cronies from Lisburn might be involved but, given the brash and drastic nature of the attacks, I don't think even they would go that far."

"I'm going to follow that up, anyway, Chief," Allen said. "I'd like to find out one way or the other if Lisburn is involved. Be good to be able to stroke them off our list, if they're not."

"Okay! Do what you have to do. The rest of you, listen up. We have a large, dark, four by four, pretty smashed up, I would think. Where is it? Where is it likely to go for repairs? Any word of one having been stolen? Any hire companies missing one? You know the drill. Connors and McCoy, make that your priority, will you?"

The two detectives nodded agreement.

"And McCullough and Miller can canvass the neighbours. The vehicle must have been sitting there for some time waiting for its chance. Big car like that, not known in the estate, maybe somebody was wondering about it and got a make or a plate."

Bill Larkin, at his usual place in front of the whiteboard, coughed and raised a finger.

Sheehan nodded. "Go ahead, Bill."

"On this business of bashed cars, just a wee update, in case anyone was wondering. We've finally traced all five of the navy E Class Mercedes we were talking about at the last debrief. All the cars are accounted for. All clean and free of damage. None of these cars, or their owners, are of any further interest to us." He caught Turner's eye. "Sorry, Mister Prosecutor, we have nothing yet on your car …"

Turner's lips tightened.

"But we're still trying," Larkin added hastily, "and we won't stop till we've recovered it."

"That's fine, Bill," Turner said. "Thank you for your efforts." He turned back to the chief. "You've probably put as much manpower as you can afford on this stalker business, Chief Inspector, but maybe these four can try to link in with what Vehicle Collision are doing." There were some nods. "It's just that there's still so much other stuff to deal with. There's Weir, his wife, Sloan … we're being dragged further and further from the murders."

"Yes," Sheehan said, a slight edge to his tone, "we hadn't forgotten. But we can't ignore what lands on our desks. We have to try to deal with it. That's police work."

"Of course. Sorry, I didn't mean to imply …"

"No worries," Sheehan interrupted. He leaned forward, his fingers interlocked in front of him. "Sloan has been passed on to Internal Security, so he's no longer our problem, but Weir remains a mystery and a problem."

He spent some minutes bringing the whole team up to speed on what had been happening with Weir, and when he had finished, Simon Miller said, "So, his alibis are crap, he blackmailed somebody into fingering somebody else, he has a real motive for offing Fitzpatrick, we know he was out of the house during the time Shaw was murdered, but, and it's a big but, do we have any connection, however tenuous, between Weir and Shaw?"

Sheehan shook his head. "No, and that gives us a problem with motive. If we can't find any motive for the Shaw killing, it'll tarnish any case we might be able to make against Weir for the Fitzpatrick killing, because the two killings are clearly linked."

"Why did he need to point the finger at Duffner?" Connors asked. "Was he paying off some kind of grudge, or did he need someone other than himself in the frame?"

"It's definitely p-peculiar," McNeill agreed. "Is he trying to cover for himself? Why would he n-need to do that if he wasn't at the scene of the crime?"

"Or if he was at the scene, what would he have been doing there, if it wasn't to commit the murder?" Allen said.

"The case against him for Fitzpatrick's murder is looking stronger now," Sheehan agreed, "but, as Simon says, what's his connection to Shaw?"

Allen said, "Somebody's gonna have to start turning over stones to see if there is any connection." He looked around the room. "We need to do a serious check into Weir's background, his contacts, his enemies, his victims. Shaw might turn up somewhere, but we might have to go way back."

"The 'somebody turning over stones', Tom," Sheehan said, "is yourself and Geoff. Dig deep and dig long."

Allen managed to grimace and grin at the same time. Then he said, "We'll need help with this, guys. Check with all your sources. Grill your informants to see what's out there. Somebody, somewhere, is bound to know something."

Turner spoke again. "While this Weir lead looks promising, I still think Sergeant Stewart's line of enquiry remains significant." He glanced over at her. "Have your investigations turned up anything new, Sergeant?"

"Not yet," Stewart replied, her expression businesslike. "I'm trying to contact a Jacqueline, no surname, who was Lynda Bell's friend. I'm also intending to go back to Queen's to look at some more student transcripts to see if I can find the third youth in the photograph."

"Intending?"

Stewart found herself blushing. "Well, I've been busy with Mrs. Weir, trying to get her somewhere safe, get her a change of identity."

Turner was smiling when he responded but the smile didn't seem to reach his words. "Far be it from me to tell you your job, Sergeant, but aren't there other units to deal with cases like Mrs. Weir's?"

"Yes, but ..."

"I mean, you're engaged in a very important investigation here, probably one of the most important of your whole career. You need to find this Jacqueline. You need to find the third person in the photograph. Research at Queen's is your best resource for that, unless your informant brings something else to the table. Although, I suppose, in fairness, I should ask if Mrs Weir is still in the hospital? And have any arrangements been made to secure her safety?"

Sheehan intervened at that point. "Sergeant Stewart was acting under my orders, Mister Prosecutor. And yes, Mrs. Weir is still in the hospital, but she'll be leaving today and the sergeant has already passed the responsibility for Mrs. Weir's safety to the Witness Care Unit. We'll keep an eye on her, of course, but Sergeant Stewart is now back on track and fully committed to finding the killer of James Fitzpatrick."

Turner held his hands up in front of him. "I'm sorry, Chief inspector, and I apologise to you, too, Sergeant, if you picked up any hint of criticism from my words. I was merely trying to point out the urgency of following whatever tiny trails we have that might lead to the killer. These things get so easily lost or side-tracked when other stuff starts piling in. I've seen it too often before. Again I apologise. I guess I am a bit anxious about seeing this killer brought to court, and perhaps I allowed that to temper what I was saying."

Sheehan said, "Aye! We're all anxious. I suppose that does tend to interfere with what we might refer to as our normally instinctive diplomacy."

Turner grinned. "Nicely put, Chief Inspector."

Sheehan turned to his notes, glanced at a page, and was about to move to the next item, when the door opened and Assistant Chief Commissioner, Peter Harrison, entered the room. He was immaculately dressed, carrying a pair of black leather gloves in his right hand, and wearing a dark, woollen overcoat over a medium grey suit and white shirt. As always, he wore his Queen's University tie, although he had barely scraped a third class pass in his degree. Not a particularly handsome man, he had presence, an air of authority, that deflected any undue attention from his rather-too-thick lips and large, heavy face. He liked to project an image of an urbane but resolute policeman, on top of events, closely linked to his men. While this persona may have fooled the public, however, it didn't fool the policemen under his command, who saw through his carefully cultivated façade to the egotistical and pompous individual that was the real Peter Harrison.

He smiled grandly at the men in the room and said, "Good afternoon, Chief Inspector ..." He suddenly noticed Turner. "Prosecutor Turner, how good of you to give up your time to be with us. Very nice to have you here."

"Thank you, Assistant Chief Commissioner," Turner smiled, "but there's a rather selfish motive behind my presence here. When this case breaks, it'll be big news. The prosecutor will ..." He beamed at the ACC. "Well, you know how the politics of the thing works. I'll be prosecuting and I intend to be aware of every nuance."

The ACC smiled back. Nobody knew more than he did about the politics of career advancement. He practically wrote the book. "Astute, Mister Turner." He took a chair beside Sheehan and cleared his throat. "Well, men, where are we with these murders? The press keep hounding me for updates, and I have a spot on UTV tonight."

"It's a case full of complexities, sir," Sheehan said, "and, although we have three promising lines of enquiry, we can't reveal information about them to the public just yet, in case it alerts the killer and causes him to flee."

"Give me the gist, Chief Inspector. You can count on me, of course, to be circumspect with the press."

Yes, Sheehan thought. *First sign of a breakthrough and you'll be right there to notify the press in order to take the credit.* Aloud he said, "Well, there are two businessmen with links to the victims and real motives for murdering them. Then there's a more complex enquiry being conducted by Sergeant Stewart, involving an event that happened at Queen's University about twelve years ago."

Harrison glanced at Stewart. "Stewart? Don't I know you from somewhere?" Dawning broke on his face. "Of course, the Kerley affair. Good job there, Sergeant. Very well done."

Stewart flushed. "Thank you, sir."

Harrison preened noticeably as he gave the pretty policewoman his most charming smile. "And what line of enquiry are you following now, Sergeant?"

Stewart gave him a brief summary of what she was doing and added, "We would rather that details of this search didn't emerge just yet, sir. We do not want to alert the killer to the fact that we might be closing in on him."

"Excellent work, Sergeant, and, of course, I'll reveal to the media only a broad hint of how the investigation is progressing." He rose from his seat and turned to the room again, now adopting the role of inspiring leader. "Good work, men. I know you've got your hands full with this one, but the higher echelons, the press, and the media are hounding me. So ..." He smiled companionably at the team, exhibiting resolution, togetherness. "I need an early result, right, men?"

There were a couple of muttered, 'Right, sirs'.

"Good." He prepared to leave. "Keep me informed, Chief Inspector." He tipped his black leather glove to Turner. "Good luck with your prosecution, Mister Turner."

As he exited the room, McCoy whispered to Miller beside him, "Pompous prat." Unfortunately, he chose a moment when the room had fallen into silence, and what was intended to be a whispered comment was heard clearly by the entire room. Some faces went down to conceal unsuppressed grins, Sheehan made a play of leafing studiously through the pages in front of him, and Prosecutor Turner carefully studied his nails.

Simon Miller put a finger up to catch Sheehan's eye. Sheehan gave him a nod to speak.

"I was thinking just now about what Prosecutor Turner was saying before the ACC came in, about Sergeant Stewart's line of enquiry. The revenge theory. Well, I suppose the other two guys could be said to be looking for revenge as well, but they're individuals. It strikes me now that the taser is significant, and we can't ignore the possibilities it presents."

"Your point, Simon?" Sheehan said.

"Well, the murders are pretty gory, and it's only natural that we might think strong, young male as the killer, or even strong, older male. But if a young woman, or even an older one, knocks on your door, you're not going to be too suspicious. She could suddenly prod you with a taser, especially if it's on 'drive stun'. With fifty thousand volts incapacitating you, you're not goin' to put up much of a fight. Basically, she can do whatever she likes to you after that."

"Woman?" Sheehan's eyebrows were raised.

"Well, has Lynda Bell got a sister, or a best friend? Maybe the father or the mother have been brooding over this for years and have finally snapped, and have decided to take justice into their own hands. Maybe there's someone else in the wings badly affected by Lynda Bell's death that we don't know about. It's the taser, sir, that has me thinking like this. It doesn't half widen the suspect pool."

"Maybe the perp is a strong, young male, or older male, who just wanted the security of knowing that he could do the deed without problems," Turner offered.

"Of course," Miller replied, "but the taser leaves these other options open as well."

"I can't see either of the parents as suspects," Stewart said. "They're quiet, heart-broken people. They were very helpful to me." She was shaking her head. "No way is either of them a killer."

"What about this Jacqueline?" Turner asked.

Stewart hunched her shoulders. "I don't know anything at all about her. Until I do, I suppose she should be on the suspect list."

There was a moment of quiet until McCullough, clearly brooding on something other than what was being discussed, said, "So, is the word out about Mrs. Weir?" He eased the front legs of his chair back to the floor as all eyes turned to him.

Sheehan stared at him with narrowed eyes. "What are you getting at, Sergeant?"

"Nothin'. It's just … well, some guy was sitting beside me in the canteen at lunch today, and he asked about her."

"What guy?"

"Just one of the ordinary uniforms. I didn't know him. He was just making conversation."

"What did you tell him?" Stewart asked sharply.

McCullough shrugged. "What could I tell him? I knew nothing about the woman until the chief told us about her a while ago."

McCoy had been wriggling about on his chair during this interlude, and eventually he raised a hand like a schoolboy asking for permission to speak.

Sheehan caught the movement. "Yes, Oliver?"

McCoy pointed a thumb at McCullough and spoke with some hesitation, sounding almost guilty. "On that point, sir. I was outside havin' a smoke yesterday afternoon, and there was one of the uniforms there, too. We chatted about this and that, the weather, you know, and then he said that he'd heard Bat Weir's missus had been badly beaten."

"What did you say to him?" Sheehan asked quietly.

"Same as McCullough. I didn't know a damn thing about her. I told him that."

Sheehan hadn't missed McCoy's guilty demeanour. "What else did you say, Oliver?"

"Well, sir, I mean, he was a fellow cop ..."

"What did you say, Sergeant?"

"Just something like we were lookin' at Weir for somethin' a lot worse than assault."

Sheehan pursed his lips, stared at McCoy for some seconds, and then spoke to the room. "Men, Mrs. Weir's position is precarious. You know that Weir has spies everywhere, and if he gets wind at all of where she's being kept, then she's pretty much dead. Anything said about Mrs. Weir in this room, stays in this room, right?"

There were nods and murmurs of agreement.

"You think this cop's one of Weir's spies?" Stewart asked.

Sheehan made no answer but turned to McCullough. "Can you give us a description of the cop you spoke to?"

McCullough stared at the ceiling for inspiration. "Mid forties, skinny, maybe five ten, dark hair, long on the back of his neck ... em ..."

McCoy cut in. "Not properly shaved …"

"Yeah, designer stubble," McCullough agreed.

"Designer? Looked filthy to me. I was going to tell him to go and shave …"

"All right, all right!" Sheehan stopped them. "Clearly it's the same guy."

Allen looked shocked. "Weir has a man in the station?"

Sheehan said, "Well, we don't know for sure, but I have awful trouble with coincidences."

"We need to pull that guy in and grill the shit out of him," Connors rasped.

There were murmurs of agreement and utterings of dire threats, but Sheehan held up a hand. "We'll definitely pull him in, don't worry about that. But right now, this is perhaps a godsend for Mrs. Weir."

"You'd n-need to explain that, Chief," McNeill said.

"Weir has contacts, spies, and henchmen all over the place. Finding a safe haven for Mrs. Weir until the trial is proving difficult. It would be useful if we could slip this dirty cop some misinformation that could get back to Weir and send his cohorts scampering off in all sorts of wrong directions."

"Devious, Chief Inspector," Turner grinned, "but clever. I applaud the idea."

Others obviously approved as well, and there was much nodding of heads.

"What we do is simple," Sheehan went on. "If anyone is approached by this guy asking about Mrs. Weir, play it like it is not a topic you're particularly interested in and don't know much about."

"Supposin' he doesn't come near any of us," McCullough said. "Do we sorta bump into him accidentally on purpose?"

"Absolutely not," Sheehan said. "Don't make things obvious. He'll suspect something right away if you do that. Just wait. Believe me, he will try to pump one of us. He'll be too scared of Weir not to."

"What exactly do we tell him?" Miller asked.

"Chat away until he steers the conversation to Mrs. Weir, and then just casually toss out that all you heard was that she is being held in a safe house or something, somewhere way down in the south of Ireland and that she is getting a change of identity. No more than that, okay? That's all you know. Just shrug off any follow-up questions and change the subject to the weather or something. Everybody clear on that?"

There was universal agreement. McCullough, slanting his chair back to balance it on its two back legs, asked, "So, where exactly is Mrs. Weir, Chief?" He shifted uncomfortably as all eyes turned to him. He assumed an expression of injured innocence. "Just askin'. What's the big deal?"

"Better not to ask," Sheehan said. "We'll leave the details to Witness Services and let Sergeant Stewart liaise with them."

Turner said, "The sooner we have the court hearing, the sooner he'll be incarcerated. He can still cause trouble from prison, but at least his wings will be severely clipped."

"His brief's pushing for an early appearance before a magistrate. He'll be going all out for bail," Sheehan told him.

Turner gave the matter a minute's thought. "Let me look into that. I'll check when he's to be arraigned and make a point of being there myself to ensure he doesn't get bail. Although there is a general assumption in favour of bail, the charges against him, his record, and the very real possibility he presents of further physical harm to Mrs. Weir, will give me ammunition enough to keep him detained in custody until the trial."

"That'd be brilliant, if you could do that," Stewart said, uncharacteristically animated.

Turner gave her a wide smile. "Delighted to help, Denise."

"It would certainly take a lot of pressure off that end of things and let us concentrate on the murders," Sheehan said. "Thanks for that, Mister Prosecutor."

"Glad to do it. My contribution to the team." He grinned at the men. "Right?"

Many of the team smiled back at him, impressed, reassessing their earlier assumptions about him. Big shots don't usually operate like this. *Maybe this guy isn't so bad.* Stewart, however, had her head down, berating herself. *That was bloody stupid. He'll think I was encouraging him.*

Tom Allen wasn't smiling either. He was looking at Stewart, wondering if there was more going on between her and the handsome prosecutor than she had led him to believe.

He had little time to ponder it, however, because Sheehan was speaking again. "Okay! That'll do for today, but things are starting to happen, and happen at speed. Go now, and carry out your assigned tasks. If you're not sure of what you have to do, Bill has a note in the Action Book. Double-check with him before you leave."

There was much scraping of chairs and loud conversation. Sheehan raised his voice to call over the top of the din, "And we'll have one more debrief on Friday afternoon before we take the weekend off … or before some of us do, anyway."

FORTY- FIVE

Not long after the debriefing in Strandtown station had ended, a civilian receptionist in the Lisburn Police Station answered the phone. "Hello, Lisburn Police Station. Who's calling, please?"

"Hi! I was looking for Inspector Chambers, or perhaps Inspector Wilson. Are either of them at the station this evening?"

"Yes, they're both here. Which one would you prefer to speak to?"

The voice at the other end of the line was suddenly muffled, and then the receptionist heard him say, "Sorry, I'm being called away here. I'll phone later. What time do they leave?"

"Sometime after five o' clock, sir. Could I have your name, please, and some indication of the nature of your business …" She stopped speaking. The caller had hung up. She looked at the phone and muttered, "Odd!" before replacing it on the receiver.

Lisburn Police Station, at first glance, is not dissimilar in appearance to the station at Strandtown. It has the same long, redbrick wall down one street, and a wire barrier on its top held in place by a series of dark green, metal posts. The entrance gate leads into a yard with more redbrick walls, and the standard protected viewing window is built into the wall at the left of the entrance.

Barracks Street, a fairly wide street with ample parking facilities, runs down along the station's wall to the town centre. At four forty-five, an hour or so after the civilian receptionist had received the odd phone call, a small, nondescript Peugeot drove into this street and parked some fifty yards or so from the station, facing in the direction of the entrance gate. Dusk was starting to fall, and visibility was becoming limited. The driver exited the car and eased himself closer to the station entrance, ensconcing himself behind a parked car from where he could observe without being seen.

The entrance gate, because of the lights around it, was visible in the gathering darkness, but as cars began to exit the station, the watcher became aware that he was unable to see their occupants. "What the hell am I doing here?" he chided himself. "This is pointless. They could drive right past my nose, and I wouldn't even know." But he continued to wait, and to watch, hoping against hope that he would catch a break.

The October breeze was freshening, and its bite, together with the discomfort caused by bursts of gusty rain squalls, made the watcher's sojourn much more unpleasant than he had anticipated. The cold was seeping into his bones now and, as he pulled the collar of his overcoat up around his neck, he debated going back to his car and attempting his surveillance from there.

Just as he decided to call it quits, he noticed two figures emerging from the station gate, one rotund and tallish, the other small and slim. "Laurel and bloody Hardy," he breathed. "And walking! *C'est mon jour de chance!*" It was to transpire, however, that luck had a deal less to do with his good fortune than something as mundane as routine.

He turned and walked slowly towards his car, keeping a vigilant eye on the two detectives sauntering down the other side of the street. Although they were hunched against the wind, they appeared to be in no hurry, and were chatting amiably as they headed towards town. Detective Allen continued to follow them at a discreet distance, rather expecting them to arrive at a parked car and drive off. Instead they turned left at the end of Barracks Street, carried on along Smithfield Street and finally turned right into

Lisburn Square where they stopped outside a bar-restaurant called The Tuesday Bell.

Even with street lights, Allen could not see the building clearly. It was two storeys high, the upper storey painted in some kind of light colour, perhaps beige or cream. He got the impression from what light the street lamps afforded, that the lower storey was dark blue. Chambers and Wilson remained outside the door, seeming to be arguing about something, and Wilson made to walk on. Chambers caught his arm and pointed into the pub with his thumb. After a few more minutes of animated discussion, they both went into the pub.

Allen looked at his watch. Five twenty-five. If they were going to eat, he could be in for a long wait. He debated going back for his car but decided against it. They might only have gone in for a quick pint. He wanted to be there when they came out. He pulled his coat closer around himself and sauntered to the corner across the road. Concealed there in relative darkness, he took a deep breath and prepared himself to wait in patience.

By seven o'clock whatever he had in the way of patience had long evaporated. He was freezing. His feet were cold, his ears were cold, his nose was cold, his hands, even in his overcoat pockets, were cold. Every part of him was cold. He was moving around on the spot, contrary to all his surveillance training, muttering to himself and wondering, for the umpteenth time, what the hell they were doing in there. People came and went, and he continued to stare optimistically as various customers left the building, hoping that this time his vigil was about to end.

Then a devastating thought, so sudden that it hit him with an almost physical thud, rendered him rigid and irresolute. Had they spotted him tailing them, put on that act in front of the pub, then slipped out through the back? His fists were curled in frustration, and he was inwardly berating himself for being all sorts of a fool, when the two detectives exited the building, chatted for a couple of minutes at the door, and left in different directions. Allen expelled a relieved breath. He considered for a moment the fruitlessness of following either of them at this time in the evening, decided against it, and crossed the street to the bar, wanting as much to get out of the cold as to seek information.

The interior was pleasantly laid out, a long bar along one wall where a few customers were chatting and drinking, well away from a central area furnished with tables and chairs, where other customers were eating. Allen went to the bar and pulled his coat open with a loud shiver. "Freezin' out there," he said to the barman. "Could you give me a hot whiskey, please?"

The barman, fortyish, black shirt, black trousers, black hair, black stubble, white pock-marked skin, brought him his drink and set it before him with a coaster and a small glass dish of peanuts. Allen made a very obvious show of gazing around as if he was searching for someone. He thanked the barman for the drink, raised it briefly in salute, and drank from it. "God, I needed that." He stared around some more while the barman wiped the counter with a cloth. "Thought I might have met up with a couple of friends of mine," he said, still looking, "but they don't seem to be here."

"Regulars, are they?" the barman asked.

"Couple of cop friends, Chambers and Wilson. Do you happen to know them?"

"Ah, you just missed them. Sure they're away home, aren't they?"

"Are they?"

"Aye! They are."

"Do you know them?"

"Sure they come in here every evening after work, don't they?"

Caught up into the rhythm of the man's mode of speech, Allen responded, fighting a grin, "Do they?"

"Aye! They do."

"Were they here last night?"

"Sure they're always here, aren't they?"

"Are they?"

"Aye! They are."

"Might be able to bump into them tomorrow evening, then. What do you think?"

The barman began polishing some glasses. "Always here till around seven, aren't they?"

"Are they?"

"Aye! They are."

Allen finished his drink and rose to leave. "Thanks for the drink. Sure I'll try again tomorrow evening, won't I?"

"Will you?"

"Aye! I will."

Allen left the bar and walked back to his car. He was grinning openly now, amused by the barman's odd conversational style, but already his mind was processing the fact that Chambers and Wilson had almost certainly nothing to do with the attacks on him and the stalking of Denise, not if they were sitting in the Tuesday Bell every evening. That was a shock. He had been sure that they were the stalkers. Now he was shaking his head uncertainly. *Where the hell do we go from here?* And he heard a faint echo at the back of his mind. *Sure your goin' home now, aren't you?* He grinned ruefully. *Aye! I am.*

FORTY-SIX

1

Stewart had just finished tidying up after her evening meal when the phone rang. Never totally at ease with the apparatus since her so-called informant appeared on the scene, she lifted the receiver somewhat gingerly and said, "Hello?"

"Hi, it's me."

Tom's voice. She grinned mischievously. "Me? Who's me?"

She got a distinctly frosty response. "Me. Detective Tom Allen."

"Oh, hello, Detective Allen," she said breezily.

"Hummph! I've got some news for you."

"Oh?"

"Yes. Laurel and Hardy are definitely not the ones who are stalking you and trying to injure me."

Her eyebrows went down. "Laurel and Hardy?"

"Chambers and Wilson."

Her laugh was sudden and spontaneous. To Allen it sounded angelic. "Oh, them? I never would have thought of calling them that." Then serious again, she asked, "How do you know?"

"I went to Lisburn tonight and followed them from the police station when they left work. They go to a pub every night in the town centre and usually stay there until around seven. I froze my butt off, and God knows what else, waiting for them to come back out. I got the info about them from the bartender after they left."

She was silent a moment as she digested this news. "I'm not sure what to feel about that. In one way it's a relief that you've discounted them, but who does that leave us with and why?"

"Hard to say. You got any jealous ex's?"

"Why do you ask?"

"Well, maybe one of them has seen us together and thinks I'm coming on to you."

She grinned again and said, "And are you?"

"Am I what?"

"Coming on to me?"

"What? Who? Me? Nooo. No way. God forbid."

Stewart was grinning into the phone, but she kept her voice serious. "Oh, so you don't fancy me? Good to get that out of the way then."

"Hold on a minute. I didn't say that ..."

"You said, 'God forbid.' I heard you. What else could that mean?"

"Look, I was trying to be ... uh ... not to be ..." He stopped talking.

"Oh, are you saying you do fancy me, then?" she said archly.

"Sarge, will you quit? You're pulling my leg, and you're pulling it very hard. I'm about to topple over."

"By the way, I hope your whatever else will be all right."

Tom stalled, momentarily baffled. "What are you talking about now?"

"What almost froze off while you were hanging around Lisburn town centre."

"Right, Stewart. I'm hanging up now. But we're going to have this conversation again, and the next time, I'll be ready for you."

She chuckled, loudly enough for him to hear. "We'll see, Detective Allen. We'll see."

2

Shortly after eleven o'clock that same Thursday night, Stewart's phone rang again. She was smiling as she answered, sure it was Tom with some plan to get his own back on her. "Hello?"

A metallic voice said, "Well, have you found Jacqueline yet?"

She stared at the phone, annoyance rippling through her. *This guy's beginning to get on my nerves.* "No," she responded, without elaboration.

"What about the third guy in the picture? Have you found him?"

"No," she said again, adding as an afterthought, "Why don't you tell me who he is?"

Her caller was silent for a moment. Then he said, "Try checking out some transcripts from the Maths and Sciences Department." He hung up, and all Stewart could hear was the eerie, metallic silence of a lost connection.

FORTY-SEVEN

1

Sheehan was sitting at his desk on Friday morning, his head resting on his clasped hands. But he wasn't praying; he was cursing the intangible nature of insight. Hunches, or sudden flashes of enlightenment, are great when they thrust themselves, unbidden, into consciousness. But when insight is sought, pursued, courted, she behaves like a coy dryad, flitting from tree to tree, sometimes barely perceptible, invariably insubstantial, never grasped. Sheehan was trying to think but his brain was simply whirling. There were so many infuriating threads to this case, and none seemed linked. What was Weir's role in the murders? He had definitely been lying through his teeth at the interrogation. Where was Lynda Bell's missing boyfriend? Was Stewart's theory about him the key to everything? Was revenge the motivation for the murders? Whose revenge? There were a number of possibilities. And who was Stewart's mystery informant? Why was he helping her? What was his agenda? And the stalker? Twice he tried to maim, even kill, Tom Allen. Where does he fit in? If he does fit in.

He sat back in his chair and expelled a frustrated breath as he stared at the ceiling. "Inspiration," he muttered, "where the hell are you?"

The phone rang, startling him out of his preoccupation. He grabbed it and grunted. "Serious Crimes, CDI Sheehan speaking."

The pleasant voice of the station telephonist said, "Chief Inspector, there's a Mister Brannigan on the phone would like to speak with you."

Weir's mouthpiece? What does he want? "Thanks, Alice. Put him on, please."

A couple of clicks and Arthur Brannigan said, "Good morning, Chief Inspector, Arthur Brannigan here."

Affecting a bonhomie he didn't feel, Sheehan said expansively, "Good morning, Mister Brannigan. How can I help you?"

"I have been instructed by my client, Mister Ronald Weir, to request a further interview regarding the evening of Tuesday the fourteenth of October."

The night Fitzpatrick was killed? Sheehan's interest was piqued. "Has he something to add to his earlier statement?"

"He has, Chief Inspector, and I think you'll find it significant."

Sheehan was silent, tapping the table with his fingers. The pause extended as he tried to conceive what possible game Weir might be playing.

Brannigan said, somewhat hesitantly, "Chief Inspector? Did you hear what I just said?"

"Yes. I'm thinking." He waited a beat longer. "Okay. I'll talk to him. Be at Interrogation Room One in forty-five minutes."

"Thank you, Chief Inspector. I'll be there. I presume you'll arrange to have Mr. Weir brought there as well?"

Holy shit! What is it with lawyers? "That would seem politic, Mr. Brannigan. I rather imagine it would be easier for him to make his statement if he was actually present in the room."

"Of course, Chief Inspector. Of course." Brannigan spoke quickly, covering his discomfiture. "I will see you then. Goodbye."

Sheehan hung up. *Wonder what all this is about?* He dialled a number. *Might as well get things moving.*

2

At the precise moment Sheehan was making his phone calls, Stewart was sitting in the Queen's University Library, studying a student's transcript. She had sucked in a breath and seemed to have forgotten to let it back out. There was a copy of the Fitzpatrick photograph on the desk beside her, and she was in no doubt that the photograph on the top corner of the transcript matched the face of the third young man in the photograph. Trying to appear calm, she went to the desk and asked the librarian to copy the transcript for her. While she was waiting, she gathered up the other transcripts in readiness to return them to the young geek in the registrar's office. Armed with this new information, she hurried from the university and headed back to the station.

3

Sheehan came out of his office some twenty minutes after Brannigan's phone call and nodded to Allen, who was on the phone looking every bit as fed up as he sounded. He waited for the young detective to hang up and said, "Weir wants us back in Interrogation Room One. I'm heading down there now. I need you with me as a witness."

Allen jumped up. "Delighted, sir. Trying to establish a connection between Weir and Shaw is driving me nuts. I'm making no headway at all."

They arrived at the interrogation room before the appointed time but Brannigan and Weir were already there.

Sheehan announced the date, time, and names of those present into the recorder, then said, "Well, Mr. Weir. You called this meeting. What do you need to say?"

"What I have to say is important. How's about a deal? Police bail for the info?"

Allen, immediately enraged, was almost on his feet. "Sir!"

Sheehan's calming hand signalled him to sit. "It's okay, Detective Allen. Mister Weir and Mister Brannigan are just leaving."

"What? You don't even want to hear …?"

Sheehan said, "If you have something to say, Mister Weir, say it. But please don't waste my time trying to do deals."

Weir hesitated a moment but, on a firm nod from Brannigan, he said sullenly, "I hear I'm strongly in the frame for Fitzpatrick's murder. I didn't do it."

"Yes," Sheehan nodded. "You've already told us that."

"And you didn't believe me."

"Uh huh! So why should we believe you now?"

"I'm not going down for a murder I didn't commit, so I want to change my account of where I was at that time."

Allen moved slightly in his seat, but Sheehan showed no reaction. He simply said, "Okay, so where were you, then?"

"At the time of the murder, or shortly after it, I was driving into the street where Fitzpatrick lives."

Now Sheehan's face did show surprise but he recovered quickly. "Oh? Had you forgotten something and had to go back for it."

"No. I happened to arrive at a time when there was a lot of activity, lights, police vehicles, cops running around with yellow tape … I didn't know what had happened. But I wasn't about to wait around to find out. I reversed quietly and got the hell out of there."

Sheehan was unsure what to believe at this point. Weir was no idiot. Was this some clever ploy, an outlandishly risky gamble, to deflect suspicion from himself? "So what were you doing there in the first place?"

"Well, I had just heard that Fitzpatrick was banging my wife. I went there to have a little talk with him."

"A little talk?"

"You know, chat with him. Find out what he thought he was playing at."

"Were you alone?"

"No, I brought along two witnesses."

"Witnesses?"

"Yes, I wanted to make sure that if Fitzpatrick tried anything, I'd have witnesses to back up my side of the story."

Good grief, Sheehan was thinking, *the guy is actually saying this with a straight face.* "Am I to be told the names of these … ah … witnesses?"

"Tommy Byrne and Graham Havern."

Sheehan recognised the names immediately. A couple of ex-loyalist thugs and well known associates of Mr. Weir. Weir's face was beginning to regain its customary smug expression. Sheehan didn't like it. "You had nothing other than a conversation planned?"

"No. I just wanted to talk to him."

"Maybe you did talk to him, and it all went haywire? Maybe you, or all of you, lost your tempers and didn't stop until you had beaten him to death?"

"No need for that, Chief Inspector," Brannigan intervened. "Mr. Weir's trying to make matters clear."

"And now you're here trying to put some sort of spin on it," Sheehan went on, as if Brannigan hadn't spoken, "in case the investigation turns up the fact that you were there at the time of the murder."

"We didn't get near his house," Weir snapped. The smug look had gone. "We just got as far as the end of the road … Look, I was driving my Rolls. Somebody living around there must have seen it. They'll tell you we barely got into the street till we were reversing out of it."

Sheehan was silent for a moment, reflecting on what had been said. He turned to Allen. "Is there anything you would like to ask Mister Weir, Detective?"

"Yes. Why did you blackmail Sloan into fingering Mister Duffner for the murder?"

"Steady on, Detective," Brannigan shouted. That's scurrilous …"

"Mister Brannigan, please!" Allen said. "I was the one who interviewed Sloan. The facts are known to me." He looked at Weir. "Care to answer the question, sir?"

"It's not that hard to figure out," Weir sneered. "I knew I was in the frame and knew Duffner was a suspect as well …"

"How did you know that?" Sheehan cut in.

"Uh … I heard it around. I think one of my men told me."

"And how did he know?"

"I didn't think to ask."

Allen chose not to push it. "So, you were quite happy to try to place the blame on an innocent person just to save your own neck?"

Weir shrugged. "It's dog eat dog out there in the real world, Detective. Every man for himself."

"So, you don't actually know whether Duffner had anything to do with the murder or not?"

"No. He was just a handy schmuck."

Allen sat back in disgust. "Nothing more, Chief."

Sheehan nodded. "Was there anything else in your previous statement that you want to redress, Mister Weir?"

The man shook his head. "No. That's it."

Sheehan turned to the recorder, stated the time the interview had ended, and switched off the machine.

"Well, do I get police bail or not?" Weir said belligerently.

Sheehan went to the door, opened it, and said to the policeman on guard outside. "Officer, could you bring the prisoner back to his cell, please."

FORTY-EIGHT

The mood in the Serious Crimes Room, as the team waited for the start of the Friday afternoon debriefing, was sombre. There was little sign of the customary ribaldry, the pockets of animated conversation, the occasional pecking at keyboards. The team members were sitting glumly in their chairs, staring vacantly in front of them or muttering the odd desultory comment to the person next to them. Sheehan was all too conscious of their mood. He shared their frustration. Two weeks after the first murder and little to show for their strenuous efforts. All they had were a couple of suspects with heavy motives but nothing in the way of facts or evidence to attach them to the crimes. And next Tuesday was approaching like an express train. *No point in hanging about,* he thought, and called the meeting to order. "Okay, men, we'll make a start …"

He stopped as Prosecutor Turner entered the room. Turner held up a hand as he took his seat beside the chief inspector. "Sorry I'm late. Got held up in court."

Allen looked up. "Feel free to miss the occasional meeting, Mister Prosecutor. We don't expect you to give us all of your time."

Sheehan glanced at him, wondering if there was a green tinge to the remark.

Turner smiled back at Allen. "Well, I was hoping I was being seen as part of the team by now, Detective Allen. For me this is a complex case, and when I prosecute it I want to have all the facts and, indeed, all the nuances, at my fingertips. It's important I attend these meetings. But, anyway, I have a wee bit of news I wanted to deliver."

"Oh?" Sheehan said, curious. "Care to share it now?"

Turner looked a little surprised. "Sure, but is it all right for me to be just throwing my stuff in out of order?"

Sheehan's mouth was turned down at the sides when he replied. "I don't think there's going to be much order here today. We're all pretty much cheesed off with our lack of progress."

Stewart raised a hand. "I might have something interesting, Chief, when Mister Turner is finished."

The team perked up. "Two bits of news," Miller said, smiling. "My day's definitely starting to brighten up."

"Yes, well, let's hear what they are," Sheehan said. He nodded to Turner. "You have the floor, Mister Prosecutor."

"As I said, I was delayed in court," Turner began, "but why I was delayed was because I was arguing at Weir's preliminary hearing." He smiled at the room. "And, I didn't seem to do too badly, as it turned out."

"He didn't get bail?" Stewart interrupted, unable to stop herself, tense, hoping for a positive response.

Turner smiled at her. "Correct, Denise. I was able to persuade the magistrate that Weir was a serious threat to his wife, having already put her in hospital for a relatively minor offence. I made the point that now that she had agreed to testify at his trial, her safety would be in considerable jeopardy if he were to be freed on bail."

"And the magistrate accepted that?" Allen asked.

"Of course. That, and the fact the he knows Weir from of old." He grinned modestly. "I think that even a newbie intern could have successfully argued the case."

"So what was the upshot?" Connors asked.

"Weir is to be remanded in custody until his trial. No possibility of bail and no appeal against that decision."

Stewart clenched her fists under the desk and gave the air a little punch.

"Any word of his trial?" Sheehan asked.

"Six months at the earliest, maybe even longer." He looked at Stewart. "I would suggest you get Mrs. Weir out of the country, Sergeant, as soon as the Witness Care Unit have set her up with her new identity and papers. She can always come back for the trial, say her piece, and disappear again immediately after it."

She nodded. "I'll see to that." She hesitated. "And thank you for the good work today, Robert."

Turner's smile was wide. "Always glad to be of help, Denise."

Allen's scowl was dark.

Sheehan looked around the room. "What about Weir's mole? Has he tried to sound anybody since that last time?"

McCoy raised his hand. "Yes, he got to me yesterday while I was out having a smoke."

"What did he say?" McCullough asked.

"I'll give him his due," McCoy said. "He takes no chances. He talked away for about ten minutes about nothing and everything, offering me a cigarette in the meantime to keep me there."

"Then what?" Sheehan asked.

"Well, he very casually said that he'd just heard in the canteen that Weir was banged up." He grinned. "I think I should get an Oscar. I just went on smoking and said I hadn't heard that. Then he said something about him being sure that Missus Weir would be relieved at the news. So I went into this routine of looking around me as if to make sure no one was listening, and I sorta whispered that I'd heard she was getting a new identity and being sent to the South of Ireland into some sort of witness protection. Made him swear that he'd tell no one."

"Did he buy it?" Allen asked.

"Yeah, he seemed to. I could see he was dying to ask me where she'd been sent, so I just said that, of course, nobody knew where she was going, that it was all very hush, hush. He actually asked me, trying to be real casual, if I knew myself where she was going. But I just gave him a sideways glance, making it look like it would be some day when the brass shared that kind of stuff with a five eighths like me."

"And that was it?" Sheehan asked.

"Aye! He just looked at his watch and said that he'd better get back in before he got into trouble."

"Right, everybody," Sheehan said. "If he approaches anyone else, just shrug and say you know nothing. Leave it at that. No more histrionics."

McCoy's pleased grin faded.

"It's fine, Oliver. It's fine. From your account, it all seems to have gone well. But those of us with lesser dramatic ability than yours might have given the game away. So that's it. The bait has been laid. Let's all forget about it." He looked at Stewart. "You have something for us, Sergeant?"

"Yes, sir. I went back to Queen's this morning hoping to look at some more transcripts. I picked Maths and Science this time," she cleared her throat, feeling guilty about the minor deception, "and after a couple of hours I found the third guy in the photograph."

This got the entire room's attention.

"Have you sp-spoken to him?" McNeill asked.

"No. His name is Finbar Kelly. I called the telephone number on the transcript but the house had been sold several years ago, and nobody knew where the Kellys had moved to."

"Another dead end," McCullough grunted.

"Not quite, Sergeant," Stewart said and went on, "Bit after your time but when we hit snags like that nowadays, the first thing we do is head for the internet. I was soon directed to the Electoral

Registry who, after I had verified my credentials, kindly gave me the man's address and occupation."

McCullough had the grace to look impressed. "Good work, Sergeant," he said.

There were other murmurs of approval around the room. Turner's smile was almost splitting his face.

"So, who is he?" Connors asked.

"I was given his home address, his phone number, and his place of work. He teaches mathematics at Bearnageeha High School. But when I tried to contact him, I was told he had already gone home. There was no answer from his house when I rang a short while ago." She looked at Sheehan. "I was hoping the chief and I could call round to see him after the debrief."

"Try keeping me away, Sergeant," Sheehan said, grinning. "That's excellent news. We can learn first hand what happened to Lynda Bell, and we can perhaps get to prevent a third murder. Great work, Sergeant. We'll head round there as soon as this meeting is over."

"Thank you, sir."

"What are we going to do about him when you're finished talking to him?" Allen asked.

"Do about him?" Sheehan responded.

"Well, not to put too fine a point on it, sir, but next Tuesday's only round the corner. Regardless of what story the guy tells us, we're hardly going to leave him sitting there high and dry for the vengeful suitor or whoever to pick him off."

"Where are you going with this, Tom?" Sheehan said.

"We'd either need to take him into protective custody or send a couple of big cops around to protect him in his house."

"When? Tonight? Tomorrow night? Tuesday night?"

"Dunno, sir, I haven't had time to think this through. Definitely Tuesday night, anyway."

Stewart, who had been listening intently, said, "We want to catch the guy, sir. Not scare him away."

"Or her," Miller chipped in.

Stewart nodded. "Or her. But I'll just stick with 'him'. If whoever it is comes on Tuesday night to finish his mission and sees cops around Kelly's house, he'll almost certainly scarper, and then we'll have lost him."

"What are you thinking, Stewart?" Sheehan asked.

"Like Detective Allen, I haven't thought this through, but I'm thinking that we might be able to bait the killer somehow. I mean, we'll definitely protect Kelly, but try to make it look like he's vulnerable, so that the killer isn't scared off."

"What do you s-s-suggest, Sergeant?" McNeill said.

"Well, my reading is that Kelly will be safe over the next few nights. Tuesday is the night when anything is likely to happen. So, we put one guard in Kelly's house each night. If the killer is true to form, there's no doubt that he'll be watching and trying to assess what's happening."

"And Tuesday night?" Sheehan said.

"Make it look the same. Make it look that I have drawn the short straw for that night. A woman sitting in the house will probably   be   less   intimidating."
"Are you mad, Denise?" Turner intervened, his voice a couple of notches louder than normal. "That's seriously dangerous. Why would you put yourself at risk like that?"

"But I wouldn't be at risk, Robert," Stewart replied. "We'd have two or three armed police hiding somewhere … we'd need to get a look at where Kelly lives before we could work out the logistics of that. I'm just putting forward the bare bones of a plan."

Turner's face was filled with concern. "Chief Inspector, you're not giving this craziness any credence, are you? It's fraught with all sorts of danger." He looked at Stewart. "I'm not doubting your courage, Sergeant, but you have to be sensible. This could be a big guy with a taser. If he gets to you …"

Allen was quick in behind him. "I agree with Prosecutor Turner. If anything went wrong, you'd be …"

"Oh," Stewart cut in with some heat, "so women cops are only good for doing research in libraries, is that it?"

Both men immediately began shaking their heads, saying, "No, no, it's not that. It's …"

"All right, all right," Sheehan quietened the incipient argument. "Any one of us in that house would be in danger on Tuesday night. Stewart's notion has merit, but nobody, no matter who it is, is going to be put at any kind of risk until the whole thing has been fully examined. We'll wait until Stewart and I have had a look around the place and see what opportunities Kelly's garden or street offers for concealment. We'll talk about this later when we know more."

Turner wasn't finished. His concern for Stewart's safety was still evident. "Chief, seriously …"

"Absolutely nothing has been decided, Mister Prosecutor, but Sergeant Stewart took the same oaths as all the rest of us. If it seems that she would be able to contribute to a resolution of this case in any meaningful way, then she'll be called upon to do so. That's her job."

Stewart didn't smirk but she was close to it. Turner and Allen looked distinctly disgruntled but neither said anything more. Certainly, as far as the chief inspector was concerned, the discussion was over. He turned to Bill Larkin who was sitting in his customary chair in front of the whiteboard, and said, "Any news on the four by four, Bill?"

"Actually, yes. The vehicle was found abandoned near Ardboe?"

"Ardboe?" McCoy echoed. "What in the hell was it doing there?"

"I've heard of Ardboe, Sarge," Allen said, "but could you just remind me where it is?"

"It's a wee village, less than a thousand inhabitants." He became aware of the eyes on him, the puzzled expressions. He raised his hands and shrugged. "I was stationed at Cookstown when I was a beat constable, wasn't I? Ardboe's only over the road from there."

"Wonder what the veh-veh-vehicle was doing there?" McNeill said. "Ass end of n-n-nowhere."

"Well, it's a pretty good place to hide a vehicle," Larkin said. "Loads of empty tracks, fields, bare land. It's a place where nobody would pass any remarks on a parked car. Lots of scenery and touristy stuff there, as well as the lonely places, but this time of year, the place would see no one for days at a time. The vehicle was only discovered by a fluke."

Larko loved this kind of limelight. More than that, he loved to pause at key points so that someone would be forced to urge him on. He waited now.

"Well, Larko," Miller said, "are you going to keep the rest of the story a secret?"

"All in good time, Simon. It happens that, despite the weather, there was a hardened hiker doing one of the trails there. The car was rather too well hidden. If it had just been on the side of the road, the guy might well have ignored it. But it was pulled in behind some overhanging branches and that, with the badly bashed wing and side door, made the guy suspicious, and he reported it to Cookstown station. And, of course, they'd seen our flier and got on to us."

Sheehan said, "Okay! Get back to the business end of this, Bill. What did forensics find?"

"Forensics have been all over it, sir, but their search has yielded little, I'm afraid."

"What's little?" Sheehan asked.

"Well, the car had been stolen, and we have contacted the owner. The fibres, prints, hairs, and other forensic data belong more or less to the owner, or members of his family. The perp was careful. However," Larkin then held up a somewhat triumphant finger, "when he crashed into Tom, he must have bumped his head back

283

against the headrest. Forensics found two hairs there that don't match the DNA of the owner or any of the family members."

Sheehan experienced a frisson of hope. "You got a name?"

Larkin shook his head. "Unfortunately the hairs don't belong to anyone on our database, so for the minute all we have are two hairs that could belong to anybody, at least, until a name comes forward that we can match them against."

"So, we're no further forward?"

Somewhat stung, Larkin responded, "Well, I would have thought the hairs … anyway, we did find something interesting on Shaw's computer."

He paused, forcing Sheehan to say, "You're going to make me ask you what it is, aren't you?"

"Oh, no, no, sir. Just gathering my thoughts."

"Well, gather them a bit more quickly. What did you find? Another copy of the photograph, or the cutting? What?"

"No photograph, no cutting. It was an email dated twelve years ago. It was found in among some flagged messages that were never deleted. I think it bears out what Sergeant Stewart just told us about the name of the third youth." Bill bent forward to his desk and picked up a printed page which he pinned to the whiteboard.

"Can't see that, Larko," Miller shouted up at him from near the back of the room. Larkin didn't see Miller's grin.

"Wait a wee minute, will you?" he said testily, fiddling with a PowerPoint viewer. "Gimme a second." A brief moment later a magnified version of the email appeared on the whiteboard. It was brief and to the point:

Hi, Petey. Did you hear about the girl? She's committed suicide. Do we do something, or let it lie, or what? Christ, man, this is terrible. Get back to me ASAP. Fin

Larkin read the email aloud, and said, "I think this Fin has to be the Finbar Kelly Sergeant Stewart was talking about."

"Looks like he was having some sort of crisis of conscience," Turner said. "Wonder if he followed up on it?"

"Stewart and I will certainly be asking him about that," Sheehan said. "Was there anything else, Bill?"

"That's all I have, Chief."

"Okay, Bill. Thanks." He turned back to the room. "Tom, Geoff, any luck on finding a connection between Weir and Shaw?"

Allen shook his head. "Sorry, Chief. It's proving difficult. We've tried pretty much everything but nothing's come up. But we've been coming at it from the Weir side. We'll go back to Shaw and see if we can find anything in his background."

"All right. Keep at it. Anyone else want to say something?"

Allen raised a hand. "Just one other wee point, sir." Getting the nod from Sheehan, he recounted the result of his surveillance of the Lisburn cops.

"Are you sure that none of the other Lisburn guys are stalking Sergeant Stewart?" McCoy asked.

"Pretty sure, Oliver. If it had to be somebody from Lisburn, I'd have said these two were our best bet."

"So we're back to being completely clueless again about the stalker?" Turner said.

"Looks like that, sir," Allen replied, "but we'll keep on doing what we always do. We'll find him, or her, sooner or later."

"Okay," Sheehan said, gathering up the papers in front of him. "We'll call a halt. I'm anxious to visit this Kelly fellow and have a chat with him."

FORTY-NINE

Even as he got out of the car, Sheehan was already studying the street around Kelly's house and, indeed, the house itself. He'd obviously taken something of Stewart's proposed action to heart. *Nothing set in stone,* he was thinking as he stared around, *but no harm in checking things out.*

Kelly lived in a three bedroom, semi-detached house in a large estate on the outskirts of Glengormley, a few miles from the city. There was room at the front for no more than a pocket-sized lawn, separated from the footpath by a two foot high wall. The incline from the gate, however, was steep although it required little more than a couple of steps to reach the front door. Sheehan's lips tightened. *Couldn't even conceal a bloody mouse here.* He looked up and down the street. The cul-de-sac ended some yards to his right. Just where it ended, there was a large detached house, obviously privately built, with a six or seven foot fence encircling the entire building. Clearly the owner treasured his privacy.

The opening door ended his reverie. Finbar Kelly, if that was the man who answered the door, was a tall, slim man in his early thirties. His thick mop of dark hair was already showing streaks of grey, and his face was prematurely lined, hinting at a life marred by some kind of hardship. He held the door half-closed, glancing uneasily right and left of the street before saying, "Hello. Can I help you?"

Sheehan held up his warrant card. "I'm Chief Inspector Sheehan, and this is my colleague, Sergeant Stewart. Do you mind if we come in to have a few words with you?"

Kelly's expression revealed more guilt than curiosity. "Police?"

Sheehan waited calmly without further remark until the man was forced to say, "Oh, yes, all right. Please come in."

He led them into a small sitting room. A small green plaid sofa and two matching armchairs sat on a polished wooden floor. A thirty-two inch flat screen television stood in a corner to the right of a small fireplace. Kelly took one of the armchairs and invited the two detectives to sit on the sofa. He was clearly nervous but he tried for businesslike as he said, "So, how can I help you, detectives?"

Sheehan elected to forego diplomacy, partly because of the contempt he felt for the man, partly because he wanted to elicit a strong reaction. His voice was almost robotic as he said, "Our investigations into the murder of James Fitzpatrick and Peter Shaw have led to the discovery that twelve years ago you three physically abused and raped a young lady named Lynda Bell who subsequently committed suicide as a result of trauma you caused."

Kelly's reaction could not have been more dramatic had Sheehan hit him in the stomach with a pile driver. He blanched, recoiled back into his seat, and stuttered, "W … what? Where did you hear that?"

"Do you deny it?" Stewart said, her tone acerbic.

The man looked from one to the other, initially searching desperately for some kind of defence. His mouth worked wordlessly before he crumpled into his chair, his expression simultaneously resigned and pleading. "It wasn't the way you think."

"Perhaps you'd care to enlighten us?" The man's state was pathetic, but Stewart had no sympathy for him.

"Neither me nor Petey had anything to do with it."

"What?" Stewart's surprise overcame her police training.

"I'm afraid that response doesn't fit with the evidence we have found," Sheehan said calmly.

"I mean ... we were sort of involved, yes, but ..."

"Perhaps you could start at the beginning, sir," Sheehan said.

The man was clearly distressed. "Oh God, we should never have let it come to this ..."

"The beginning, sir?" Sheehan prompted.

Wringing his hands and unable to stop fidgeting, Kelly said haltingly, "We were at a students' party ..."

"Would this have been on a Tuesday evening?" Stewart asked.

Kelly looked at her, hopelessness seeping into his every expression. "Yes," he said after a few seconds reflection, "It could have been. It was definitely a mid-week thing, shortly after the summer break, sometime in October."

"What time in the evening did the incident you were sort of involved in occur?"

Kelly was puzzled by this line of questioning but he gave the query some thought. After a moment he said, "I think it was sometime round eleven."

"So, what happened?"

"We were there with Jamsie ... he was our mate, supposed to be. But he was more of a ... I don't know, a Svengali figure for us. He was big and powerful, uni rugby player, popular with everybody. He could put on this great show, but God, if only they knew ..."

"Sir," Stewart cut in. "You're not making much sense."

The man was almost weeping. "Nothing has made much sense since then."

"Try just telling us the simple facts," Sheehan suggested.

"We were drinking. Jamsie said he'd get us a couple of birds. He told us to go upstairs and find an empty bedroom ..." He folded his arms across his chest and, with his eyes squeezed tightly shut, he leaned forward shaking his head from side to side as if to block out the memory. "He came up with this girl, oh God, she was lovely, and threw her onto the bed. He told me to lock the door and when the girl started to scream, he began whacking at her. We tried to stop him. This was not what we wanted. He climbed on to the bed and started opening his belt. The girl began to scream, and he started into her, trying to stop her. It was terrible. He didn't care where he hit her, body, breasts, face, until she was silent. We tried to stop him, but he was too strong. He threw Petey across the room. Jesus, he went flying against the far wall like a toy. Then he caught me by the throat. I'll never forget his eyes. He was beyond control. 'You can have some of what she's getting," he said, "or you can get some of what I'm getting. Take your pick.' And then he stood there with his hands on his hips." Kelly stared at the police officers, his eyes agonised.

"Well? So what did you do?" Stewart asked, mesmerised by the man's tale.

Kelly's voice was so low that the detectives could hardly hear his reply. "We just backed away from him and ran out of the room."

Incredulity vied with disdain for control of Stewart's voice. "You left that poor girl alone with that … that animal?"

Her eyes were blazing, and Kelly cringed, surprised by the depth of her anger. "We were terrified of him." He sagged again. "But, yes, I know. We should have done something."

"Why didn't you report him, for God's sake?"

"We heard him shouting after us that if we told anybody, he'd make sure that we'd be fully implicated in everything, that we'd go to prison."

Understanding cowardice was difficult for Stewart; empathising with it was impossible. Her tone was scathing as she said, "So you were only concerned with your own skins? You were prepared to let that poor girl suffer abominable sexual and physical abuse just to save yourselves?"

Sheehan touched her arm. "Sergeant."

Stewart practically had to bite her tongue to stem the tirade that threatened to surge from her.

Kelly, openly crying now, "Not a night has passed since, that I don't regret that cowardice. Twelve years of tortured, guilt-wracked nights. I wish we had gone to jail. We waited days, weeks, expecting the dean to call us in, but there was nothing. The girl left Queen's, and we heard nothing more until she committed suicide. That nearly killed us …"

"But you still chose not to report it," Sheehan said quietly.

"I know. I know. We almost did report it. We were sickened by the news. But we were two scared kids, terrified of prison, even more terrified of Fitzpatrick. We kept well away from him after that."

"Bully for you," Stewart hissed.

"Sergeant, please," Sheehan said. He turned back to Kelly. "You know that Fitzpatrick was murdered two Tuesdays ago, and Shaw last Tuesday?"

"I do, and I can do the math," Kelly said stoically. "I'm next, and it'll likely be next Tuesday."

Sheehan's eyebrows went up. "And you didn't think to come to the police for protection?"

"I thought about it. But a story like mine, I figured the police would probably shoot me before the killer ever got near me." He emitted a weary sigh. "I decided that I'd barricade myself in and try to protect myself as well as I could. I reckoned being prepared would make the difference." He stared at Stewart. "And if it didn't, well, there's always the question of justice. Maybe I deserve to be killed."

Sheehan let that sit. "There's not a lot of room at the front of the house. How would anyone break into the premises without alerting you?"

"Only through the front door. The door from the kitchen leads out to the back but the estate runs very steeply downhill and there are high stone walls separating the back of each house. There's a twenty foot drop from the top of the small wall at my back to the garden of the next house down. There's no way anybody could get in from the back."

"Can we have a look?"

Kelly shrugged and rose from his chair. "Sure. It's this way." He led them down a short hall and into the kitchen. The back door was at the far wall. When the detectives went into the small back garden, they saw a small three foot high brick wall with a long drop immediately behind it. Beyond that were rows of houses, falling ever downward. Kelly had been right. Only someone with ropes and a grappling hook would be able to ascend the other side of the wall to the back of his house.

They went back into the sitting room again and Sheehan asked, "Who owns that big detached house at the end of the cul-de-sac?"

If Kelly was surprised by the question he didn't show it. He looked emotionally drained. "That belongs to Mister Owens, Tony. He's a retired chemist."

"Does he live alone?"

"Yes. His wife passed away a couple of years ago. He has two children, but they both live and work in London."

Sheehan grunted a response, lost for a moment as he considered the possibilities that were available to him. Then he said, "I take it you wouldn't mind some police protection next Tuesday night?"

The man's mouth dropped open, his relief palpable. "Oh, God! Would you?"

"We have the bare bones of a plan, nothing definitive yet," Sheehan told him. "We'll be fleshing it out at our team meeting on Monday. It might involve you taking a little risk, but Stewart here will be with you on Tuesday night and we'll have a couple of men stationed nearby as well."

"Oh, thank God. I'll co-operate in any way you want."

"Okay! I need to go and have a chat with Mister Owens. Stewart here will give you a rough indication of the way our thinking is going."

"Sir!!"

Sheehan glanced at her as he left and said quietly, "To protect and serve, Stewart. To protect and serve."

FIFTY

1

*E*n *route* to home for his evening meal, Sheehan detoured to St. Malachy's Church on Alfred Street. Three and half million pounds had been spent on its restoration in 2009, and it was now an impressive but peaceful place to sit in. Visiting St. Malachy's was something that Sheehan had started doing after he had attended a funeral Mass at St. Peter's Pro-Cathedral a year or so earlier to hear Margaret play. It had been in the early days of their relationship, and hearing her on the organ had been his sole purpose for attending the Mass. But his friend, Monsignor Keenan, had been preaching that day, and something silent, a tiny seed of grace, perhaps, had entered his soul while he watched the drama of the Mass unfold. Now, from time to time, he would drop into St. Malachy's just to sit there. He didn't pray. He did not engage in any serious meditation. He would just sit there. He still didn't really know why he did this, but the good monsignor had told him not to worry about reasons, or about praying, or about meditating, but simply to '… follow the grace' at his own pace. Often he thought about going on home and forgetting the whole thing, but somehow his car would bring him to the chapel, even when he had fully intended to pass it by.

Now here he was again. He was remembering a story the monsignor had told him about an old guy who used to come into the chapel every day and sit at the back. Asked if he was praying for something special, he replied, "No. Sometimes I come in, and I sits and thinks. Sometimes I come in, and I just sits." Sheehan's mouth spread in a grin. *That's me. No prayers, just sittin'.* But occasionally he would address the Lord in a casual way. Like now, for example. *God, this case is driving me up the walls. How's about some inspiration?* He waited in silence, but if God was listening, he wasn't ready to answer.

Sheehan arrived home shortly after six. Margaret was watching the Ulster News on television. He kissed her 'hello', and sat down to join her. Assistant Commissioner Harrison's thick face filled the screen. His expression was both earnest and sincere. "Our best brains are working day and night to bring this miscreant to justice," he was saying with a smile to the pretty blond reporter who was interviewing him. "Chief Inspector Sheehan has assured me that he is following two good leads, and that he is expecting a break in the case at any time. And our rising star, Sergeant Denise Stewart, is following up on a promising lead that dates back to a serious crime at Queen's University some twelve years ago. She assures me that there is a definite connection between that event and the current murders." He smiled benignly at his interlocutor. "I'm sorry, Brenda, that's all I'm prepared to divulge at this point."

"Can you tell us what happened at Queen's twelve years ago?" the girl persisted.

Harrison was already removing the earpiece from his ear. "Come now, Brenda," he said, with a patronising smile. "It would hardly be discreet of me to divulge these kinds of details before the perpetrator has been apprehended, would it now? Perhaps in a couple of days."

The camera panned to the anchor woman who said, "That was Assistant Commissioner Harrison with the latest updates on the recent brutal murders of two Belfast men. Now, some news just in …"

Margaret switched off the television. Sheehan said, "Smug bastard. Always trying to pretend he knows far more than he does."

Margaret got up, went to the kitchen, and came back with a newspaper. "Wait till you hear what I saw in the *Daily Mail* today." She searched through the pages for a minute. "Here we are." She shook the page a bit and read aloud, "According to crime scientists at Birmingham University, the key characteristics of serial killers are: One, an addiction to power; two, a desire to manipulate; three, a huge ego; four, superficial charm; and, five, high standing in the community." She looked up, grinning. "So, who does that remind you of?"

He grinned back. "I'm not playing this game."

"It's him." She nodded towards the television. "Never liked that man. Always felt there was something fishy about him."

"Dear, oh, dear, Margaret. Talking like that and you a Christian woman."

"I'm just saying. And here we find out that he has all five characteristics of a serial killer." She handed him the paper. "There," she said with a triumphant smirk. "I've solved your case for you."

He dropped the paper on the sofa and took her in his arms. "If only it were that easy."

"Sometimes easy is hard to see," she smiled, putting her arms around his neck. "You should give this some thought."

He laughed aloud. "Will you quit! Even the Lord's puzzled by this one. I dropped into St. Malachy's this evening and asked Him for some help but he had nothing to say."

Margaret smiled. "The Lord's timetable is different from your timetable. Give it time. You'll get the inspiration when you need it."

"Whatever! Right now I'm trying to think about stalkers. What do you know about them?"

She frowned. "Stalkers? Nothing. Are you talking about the guy who tried to run down Tom?"

"Aye!"

"Why don't you phone Nigel? You know how he loves it when you consult him."

"Maybe I'll give him a call after tea."

"Oh, a hint, is it?" She laughed. "Read the paper. I'll call you in a few minutes."

2

Professor Nigel Greenwald, Professor of Psychology at Queen's University, was jerked out of a doze in front of his television by the insistent ringing of his phone. Greenwald, a stout man in his late fifties, was wearing a grey sweater and jeans. His long, silvery hair was tied behind him in a ponytail. He staggered out into the hall and, stifling a yawn as he lifted the receiver, he said, "Hello?"

"Hi, Nigel. Jim Sheehan."

"Jim, my boy! How are you?"

"Grand, Nigel. Grand. What about yourself?"

"Suppose I should say I can't complain. But I can, and I can complain bitterly. Liver's acting up, and that damn doctor has barred me from all my favourite tipples. Coffee doesn't just do it for me."

Jim grinned. "But sure look how sharp your mind is becoming again."

"Funny! Well, I know you're definitely phoning to ask about my health, and I appreciate the call. No way are you remotely interested in anything that my sharp mind has to offer."

"Well …"

"All right. All right. This call might take a wee while, then?"

"Probably."

"Okay. Let me get comfortable." Nigel took the cordless receiver with him and went back to the lounge. Settled again in his armchair, he said, "Well, what's the problem this time?"

"I don't know enough to ask a specific question, Nigel, so I'll just go with what do you know about stalkers?"

Nigel grunted. "Stalkers? Let me think." There was silence on the line. "Broader subject than you might imagine. For a start, there are two main categories of stalker."

"Yes?

"Uh huh! Psychotic and non-psychotic. Any idea which category your stalker fits into?"

"Not a clue."

"That's helpful."

"Well, he's violent."

"Violent? How violent?"

Sheehan told him what had happened to Allen.

"Hmmm! There are various typologies of stalker offered by researchers such as Mullen, Purcell et al. We can ignore broad classifications like terrorist or political stalkers. This sounds like a 'resentful stalker' or maybe a 'predatory stalker'. These types tend to pursue a vendetta because of a sense of grievance against the victim. They're usually motivated mainly by the desire to frighten and distress."

"Oh, no. Tom isn't the stalker's target."

"He's not?"

"No, the target, we believe, is my sergeant, Denise Stewart."

"Oh? Never heard you mention her before."

"She's new."

There was a moment's silence on the line. Then Nigel said, "Well, she's not new to the stalker."

Sheehan was startled. "Why do you say that?"

"The level of violence you describe. It wouldn't have escalated to that in just a couple of weeks. Early stalker violence is more nuisance stuff … like phone calls in the middle of the night with silence on the end of the line, or maybe making a scrape on your car with a nail. Not this. This stalker has had his focus on your sergeant for quite a while. At least a couple of years, I'd say."

"Huh? That doesn't make sense."

"Maybe it's somebody from her previous posting?"

"Well, I suppose that's possible." Jim was puzzled. "Strange, though. You're sure it has had to be going on a long time? It's only recently she's become aware of him."

"Mmm." Greenwald in turn was puzzled. "Can't explain that."

Sheehan gave the matter a few seconds' thought. "I might have to contact the station commander at Lisburn then. Are there any signs that might give the guy away?"

"Not really. Many stalkers do good, or even excellent, work in their organisations. They would have just the one focus of tenacious obsession, and unless they suffer from a delusional disorder, or perhaps a schizoaffective disorder, they could function normally in social settings, and none of their colleagues would be any the wiser."

"No help there, then."

"What has he done to alert your sergeant about his existence?"

"Not much. She just senses his presence occasionally."

"Oh? She's psychic?" Greenwald's tone was sceptical.

"Gimme a break, willya? She's had a feeling … we all get them. The attacks on Allen show that she wasn't wrong."

"All right. All right. So, he's there. But you say he's only attacked young Allen. Hmm! These two close, by any chance?"

Sheehan's eyes narrowed. Nigel never failed to impress him. "I think there might be a budding romance there, yes, but it hasn't got off the ground yet."

"Your stalker might be an 'intimacy seeker' hoping eventually to establish an intimate, loving relationship with your sergeant. Such stalkers often believe that the person they focus on is a long-sought-after soul mate, and they were meant to be together."

298

"I'm quite sure Stewart has done nothing to encourage this kind of belief in anybody. In fact, she's quite prickly when guys try to approach her."

"Intimacy seekers need no encouragement. This type of stalker believes that they are loved by the object of their desire even though their target has done nothing to suggest this is true. Even in the face of aggressive denial from their target, they would reinterpret what they heard and twist its meaning to support their morbid fantasy that the target loves them."

"How long can this go on before the stalker takes some sort of action?"

"Good point. Intimacy-seeking stalkers often have disorders involving **erotomanic** delusions. These can grow to the point of needing physical satisfaction. There could come a time when they'll want to act them out. Kidnapping the victim wouldn't be unusual in cases like this."

"Whoa! We'd need to keep an eye on Stewart, then."

"That would be advisable."

Sheehan was nodding even though Greenwald couldn't see him, but his expression remained puzzled. "This is all very impressive stuff, Nigel, but it isn't ringing any bells for me."

Greenwald laughed, and his voice boomed across the phone. "Do what you always do, my boy. Tuck it away in that creative mind of yours. If there's a link with someone, you'll see it eventually."

"Hummph!"

"Oh, one other point. Remember this. Even though there are general categories of stalkers, that does not mean that every stalker will fit neatly into a category. Stalkers can have any characteristics and come from any type of background."

"Of course they do. Great. Any more complexities?"

Greenwald took the question seriously and spent a while in thought. Sheehan waited patiently, glad of the brief respite.

299

Greenwald spoke again. "Tell you what, Jim. You had me focused on stalkers, but now that I think about it, your stalker's behaviours seem to exhibit what we call 'obsessive love'."

"Okaayyy? The words seem easy to understand, Nigel, but I suppose you psychologists have fitted a lot more into their basic meaning?"

"Of course we have. How else can we sow confusion and bewilderment?"

"All right, hit me again. And go a bit slower. I'm trying to write notes here. My wrist's nearly broken trying to keep up with you."

"Man in your job, you should learn shorthand."

"Thanks. I'll keep that in mind. So, obsessive love?"

"It's a hypothetical state in which one person feels an overwhelming obsessive desire to possess another person toward whom they feel a strong attraction. This would be accompanied by an inability to accept failure or rejection. I was just thinking about what happened to young Allen. Obsessive lovers often feel entirely unable to restrain themselves from extreme behaviours such as acts of violence. Even if Allen is only accompanying Stewart home, the guy's obsession, fuelled by the persistent jealousy of the paranoid personality, could trigger all sorts of violent reactions."

"All right, Nigel. I quit. My brain's wilting here. I'll let this stuff simmer for a while. If I need further clarification, I'll get back to you."

"Why don't you get back to me, anyway, and go somewhere for a cup of coffee … yeucchh! Maybe have a normal chat."

"Definitely, Nigel. I will. Soon as this case is over, we'll go out for a meal somewhere."

"And bring that lovely wife of yours."

"Absolutely. Thanks, Nigel. I'd love to say you've been a big help, but all you've managed to do is hurt my brain. But you never know."

Greenwald chuckled. "'Night, Jim. We'll talk again soon."

FIFTY-ONE

D enise Stewart had always wanted to be a police officer. Her father, and his father, had served with distinction in the old Royal Ulster Constabulary, and from early childhood she had been imbued with a fascination for what they did. Both men were dedicated officers, and Stewart had always sensed their passion. Thus she grew up with a desire to emulate them. The RUC, following civil rights marches, terrorist violence, and political wrangling, became the Police Service for Northern Ireland in 2001, bringing with it a more tangible equality base, offering greater opportunities for both Catholics and women to serve and protect. The PSNI was well established as Northern Ireland's police force when Stewart finally signed up. Her graduation day from the academy was the proudest of her life, although it would be hard to say whether she or her father had been more proud; and of the newly qualified officers, hers was the hat that flew farthest into the air at the final moment of the ceremonies.

Her time at Lisburn had been a horrific and unexpected introduction to the life of a police officer, but despite the sexual discrimination and abuse that she had suffered there, her passion for the service never wavered, nor did the ideals that had prompted her to follow her father's footsteps. Now in Belfast, serving under Chief Inspector Sheehan, working in an environment that recognised her qualities as a police officer, she so loved her work that she could scarcely allow herself time to live a life outside of it. She was perfectly happy to work long hours outside her allotted timetable, to follow up on investigative leads, even to do dull paperwork, without ever experiencing the ennui that can sometimes settle on the spirits of even the most dedicated of employees. Nor was she interested in seeking additional reward for the extra hours she worked. On two occasions since she had joined his team, Sheehan practically had to force her to submit claim forms for overtime.

Thus on the morning of Saturday, the twenty-fifth of October, it did not occur to Stewart to go shopping with friends, to lie on an extra hour in bed, or even to lounge about her house enjoying the relaxation of a day off. Instead she rose at her normal time and went to the station to continue making the phone calls and laborious searches that might finally lead her to the Jacqueline who was Lynda Bell's friend.

Her first two calls deadened her hopes. Again she found herself having to speak to parents who did not know about "any Lynda", to ask for their daughter's current whereabouts so that she could double check, to make calls that rang into empty space, to speak to Jaquelines who were "... sorry, but couldn't offer any help."

Then she got lucky, the kind of luck that makes the grind an easy price to pay. And she knew again, as she experienced the surge of elation that comes with those moments of sudden success, why she so loved being a police officer. The lady who answered this third call, Mrs. Brenda McCabe, recognised Lynda's name immediately and spent some moments talking about the tragic end to such a young life. Stewart listened to the woman's reminiscences, concealing the impatience she felt, waiting for an opportune time to cut in and ask for Jacqueline's current phone number.

"And it took Jacqueline such a long time to cope with the loss of her best friend, especially under those circumstances," Brenda was saying tearfully.

Stewart cut in, but with as much empathy as she could muster, "Could you tell me where your daughter is now?"

"Oh, Jacqueline works in Edinburgh now." The woman's voice revealed her pride. "She's office manageress for a big accountancy firm ..." She was silent for a minute. "Oh, I forget their name just now, but it's a very important position. Let me just go and …"

"No, it's all right, Mrs. McCabe," Stewart interjected quickly, wanting to stop the woman from going off to search for information she didn't need. "If you could just give me Jacqueline's phone number, please, I'll be able to talk to her myself."

"Yes, I have it here in 'our wee brown book', as we call it." Brenda emitted a little chuckle, and Stewart could hear the faint rustle of pages being turned. "Ah, here it is." She hesitated again, "Oh, they're probably closed on a Saturday morning. Maybe I should give you the number of her mobile?"

"That'd be great." Stewart tried to sound calm but her mind was desperately urging the woman to *speed it up, for God's sake.*

Mrs. McCabe gave her the number and, in spite of her anxiety to get to the crucial phone call, Stewart took the time to thank the woman politely for all her help. She could hardly dial the number she was given, so tense was she. Was now the time she would finally get the answers she was looking for? She waited, scarcely daring to breathe, as the dialling tone went on … and on … and on. She was about to hang up when a sleepy voice said, "Hello?"

"Jacqueline McCabe?"

"Uh huh!" This was followed by a poorly concealed yawn.

"My name is Sergeant Denise Stewart, and I am speaking from Strandtown Police Station in Belfast."

That got Jacqueline's attention. Her voice suddenly alert, she said, "Oh! How can I help you?"

"I was hoping I could ask you a few questions about a friend of yours at university."

"Of course. Which friend would that be?"

"Lynda Bell."

"Oh, my God!" Jacqueline's voice was hushed with something akin to shock. "Lynda?"

"Yes. Were you present at the party where Lynda was assaulted?" Stewart winced as soon as the words were out. She had not meant the question to be so abrupt. *Patience, woman*, she admonished herself.

Jacqueline, however, didn't seem to notice the gaffe. "Oh, God! Poor Lynda. That awful night. Yes, I was there."

"Can you tell me what happened?"

"I can't really tell you what happened to Lynda," Jacqueline said, adding darkly, "but I could make a good guess."

"Maybe you'd just run through the events of the party as you remember them?"

"Well, again I can't tell you much because I was assaulted too."

"What?" Stewart couldn't keep the surprise out of her voice.

"Not like Lynda," Jacqueline added hastily. "I went upstairs to go to the toilet and, the next thing, I felt this awful thump to the side of my head. I was knocked unconscious, and when I woke up I was lying bound and gagged in an airing cupboard on the landing. It was terrible. It was two hours before anyone came to release me."

"That's awful. Do you know who struck you?"

"No. Whoever it was sneaked up on me from behind."

"I understand. So, you don't know what happened to Lynda?"

"Not as far as that night was concerned. Lynda was gone by the time they found me. In fact, she went home the next day. Left the university without a word to anyone."

"What do you think happened?"

"Lynda was a lovely girl, such a wonderful and reliable friend. But she was terribly shy and introverted. She was also a virgin. If what happened to her is what I think happened to her, then she'd have died of shame and embarrassment. She would never have told anybody what happened."

"Did she tell you?"

"No. As far as I could make out she was completely traumatised by what happened. When I tried to contact her over the next few days, even though she knew it was me, her mother kept telling me that Lynda wasn't taking any calls."

"Did you never try to visit her?"

"I did, a couple of times. Once she relented and let me in. I couldn't believe it was her when I saw her ... gaunt, lack-lustre, all the light gone from her eyes. She was a totally different person. She thanked me for my concern but asked that I didn't contact her again. The whole visit broke my heart."

"She didn't say anything at all about what happened at the party?"

"No. I tried to talk to her, but she was so dead, so unresponsive."

"What did you mean when you said you had your suspicions?"

"One of the girls I was with saw a student talking to Lynda just before she left the room."

"Do you remember the student's name?"

"Yes. It was James Fitzpatrick."

"Did you know him?"

"Only by sight. He was a popular figure about the campus."

"Do you think he had something to do with what happened?"

"I did at the time. He was one of those charismatic types, talented but very full of himself. When I heard that he'd been seen talking to Lynda, I made a point of talking to him. But he denied having had any contact with Lynda. He had this sincere expression, but I didn't believe him. There was something fake about him."

"Did you do anything about your suspicions?"

"I asked about a bit. I learned that there were rumours about him but nothing definite."

"So what happened?"

"Nothing. Lynda never made a complaint. There was no enquiry of any kind. Apart from Lynda, her family, and, I suppose, myself, no one was aware that anything had happened. That was it. It was all so heartbreaking and frustrating." Then she said, "Sergeant, can I ask why you're asking these questions?"

Stewart thought about palming off the woman with the usual pat euphemisms about following leads but then she thought, *what the hell! Lynda's grieving friend? She's entitled to some closure.* "We believe that three people were involved in the assault on Lynda that night. Two of them have been murdered. We're investigating those murders. One of them was James Fitzpatrick. We believe there's a connection between these deaths and Lynda's assault."

Stewart could hear the woman's sudden intake of breath. "God forgive me, Sergeant, but I can't help saying the bastard deserved it."

Stewart let that go and tensed as she prepared to ask her next question. "Do you happen to know if Lynda had a boyfriend?"

"You think he might have something to do with the murders?"

"It's just a line of enquiry."

"She did, but Lynda being Lynda, she would never say much about him. Even her parents didn't know about him."

"Did you ever meet him?"

"I was never introduced to him, but I did bump into him some months after Lynda died. Seems she had ignored him, too, after that night. He hadn't known about her death. I could see he was devastated when I told him. He was nice, Sergeant. I can't see him being your killer."

"What can you tell me about him?"

"He was a very handsome, black man, dressed well. That was my first impression." Stewart's heart almost stopped. All she could do was listen as the woman went on. "But when he spoke to me, I almost laughed in his face ..."

"Laughed?"

"Yes. Lynda was so in love with him, but she would never talk much about him." Stewart could hear a sad chuckle at the other end of the line. "But, dear God, the odd time she did talk about him ..." The sad chuckle came again. "Lynda was studying English and always wanted to be a writer. She had such a way with words ..."

Anxiety about the conclusion that her mind was forming eroded Stewart's customary delicacy. "Jacqueline, please, what can you tell me about the boyfriend?"

"I was just about to say," the woman's tone sounded slightly miffed. "I remember asking Lynda to tell me at least one thing about her boyfriend, and she told me that his voice would cover her in goose bumps. She said, God help her, she loved playing with words, she said that his voice was, I remember it like it was yesterday. In fact, I loved the description so much that I wrote it down and learned it off by heart."

Stewart's knuckles were white as she clung to the receiver. This woman was worse than her mother. She desperately willed the garrulous woman to get to the point. "Do you remember it now?"

"Of course I do. She said his voice was, 'gloriously mellifluous, a vocal evocation of melting chocolate'." And again there came the chuckle, but with more life in it this time. "And when he introduced himself to me, I nearly melted myself. God, that voice, that big, round, deep voice. The only thing I could think of when he spoke was Lynda's description. It was so brilliantly apt. That's why I almost laughed in his face." Stewart heard Jacqueline laugh now, but it was a laugh that died almost at birth, replaced immediately by a tear-loaded choke. "God, Sergeant, she was so shy, and so kind, and so lovely, and such a great friend. She ... she didn't deserve what happened to her." The woman was sobbing openly now.

But Stewart was immune to the woman's sadness. Her blood had frozen in her veins. *Doctor Jones!* She commiserated with the woman as best she could, thanked her for her help, and ended the call quickly. *Doctor Jones! My God!* She took a second to compose herself, but her hand was shaking as she reached again for the receiver to call the chief's mobile.

FIFTY-TWO

1

Sheehan was not prepared to wait until Monday to question Jones. Immediately after receiving Stewart's call he phoned Dick Campbell to ask for Jones's address. He didn't need it. There were three suddenly deceased that required urgent post-mortems that Saturday morning, so both Jones and Campbell were working at the mortuary when Sheehan called.

"Could you please stay there, Dick, until I get to you," Sheehan said, adding, "and please make sure that Doctor Jones remains there as well."

Campbell's response was half-amused, but he sensed that this time there was no levity in Sheehan's call. "What's up, Jim?"

"I'll tell you when we get there, Dick." He hung up before Campbell could question him further. He then phoned Stewart telling her that he would pick her up at the station gate in ten minutes.

Once Stewart was in the car, Sheehan said, "And nearly the first thing I said about the guy was how well-dressed he was. Little gold cufflinks … the lot. Why didn't that make a bell ring somewhere?"

"It didn't with me, either, Chief. I mean, the medical examiner? You don't even think … but then, young, professional and in an important job. You'd expect him to dress well. Look at Robert

Turner. He's about that age, and he dresses immaculately. You're not kicking yourself because you should have suspected he was the boyfriend."

"Yeah, I suppose." Sheehan's subconscious was annoying him again, but he didn't know why.

"And, sir, just because Jones is the missing boyfriend, doesn't necessarily mean he's our killer. I mean, he was reserved and all, but he doesn't seem the type."

"Well, the very least he has to do is to answer some trenchant questions. Why didn't he comment on Fitzpatrick when he arrived at the crime scene? Did he know him? Or did he just elect to remain silent?"

"Yes, there's that."

Both sat in silence, each reflecting on the situation. Sheehan's mind drifted back to what Nigel Greenwald had been saying. He said, "Let's see what he has to say when we talk to him. There's something I'd like to ask you."

"All right, sir." Stewart's tone was slightly puzzled.

"Did you have any consciousness that you were being stalked before you came to Strandtown?"

Not sure what her boss was getting at, Stewart shook her head and said simply, "No sir."

"Not an inkling?"

"No. It was only a few nights ago I began to get this sense of being followed. I had to put up with all sorts of crap at Lisburn, forgive the language, sir, but I had no sense of being stalked."

"That's very strange. I was speaking to a psychologist friend of mine last night, and he is convinced that your stalker must have had you in his sights for at least a couple of years. He's not usually wrong about these things."

Stewart experienced an inner frisson of dread. "God, that's disturbing. But no, sir. This is all new as far as I'm concerned."

"I don't get it. Greenwald was very positive."

"I'm sure I would have noticed, sir. Stalkers are not notorious for being discreet. Whoever it is couldn't have kept that from me for two years."

Sheehan nodded. She made sense. "Ah, well. Some explanation might turn up."

They had arrived at the hospital grounds now and Sheehan found a completely illicit parking spot near the mortuary. He threw his 'Police on Duty' card on the dash, and they went into the building

Doctor Campbell was waiting for them, his mien unusually tense. Something about Sheehan's call alerted him to the fact that this was not just an ordinary information-seeking visit. He strove for something of his usual bonhomie, however, as he said, "Well, Jim. Pretty cryptic phone call. What are you up to?"

"Good morning, Dick." He looked at his watch. "Oh, it's just gone afternoon. Good afternoon, Dick."

"Well?"

"We're here to have a word with Doctor Jones, Dick," Sheehan said seriously. "I'm going to have to ask you to go to another room for a few minutes."

Campbell immediately began to bluster. "Come on, Jim. You can't exclude me from this, whatever it is. How long have we known each other, for God's sake? What's going on, man?"

Sheehan stared at him, tight-lipped. "All right. All right. You can stay, but you can't interfere. Sit over there somewhere."

Jones in the meantime was standing just to one side of Dick, his expression neutral, almost as if he had no interest in the proceedings.

Sheehan said, "Good afternoon, Doctor Jones." Stewart pulled out her notebook as Sheehan was speaking, giving the doctor a nod of acknowledgement as she did so. Sheehan continued, "We need to ask you a couple of questions in relation to this case we're working on."

The man nodded, unperturbed. It seemed that he had no inkling of what questions he might be asked. Sheehan took the colour photograph of Lynda Bell from his briefcase and placed it on one the stainless steel table in front of the doctor. "Do you know this person?"

Jones's initial glance was casual, but when he focused on the photograph, his reaction was almost violent. He jerked back in shock for a second and then moved forward to study the photograph again. The neutral look had left his face to be replaced by one of intense sadness. Sheehan was slightly deterred by this, but he pursued the point. "Well, do you know her?"

Jones nodded slowly, seeming unable to take his eyes from the photograph. "Yes," he said, a short, sad word, nothing like his customary rumble.

"How do you know her?"

"She was my girlfriend for a while at university."

Campbell couldn't keep still. He had been standing a few paces away, his head following Sheehan's every move. "For God's sake, Jim. What's this all about?"

"Please, Dick. You can't interfere. It's police business." He placed a crime scene photograph of James Fitzpatrick on the table. "Do you know this man?"

"Yes, he's one of the bodies brought into the mortuary a week or so ago."

"Did you know him before he was brought in?"

"I saw him at the crime scene."

"I mean before that."

"No."

"Are you sure?"

Jones gave him a tired look. "I'm sure."

Sheehan showed him a photograph of Peter Shaw. "Did you know this man before you saw his dead body?"

"No."

"You stick to that answer?"

Jones looked at him askance, and said, "Yes."

"Do you know a Queen's graduate called Finbar Kelly?"

"No."

"You're sure?"

"I'm sure."

Sheehan placed two small plastic evidence bags on the table, each containing one of the broken cufflinks found at the crime scenes. "Have you ever seen these before?"

Jones studied them for a long time, his expression changing from puzzlement to wistfulness. "Yes."

"Well?"

"They were a present to me from Lynda."

"Uh huh! Can you explain to me why they were found at the crime scenes of Fitzpatrick and Shaw?"

Jones looked genuinely puzzled. "No."

"No? Just no?"

Jones, showing a little annoyance for the first time, separated the words of his response. "I ... can ... not ... explain ... it. I lost them years ago."

Sheehan looked frustrated. "All right. This is getting us nowhere." He turned to Stewart. "Sergeant, cuff him."

Campbell, who had been fidgeting like someone demented at the other side of the table, shouted, "Jim! Are you mad in the head? You have to be mixing Andrew up with somebody else."

"I'm sorry, Dick. No mistake. I'm not satisfied with Doctor Jones's answers. We're taking him back to the station for questioning."

"Have a heart, man. Cuffs? And what if he's innocent?" Campbell was almost screeching. "His reputation will never recover from being marched out of here in handcuffs. Come on, man. How long have we been friends?"

Stewart hovered uncertainly, not moving towards Jones, waiting for Sheehan's response. Sheehan nodded to his friend. "Fair enough, Dick. No cuffs. But we still go to the station."

2

When Sheehan and Stewart entered the interrogation room, Jones was sitting calmly at the table, his hands clasped before him. Sheehan set a file on the table as he sat down, while Stewart placed some blank sheets of paper in front of her. She would be taking notes as Dr. Jones made his statement.

Sheehan switched on the recorder. "Saturday, twenty-fifth of October, fourteen ten. Chief Inspector Sheehan and Detective Sergeant Stewart present with Doctor Andrew Jones from the State Forensics Pathologist's Office." He then spoke directly to the suspect. "Doctor Jones, you understand that it is your right to have a solicitor present with you during this interview?"

Jones said quietly, "I haven't done anything. I don't need a solicitor."

Sheehan said, "Let the record show that the witness has waived his right to have a solicitor present while being questioned." He opened one of the files in front of him and showed Jones photographs of Fitzpatrick and Shaw. "According to your preliminary statement, you had no knowledge of these two men until you saw their bodies at their respective crime scenes?"

"That's correct."

"You didn't know them when you were a student at Queen's University?"

"No."

313

He placed a photograph of Lynda Bell on the table, the colour portrait Stewart had been given by the girl's mother. "But you knew Lynda Bell?"

Jones looked at the photograph for some time, his lips tightening.

"Doctor Jones?"

Jones's deep voice sounded suddenly constricted. "Yes, I knew Lynda Bell."

"In what capacity?"

"I have already told you."

"For the record, please. We are recording this."

"She was my girlfriend for a while."

"For a while? The relationship ended how?"

"We'd been seeing each other for a few months. She invited me to go with her and a couple of friends to a party at someone's house. I said I would, but at the last minute I was called home. My mother had taken a stroke. My parents lived in Limavady, so I had to leave immediately I received the news. I told Lynda to go ahead with her friends and that I'd see her when I got back."

"How long were you gone?"

"A few days."

"Were you jealous that she had gone to the party without you?"

"No ... uh ... no, I wasn't jealous. Although I had not known her long, I believed that I could trust her."

Sheehan noticed the hesitation. "Was there any other reason you didn't want her going to that party?"

Jones seemed to drift to another time. After a moment's reflection, he said, "I was worried about a stalker."

Stewart's head lifted, but she didn't speak.

"Stalker?" Sheehan said.

"Yes. She told me that she often felt that she was being followed but that she had never actually seen anyone. We talked a lot about it. She also used to get phone calls when the caller would simply listen at the other end of the line but never speak. Got to the stage she was terrified to answer the phone."

"Was she ever physically threatened by this … stalker?"

"No, but I was."

"You were?" Sheehan's voice expressed surprise.

"Yes. I got phone calls warning me to stay away from Lynda. I found notes, too, in my coat pockets, however they got there, threatening me with all sorts of dire consequences if I didn't end the relationship. Some of the phone calls were seriously manic, definitely unhinged. He would sometimes end the calls screaming all sorts of vile invective down the line at me. The guy was clearly obsessed with Lynda. But when Lynda and I discussed it, I convinced her that she was safe from real harm, that I was far more likely to be the target of his insanity than her."

"And she had no idea who it was?"

"None."

"So, why didn't you end the relationship? If the stalker was as unhinged as you say, he might well have escalated to physical violence towards you?"

Jones was again silent, staring at the girl's photograph.

"Please answer the question, Doctor Jones."

"I loved her. I thought the relationship was going somewhere. No idiot stalker was going to interfere with that."

"But you ended it?"

"I did not."

"So how did it end?"

"While I was at home with my mother, I phoned constantly and left messages for her but never received a reply. I was hurt, so I decided to let it cool for a while."

"Weren't you anxious to know why she didn't contact you? Were you not worried about the stalker?"

"To be honest, I presumed that she had met someone at the party and that this was her way of giving me the brush off."

"You didn't know that she had been attacked at the party?"

Jones's eyes bleared. Clearly he was in the grip of strong emotion. All he said was, "No."

"No? That's it? No?"

Jones cleared his throat. His voice cracked when he spoke. "No, I didn't know a thing about it. I was a student in the medical faculty. I would not easily have run into her. I was probably immature at the time, but I stubbornly decided that since she was the one who stopped communicating, she would have to be the one to make contact again. In fact, in my stupid pride, I deliberately avoided being anywhere there was a chance we might meet. I thought that, since none of my calls were answered and the letters I wrote were returned unopened, she no longer wanted to have anything to do with me." He paused and looked directly at Sheehan. "To tell you the whole truth, I thought somebody might have got at her about my colour." His eyes blurred again. "God, I should have trusted her. She never would have allowed that to be a factor."

"You were angry?"

"Hurt, disappointed, angry, stubborn, heartbroken … you name it, I experienced it. And because I avoided contact with her or her friends, I had no clue that Lynda had left Queen's. I buried myself in my studies, and I didn't even hear of her death …" He stared at the photograph, tears clouding his eyes. "… until … until several months after she had been buried."

Sheehan believed him. *No way the guy could be lying.* "How did you finally come to hear about her death?"

"I bumped into her friend, Jacqueline, one afternoon by chance. She didn't know me, but I had seen her around in Lynda's company. I was going to ignore her, but something made me introduce myself …" Sheehan gave the man time to collect himself. Regardless of his guilt or innocence of the murders, these memories

316

were devastating for him. "That's when I first heard about Lynda's ... death."

"How did that make you feel?"

"How do you think I felt? I almost lost my mind. I ended up in counselling for a long time."

Sheehan spread his hands. "I'm sorry to hear that but, you have to admit, it sounds like motive for murder, that."

Jones's eyes narrowed. "I think I might well have killed the culprits, had I been able to find out who they were."

"You never learned who molested her at the party?"

"No. I did try to find out, but I didn't know where to go or whom to ask."

Sheehan leaned forward and said, "But you did find out years later, and finally got your revenge, didn't you? Why don't you admit it and get if off your chest?"

Jones shook his head, although he did not seem surprised by the accusation. "No. I never did find out who they were. After a time, my counsellor finally convinced me to move on and let it go. I devoted myself to my work, gave up on any social life, and tried to forget."

"You never went with any other girl, got married?"

"There's been no one since Lynda."

"In twelve years. Wow! That's pretty intense."

Jones regarded him, unmoving, and didn't respond.

"So you've been carrying that anger all this time?"

Jones seemed to reflect. "No, not anger. Ah ... regret ... anguish ... heartache ... and something close to despair for a while. I was more suicidal than murderous, if the truth be told. I mean ..." His voice cracked again. "I should have been there for her. Don't you see that? I was mooning around angry and stubborn, and all that time she was ... she was going through ..." He put his head in his hands and kept shaking it from side to side. Tears plashed on the table.

Stewart, taking notes, found her own eyes filling. She could hardly see the page and blinked rapidly, trying not to show any emotion. This story was breaking her heart. Yet her boss seemed unaffected.

Sheehan was not immune to the man's obvious suffering, but the fact was that the more he heard, the more convinced he became that the murderer was sitting in front of him. Prolonged grief, the frustration of having had no closure, the fact that he had cut himself off from Lynda at a time when she was suffering to the point of suicide, must have played havoc with the man's psyche over the years. It was a wonder he was able to function in society as well as he did, even if he did exude an aloof and solitary mien. Men, good men, have killed in the past for far less reason than Jones had. And every word he was speaking was digging a bigger and bigger hole for himself. The suspect was in serious need of a solicitor at this point. Sheehan's innate charity made him say again, "Look, are you sure you don't wish to have us suspend this interview until you have a solicitor present to advise you?"

"No." Jones's eyes were as dead as his voice.

"But surely you must know that your answers reveal that you had a monumental motive to seek revenge on these people?"

"That may be so, but I had nothing to do with their murders."

"And you didn't know that there was a connection between the bodies coming into the mortuary and Lynda."

"No."

"Seriously, Doctor Jones? I find that hard to believe."

"Why? Doctor Campbell never made any mention of Lynda Bell. I doubt if he, too, had any awareness of this connection you refer to. And where else might I have heard it?"

"Many of the detectives on the team were looking into the connection. We thought it important and talked about it quite a bit. How did you miss that?"

"None of your team spoke to me about it. In fact, apart from yourself and the sergeant here, no other policeman has spoken to me about these murders."

Jones spoke calmly, without inflection, but there was something convincing about his words. *This guy's some actor,* Sheehan was thinking. He sat back, exasperated. "Why don't you just come clean so that we can get this thing tied up and dusted? We'll get to the truth eventually, you know."

"I've already told you the truth."

Sheehan raised his eyes to the ceiling as if seeking support. He ploughed on. "Very well. Where were you between ten-thirty and midnight on the night of the fourteenth of October?"

"I was at home," Jones responded immediately

"You answered that without much thought. Would you like to try again?"

"I was at home."

"Do you have any witnesses who can confirm that?"

"No. I live alone."

"How can you be so sure that you were at home on that particular night?"

"I am engaged in doctoral study into clinical microbiology. My dissertation is due for submission in a couple of months. It's taking up all my time at the moment. I'm at home working on it every evening."

"Where were you between ten-thirty and midnight on the evening of the twenty-first of October of this year?"

"At home, alone, working on my thesis."

"Not a very convincing alibi, is it?"

"It's the truth."

Sheehan sighed. He pushed forward a colour glossy of the two cufflinks. "You admitted when first approached that you recognised these?"

"Yes. They were a present from Lynda."

"And you lost them?"

"Well, they were stolen, I think."

"You think?"

"Yes, my room at my college digs had been broken into one evening. The room had been badly tossed about, ransacked. My first feeling was panic about losing my study notes, my books, that sort of thing. The place was a mess, but after I had managed to put it back together, I couldn't find that anything was missing. I put it down to some idiot who thought wrecking my room was a prank. It was only a week or so later that I noticed the cufflinks were missing."

"Somebody wrecked your room, had access to your belongings, and all he took was a pair of cuff links? Have you any idea how lame that sounds? Isn't it the truth that you never thought that the cufflinks could be traced back to you, and you deliberately left them at the crime scenes as a ... what? A kind of karma thing? Whatever it was, you were letting your victims know that what goes around, comes around."

"No. I didn't have them. They were stolen years ago."

"Why on earth would somebody steal those cufflinks and nothing else?"

Doctor Jones said quietly, "If you factor in Lynda's stalker and his obsessive jealousy, it would tend to make sense. Even a basic study of obsessive fixation, or perhaps a brief examination of what's sometimes referred to as 'obsessive love disorder', will confirm everything I'm saying."

Sheehan's lip curled as he tried to remain cynical in the face of the man's psychosexual babble, but it had the ring of Greenwald about it and made a horrible kind of sense. Nonetheless, he was convinced Jones was his man, and he was not about to be bamboozled by his jargon.

"Very interesting, Doctor Jones. But the cufflinks ...?"

"The only thing I had of Lynda's in my room at that point in our relationship was those cufflinks. There's no question he would have wanted to deprive me of them."

"Oh, I see." Sheehan plainly didn't see. "And how would he have known about them?"

"I've no idea. I did try to learn something about the behaviour patterns of obsessional stalkers. It seems they're capable of ferreting out uncannily detailed information about the object of their delusion."

"Of course, Doctor Jones. Why didn't I think of that? Great answer. Almost sounds convincing."

Jones shrugged and said, "I've had plenty of time to study it."

This man is hard to break, Sheehan was thinking. *He's been stewing on this for twelve years, getting blacker and blacker in the heart, and now that he has achieved his revenge, or two thirds of it, he doesn't care what happens to him. He's just going to sit there and stonewall.*

He decided to push a bit harder. "All right. So let me get this straight. Your alibis for the times of the two murders are as thin as a dud banknote. You're one of the pathologists on these cases, but you claim that you knew nothing about the connection between the victims and Lynda Bell, despite the fact it was a key aspect of our investigation. You admit openly that you almost lost your mind with grief and rage when you heard what happened to Lynda and instigated a search to find the perpetrators. You say you couldn't find them, but we only have your word for that. Then there's the fact that you allowed no other woman into your life since then, which means that you must have been obsessing about Lynda's death for the past twelve years. You talk about obsessional stalkers, huh? The kind of obsession you've been experiencing is bound to lead to all sorts of disturbing behaviours." He sat back in his chair and gestured to the files. "I have to tell you, Doctor Jones, this is not looking good for you. I strongly advise you to hire yourself a solicitor."

"I have told the truth," Jones said stolidly. "I have nothing more to say."

Sheehan emitted an exasperated breath, gathered the photographs back into their files and said, "Stewart."

Stewart was far less convinced than her boss of the suspect's guilt. She felt sorry for him, and she found his story disturbingly convincing. But duty was duty. She handed the pages she had been writing on to the suspect. "Are you satisfied that what I've written here," she said, "is an accurate account of what you've told us?"

Expressionless, Jones read through the notes and said, "Yes. This pretty much reflects what I said."

Stewart felt numb. The man seemed so genuine. But her boss was more experienced in dealing with these kinds of interrogations than she was. Maybe she was falling for the kind of convincing lies that most guilty suspects seem capable of manufacturing. Nonetheless, her tone was compassionate as she said, "Could I ask you to sign each page, please, Doctor?"

Jones reached into the inside pocket of his jacket and took out a fountain pen. Stewart stared at it. It was heavy, almost bulbous, with a gold top and a brownish onyx barrel, not dissimilar in pattern to the cufflinks found at the crime scenes. She watched as Jones unscrewed the top with his right hand and signed his name at the bottom of each of the pages. The nib was gold, squat, but because the doctor's fist obscured her vision, she was unable to tell if the handwriting matched the distinctive pen.

His fist was obscuring her view! Realisation struck Stewart with the force of a hammer blow. And with the sudden awareness came a vision of Jones in the mortuary, holding a large organ aloft in his right hand as he adjusted a weighing machine with the other. She turned to Sheehan, almost breathless. "Sir, could you suspend the interview, please. I must talk to you outside."

Sheehan gave her a puzzled look but made no demur. He bent over the machine and intoned, "Interview suspended at fourteen fifty-six. Chief Inspector Sheehan and Sergeant Stewart leave the room."

Once outside the room, Sheehan said, "Okay, Sergeant, what has you so fired up?"

The corridor outside the interrogation rooms was empty and, even though there would be occasional movement around the other interrogation rooms, Stewart felt it was safe to conduct the conversation where they were. "Sir, do you have Doctor Campbell's mobile number?"

"That's personal, Stewart. I can't give that to you."

"I don't want it, sir," Stewart said earnestly, clearly wrought up about something. "I just need you to phone him right away."

Sheehan gazed at her. "And what? Have a chat with him about the weather?"

Stewart ignored the chief's caustic wit and rushed on, "I need you to ask him to review the photographs of the two autopsies, maybe even look at the bodies again."

"He's going to need a helluva good reason to revisit those cases," Sheehan stalled. "Without Jones's help, he's probably way behind on his work schedule already. What's going on, Stewart?"

"Don't know how I missed it, sir, but when we went into the mortuary the other day, Jones was standing with an organ held in his right hand and working on the weighing machine with the other. And just now, I couldn't see him signing his statement because his fist was in the way."

"What are you talking about, Stewart?"

"If it had been me or you, sir, we'd have the organ in our left hand while we adjusted the weighing machine with our right. That's because we're right-handed. Jones is left-handed, sir. That's why I couldn't see his writing."

Sheehan immediately caught her reasoning. "Holy crap! You want to see if Campbell can determine from the cuts whether the killer was left-handed or right- handed?"

"Yes, sir. Usually, if a perp is right-handed, nobody at the crime scene passes any remarks, but if anything about the scene indicates the perp is left- handed, it always tends to get mentioned. Because Doctor Campbell didn't bring the issue up, I have a feeling this killer might have been right-handed."

Sheehan's brain was racing as he considered the implications of what Stewart was saying. He had to admit that Jones's testimony had the ring of truth almost from beginning to end. But that was easily explained. Ninety-five per cent of it was true, and the man had lived with it for twelve years. His thoughts and responses needed no fabrication or elaboration. The only lie was his denial of the murders. His motive was overwhelmingly obvious and, almost certainly in the man's mentally fragile state, overwhelmingly compelling.

And yet, there was something about his calm demeanour. Or was he just fatalistic? He did not seem to care one jot whether Sheehan believed his denials. He simply made them and left it at that. Could there be something to Stewart's insight? Was there a possibility that Jones, despite the prodigious provocation, was innocent of the killings? Sheehan was torn. He was reluctant to let go. But, bloody hell, what if the killer had been right-handed? That could change everything.

He reached into his pocket for his mobile. "Jones might well end up owing you some serious gratitude, Stewart. I'll call Dick and see what he says."

Stewart stepped to one side, waiting tensely while her boss made the call. When Campbell answered and Sheehan asked for a review of the autopsies, Stewart could hear some strenuous squawking at the other end. This morphed to silence very quickly when Sheehan explained what was wanted. Sheehan was staring at Stewart while he listened to what the doctor was saying. He muttered an "Okay!" as he ended the call, and said, "He'll try to get back to us within the next half hour to forty minutes. He's up to his armpits in blood and no one to help him. He blames me for it. He wants to examine the two bodies again before he commits himself." Then the corner on his mouth twitched. "He says if you're right, he's going to give you one massive hug the next time he sees you."

Stewart had the fingers of both hands crossed as she raised her head to the ceiling and blew out a tense breath. "Oh God, I hope we're right, sir ..." She paused suddenly, then continued somewhat awkwardly, "I mean, not because the doctor has promised me a hug or anything, sir. It's just that Doctor Jones is so nice, so civil. I could never see him as the killer."

"Calm down, Sergeant. We don't know yet that he's innocent."

"What do you mean, sir?"

"I keep thinking about the way he tried to deflect us from talking about the cut to Fitzpatrick's throat. It was almost as if he didn't want us thinking about it."

"But it's the cut that's going to get him off the hook, sir."

"Is it? Think about it. This guy's smart. He's doing a doctorate. What if it was him who did the killings? Perhaps the first thing he thought about was that if he sliced the victim's throat with his left hand, it would be picked up immediately. So he used his right but, not being ambidextrous, he made a bit of a mess of it. It would fit Campbell's notion that our guy knew where to cut but didn't have the expertise to make a decent job of it."

Stewart waited for a uniformed constable carrying a sheaf of papers to walk past them before saying, "God, Chief. Is that not a bit tortuous? And why would he not have drawn attention to the fact that the cut was right-handed?"

"Ace in the hole, Stewart. He wasn't going to waste it at this point. He would want us to find that out for ourselves. More impact. You could say he was betting that one or other of us would notice he is left-handed and draw the relevant conclusions. Happens you did. By the way, good call, good instincts."

Stewart flushed. "Thank you, sir, but supposin' I'd missed it?"

"Then he'd have had to draw our attention to it some other way. But I bet it would've been subtle."

"I believed him, sir," Stewart said, suddenly downcast.

"And maybe you're right to do so, Stewart, but you have to admit, it's a scenario we can't ignore."

"So what about Weir? And Duffner?"

"Don't worry. I have tortuous scenarios for them, as well."

"I thought Duffner was off the hook?"

"So did I, until I started to think about it. We were impressed by Duffner's certainty that Sloan was lying, and so it proved to be. But the certainty came from the fact that he knew Sloan hadn't seen him under that lamppost. That need not necessarily mean that he wasn't there. He just wasn't under the lamppost. He could have committed the murder and slipped out to a waiting car driven by his brother. They could easily have sped off in that."

"And Weir? What about his admission that he was there with his two henchmen? And why did he try to frame Duffner?"

"Well, we're short on facts, obviously, and working with loads of lies. Weir is a compulsive liar. Maybe he thought up this story of putting himself at the scene of the crime in such a way as to account for being there but to make himself look innocent of the murders. It's a clever story, and the two thugs who were with him would swear on their mother's grave anything Weir asked them to. He could well have committed the murder and then decided to point the finger at Duffner. Maybe he has a history with Duffner. Or maybe it's just what he said, that he knew Duffner was a suspect and would make a good scapegoat."

Stewart was shaking her head in mystification. "How do you cope with all the devious stuff that goes on in that head of yours, Chief?"

Sheehan grinned. "The job does that to you."

"You've got me totally confused now. So where are we with all of this?"

"Short of facts, like I said. If it was Weir, we've no connection between him and Shaw yet. Duffner has clear connections to both Fitzpatrick and Shaw but, so far, not to Kelly. And we need to find out if Kelly has connections to either Weir or Duffner. And there's Jones. He is the one candidate whose connections definitely stretch to all three."

"You still think it's him, then?"

"Too early to say. I'm just conjecturing to see where it takes me, but if it's Jones, what's his connection to the stalker? And, even more unlikely, what's his connection to your informant. These are the sort of questions that can throw all this clunky thinking out of whack."

"This is crazy, Chief. How are you going to know what way to leap?"

"Like I told you before, Sergeant, if you develop a theory and try to fit the facts into it, you're in trouble. You'll almost certainly ignore some important issue. If we are going to accuse anybody, all the parts must fit into that person's scenario. But where does your stalker fit in with any of these three at the moment? Or is the stalker even connected with the case? And where does your informant fit in? He's definitely connected, but what's his game?" He spread his hands. "And we haven't even taken into account the possibility that there could be another person we haven't even met yet who's the real killer."

Stewart was shaking her head, her expression confused.

Sheehan smiled. "Look, what we need is one fact, one key fact, that can bring us that eureka moment. The fact might even be sitting on the whiteboard already, but one of us has to see it, see its significance, and then all will fall into place."

Sheehan's mobile rang, and he pulled it from his jacket pocket. It was Campbell. Sheehan listened for a few minutes and said, "Thanks, Dick. I'll get back to you."

He put the phone back in his pocket and said, "Dick's convinced that the cut was right-handed. He also says we should release Jones immediately. He's bawling at me that there is no way Jones could have done something like this."

"What do you think, Chief?"

"Don't know. Maybe I'm overthinking this. Jones came across like he doesn't care what happens to him, but he was adamant that he didn't commit the murders. Hard to know what to think. Bring him a cup of coffee … but don't tell him anything. I'll have to think about it, but we'll probably let him out on police bail."

FIFTY-THREE

It was evening now. Stewart was sitting on an armchair with a newspaper on her knees and the television on. She had no idea, however, what was in the paper or what was happening on the screen before her. Her mind was still filled with the events of the day. On the basis of her observations, Sheehan had decided to release Jones on police bail. He had dropped her off at home after that, and she had spent the rest of the evening doing some desultory housework. Her mind had not stopped racing since she came home. *Jones and Lynda? Who would have thought?*

The phone rang. She jumped up with alacrity and almost danced to it, hoping it was Tom. "Hellooo!" she carolled.

The metallic voice of her informant replied, "What the hell did you do?"

"What?"

"Jones has been released." Despite the emotionless tones of the electronic voice, Stewart could easily hear the anger of the speaker behind it.

"We believe he's innocent," she said flatly.

"Innocent? You stupid woman! He is not innocent. He's as guilty as sin, and all your fancy deductions about left hands change nothing."

"How did you know about that?" Stewart snapped.

"You have no idea what's going on. You've made a complete mess of things." There was a pause on the line. Then the robotic voice came again. "I can't speak to you when I'm this angry. Do nothing until I get back to you."

Again Stewart found herself listening to the hiss of empty static.

FIFTY-FOUR

The team was fully assembled in the Serious Crimes Room several minutes before the Monday meeting was due to start. Strain was showing on everyone's face. Whatever tomorrow night might bring, all were hoping that it would bring the arrest of the killer of Fitzpatrick and Shaw and perhaps some answers to the mystery surrounding Lynda Bell. Even Turner was there, sitting with the chief as usual. Stewart was sitting at her own desk, as was Allen, but they had found time for a brief chat before sitting down, just an ordinary chat about ordinary things. But to Stewart it didn't feel ordinary. It felt special and, although her expression was solemn, her heart felt light.

Sheehan looked conspicuously at his watch. He cleared his throat and said, "It's a bit early, but since we're all here we might as well start." He pulled some papers on the desk closer to him. "Right, by now the news about Doctor Jones will have filtered down to all of you."

"You let him go, Chief," Miller said. "Does that mean you're satisfied he's not the guy we're looking for?"

"Not necessarily. There still remain some questions around his involvement, but Stewart made a very significant deduction about his left-handedness that, on the surface at least, would seem to point towards his innocence."

"On the s-surface?" McNeill interjected.

"Well, depends how devious he is," Sheehan said. Then he smiled. "If his mind's half as devious as mine, the left hand thing isn't a total let off." This earned him a few grins.

"And Weir?" McCoy asked.

"Still in custody. But we can't find any connection between him and Shaw yet. He may well have nothing to do with the two killings."

"And Duffner the same?" McCoy again.

Sheehan shrugged. "There are still questions about all of them. Nothing's off the table."

"What about Weir's mole?" McCullough's uncharacteristic contribution raised a few eyebrows. "Now that Weir's out of the picture, do we sort out his man?"

"We'll get today and tomorrow out of the way first," Sheehan answered. "But he's definitely on my agenda for next week."

Connors, somewhat impatient with what he thought was 'this tippy-toeing about', asked the question that was in everyone's head. "What are we doing about tomorrow night? Are we laying a trap for the killer or what?"

Sheehan leaned back in his chair, hands behind his head. "You've had the weekend to ponder it. What does anybody think?"

Several eyes, under lowered eyebrows, glanced in Stewart's direction, but there was no immediate answer to the chief's question. Allen was the first to speak. "If you're still thinking of using Sergeant Stewart as bait, I'd like to declare my opposition to that plan right away."

Turner was right in behind him. "I'm very much of the mind of Detective Allen," he said. "I, too, have been pondering this over the weekend and, should things go wrong, the consequences for the sergeant don't bear thinking about."

Connors chipped in again. "Be very hard for them to go wrong. We could place two burly policemen behind Mister Owens's fence.

They'd be well hidden but only a step or two away from Kelly's place. If the killer turns up, they'll be on him in seconds."

"And there's a couple of side streets very close to the place as well," Miller added. "We could have a couple of cars there, waiting for any signal. The two uniforms could have radios linked directly to us. Two seconds would bring us to the house if we're alerted to anything."

"And I could have all sorts of radio devices all over the house," Stewart said, "all ready to hand. I'd be able to kick up some sort of alarm at the slightest sign of trouble. It wouldn't be hard to reach out a hand if there was any kind of noise at the door or wherever. And, don't forget. We'd be expecting trouble, so it wouldn't be as if I wasn't prepared and waiting."

"This miscreant has shown himself to be devious and ruthless so far," Turner argued, his concern evident. "Being ready doesn't mean that you will be able to circumvent some insidious approach that we just can't foresee right now. I still think the whole idea of using you as bait is extremely foolhardy."

"I agree," Allen said, nodding vigorously.

"We've got to catch this guy," Connors said. "Does anyone have any other kind of a plan?"

No one answered.

"I didn't think so." He looked at Stewart. "I hate the idea of using the sergeant as bait, too, but Kelly's almost certainly his next target, and we're not likely to get a chance like this again to stop the guy. I've been racking my brains about this all weekend, and I've come to the conclusion that Stewart's plan is as good a one as we're likely to come up with."

Stewart smiled at him. "Thank you, Declan."

Connors smiled back. "You're welcome, Sergeant."

"What kind of logistics are involved?" Miller asked.

Connors had been giving the matter a lot of thought. "Well, this guy will be checking the place out; there's no doubt about that. If we're using cars, they'll have to be parked in that side street with the bend in it so that the cars can be hidden. If the guy comes up towards the house, we don't want him spotting us parked in a side street like two big sore thumbs."

"And we'll b-be in radio c-contact with each other the entire time," McNeill threw in.

"Yes," Connors agreed, "but there'd have to be complete radio silence from ... when? Maybe from ten-thirty to eleven thirty. That's the longest window we'd need. We want no alien sounds in the area during that time that might scare the perp off."

"The cops behind the fence will have to be well warned as well," Stewart said. "They can keep their radios with them, but they can't use them during that hour. Nor should they be allowed to talk. Conversation of any kind carries a long way in the silence of the night."

Allen looked up at her, grinning. "Poetry now, is it?" But he wasn't feeling as light as he sounded. His was filled with an inner dread. *What if Turner was right about the perp being able to come up with something devious? God knows what might happen to Denise.*

"We'd need everybody in place by around eight o'clock, or eight thirty at the latest," Stewart said. "Myself, the uniforms, the two cars. We don't know when the killer will begin his reconnaissance, so we'd need to be well settled before that."

"Good point," Connors said. "And definite radio silence on the dot of half ten, okay everybody?"

Everyone was nodding now. The plan seemed to be coming together. McCullough must have been feeling garrulous, or perhaps even he was caught up in the precariousness of the situation. "You're not saying much, Chief," he said. "What do you think about any of this?"

"Prosecutor Turner's right," Sheehan said. "This killer has shown himself to be calculating and guileful. Even if he suspected we were hovering about the area— in fact, he's bound to know we will be—he might still devise some sort of way to execute his plan."

"Execute Kelly, you mean," McCoy said. Gallows humour. Acceptable in this situation. There were a couple of chuckles and a few grins.

"Exactly. But, frighteningly, maybe Stewart as well." He turned to Denise. "Are you sure that this is something you can genuinely feel comfortable with, Sergeant? There are definite risks to it, no matter how carefully we plan."

"I think we should do it, sir," Stewart said forcefully. "We cannot leave him out there killing whoever takes his fancy. We can't know if Kelly's his last target. We only know that he's the next one and, as Declan said, this is definitely our best opportunity to catch him."

Sheehan still looked apprehensive. He sat silent for a time while all eyes watched him. "This is a serious matter," he said. "I don't know if I can take it on to myself to make this decision."

"Put it to a vote, then," Connors suggested. He raised his hand. "I vote in favour."

Stewart's hand was up immediately. More slowly, but positive nonetheless, there followed the hands of Miller, McNeill, McCoy and McCullough. Only Turner and Allen abstained.

Connors looked at Sheehan. "Sir, the vote's in favour."

"Very well," Sheehan said, looking more depressed than pleased. "Connors, get two big uniforms and brief them thoroughly. Stewart, sort yourself out with whatever radio devices you think you'll need. I'll talk to Kelly and to Mister Owens. I'll make sure the old guy's in bed before anything goes down."

FIFTY-FIVE

Two large policemen, safely ensconced in Mr. Owens's front garden, stood peering into the gloom through the slats in the fence. Another chilly October evening but, thank God, there was no rain. They shifted their feet slowly, moved their arms about, trying to keep the blood circulating through their bodies in the nocturnal cold. One turned to say something, but the other raised a swift finger to his lips, shaking his head. The first mouthed an apologetic, "Oh!" and placed a hand in front of his mouth with a slight grin. They shrugged at each other and went back to staring through the fence again. Stakeouts such as these were normally excruciatingly boring, but both men were acutely aware of the significance of their role here tonight and the customary ennui had been replaced by tense trepidation.

A noise nearby caused them both to start poking their heads apprehensively at different sections of the fence, trying to locate its source. It was caused by one of the neighbours a house or two down. He was coming out of his door, dressed in a heavy overcoat, and wheeling out what seemed to be a long bicycle. They watched him push the bike out on to the road, expecting him to climb on and ride away. Instead he stopped, looked around as if puzzled, and then his eyes focused on Owens's fence. His head moved forwards as if he was trying to see through the chinks. Leaving the bicycle on the road, he began to walk towards the Owens residence, and stopping a few feet from the fence, he called, "Is there somebody in there?"

The policemen, not briefed for an eventuality such as this, were unsure as to how they should respond. Both stood stock still, maintaining silence as ordered.

"There's somebody in there," the neighbour shouted. "I saw you moving. I'm calling the police."

"Shit!" one of the policemen said under his breath. He called back to the man, "We *are* the police. You're interfering with a police operation here. Go on about your business."

"A likely story," the man said. "Show me your warrant card, or I'm going to raise an alarm."

The policeman raised his hands and eyes heavenwards in frustration. The last thing Sheehan wanted at this precise time was any kind of disturbance. If this guy ...

"For God's sake," his companion gritted, opening the fence gate. He stepped out, grabbed the nosy neighbour by the collar of his coat, and dragged him in beside them. "Here you are, for crying out loud."

Both policemen began opening their coats, searching inside their inner jackets for the warrant cards. While they were thus occupied, the neighbour swiftly and accurately applied a stun gun to each of their necks, causing them to slump to the ground, their eyes wide with shock and pain.

While they were jerking spasmodically on the lawn, the neighbour calmly and silently removed his overcoat and threw it across the top of the fence. Underneath he was wearing a white, protective coverall. The stricken policemen watched helplessly while the man bent to pull the legs of the suit, which had been tugged up to his knees to conceal them from sight, down to his feet. As he did this, they could see a large watch attached to the man's wrist on the outside of the protective sleeve. The 'neighbour' reached into the pocket of the overcoat hanging on the fence and pulled out a pair of matching Tyvek bootees which he pulled on over his shoes. Finally, he pulled the suit's hood up over his head so that only his face was showing, and reached again into the pocket of the overcoat.

The eyes of the gasping policemen bulged when they saw the hand had withdrawn holding a knife. Swiftly the man stepped forward, knelt behind one of the policemen and pulled him into a sitting position almost on to his lap, facing away from him. Without compunction or empathy, he dispassionately cut the policeman's throat, a hacking slice that did not fully sever the carotid artery. The nick to the blood vessel thus caused the blood to squirt out under pressure and a long arterial spray spouted onto Mr. Owens's immaculate lawn. The killer, maintaining an eerie silence throughout, threw the policeman aside as if he was useless baggage.

He rose to his feet and walked over to the other policeman. Wheezing desperately, scarcely able to breathe, his eyes filled with terror, the second man tried to move, but his muscles were unable to heed any of his brain's commands. The assailant dispatched him, too, with the same cold ruthlessness, wiped the knife and his gloved hands on the man's overcoat, and stood up. He returned the knife to his own overcoat, took off the bootees, and put them into his overcoat pocket as well. Then he rolled the overall legs back up to his knees, pushed back the hood, squeezing it down to the back of his neck, and put his overcoat back on. No trace of the protective suit could now be seen.

He looked at the large watch on his wrist. *10:50. On time.*

He let himself quietly out through the gate without a backwards glance at the two dying policemen. Once outside the gate, he paused for a second to survey the street before him. Nothing stirred. All was silence. Moving purposefully forward, he went to retrieve his bicycle. It wasn't an ordinary bicycle. It was a tandem with a strangely constructed bucket seat where the second saddle should have been. The man wheeled the bicycle quietly to the door of Finbar Kelly's house and leaned it against the low wall. He removed the glove from his left hand and took something from his pocket. He fiddled with it for a moment and, putting both the object and his left hand back into his pocket, he walked down the slope to Kelly's door and gave it a gentle rap.

After a minute's silence, Stewart's voice sounded from behind the door. "Who's there?"

"It's me," came the whispered response.

Stewart, thinking it was Allen, opened the door. "You?" Surprise filled her voice. "What are you doing here?"

The man looked searchingly down the street before turning to her again, whispering urgently, "Chief Inspector Sheehan wants me to give you a message."

"What is it?" Stewart whispered back.

"This." The man withdrew a syringe from his left pocket, stuck it into Stewart's neck, and depressed the plunger. Stewart's eyes widened with confusion but almost immediately the pupils rolled up until only the whites were showing. The man caught her before she could fall and lowered her gently to the ground.

He looked at his watch. *10:54. On time.*

Kelly came into the hall a second or two later, saying, "What is it, Sergeant? Is everything all right?"

The man stepped forward, extending his right hand. "Everything's fine, sir. The chief has decided that it's too risky to leave Sergeant Stewart here. I'm her replacement." Kelly unthinkingly took the man's hand, wondering vaguely why it was gloved in plastic. As soon as the man had Kelly's hand, he pulled him suddenly forward and applied a taser to his neck. Kelly dropped to the floor with a tortured moan. The man bent, seized him under the armpits, and dragged him back into the sitting room. Leaving Kelly wheezing and jerking on the floor, he took off his overcoat, and went again through the routine of covering his feet, legs, and head with the protective clothing.

He threw his overcoat out into the hall and again glanced at his watch. *10:56. On time.*

He knelt beside the supine figure, looked into the terrified eyes, and hissed, "Remember Lynda Bell, you fuck? Do you? Well, think of her now because she'll be your last thought."

As he did with the two policemen, he knelt behind Kelly, pulled the shoulders up on to his knees, and coldly sliced the hapless man's throat. The cut was less than proficient, but it was more than effective. This time the carotid artery was fully cut and the blood emerged in a heavy flow, barely spurting six inches high. The killer watched the man's dying struggles, listened impassively to the gurgles and wheezes, until the body was still. Quickly he rose, bent again and pulled down the man's trouser and underpants. He seized the man's penis and sawed at it without emotion, like a butcher cutting a piece of fat off a side of beef. Although the victim's heart had stopped, some blood spilled from this new wound. The killer, making no attempt to clean off any of the blood, stuck the knife between Kelly's clenched teeth to force down the lower jaw, and roughly shoved the now detached penis into the dead man's mouth.

He looked at his watch. *11:03. On time.*

He grabbed Kelly's limp left wrist, noted that the watch showed three minutes past eleven, reset it at eleven-o-five, and pulled out the winder. Rising swiftly, he surveyed the scene, nodded once briefly, and began divesting himself of the now-bloodied protective suit. He rolled it into a small ball and strode quickly into the hall. He took a plastic bag from a pocket of his overcoat, put the coverall in that, knotted it, and put the overcoat back on. Holding the handle of the plastic bag with his little finger, he picked up Stewart from the floor and carried her out to the bicycle. He held the tandem steady with one hand and managed to squeeze the policewoman into the bucket seat at the back. He bent and pushed her feet into the guards on the back pedals and then handcuffed her. Mounting the front part of the tandem, he pulled Stewart's cuffed hands over his head and around his neck and prepared to pedal off.

He looked again at his watch. *11:11. T plus two. No matter.* He had allowed a margin of five minutes. He was well inside that.

Still, he hurried a little. The street sloped downwards towards the entrance to the estate with quite a steep incline, so pedalling the tandem gave the killer no trouble. By the time he passed the entrance to the side street where Sheehan and his team were parked, he was racing at speed, a silent, flying ghost.

Even as their quarry was passing them unnoticed, Allen, sitting beside Sheehan in the front seat of the car and showing obvious signs of distress, was saying, "It's ten past eleven, Chief. What's going on, do you think? Do you think something might be happening? Maybe we should …?"

The chief's raised hand silenced him. "Stick to the plan, Tom. We want to catch this guy."

The man on the tandem sped to the end of the street, turning left towards a roundabout. Less than fifty yards beyond the roundabout was a lay-by where he had left his car. He stopped beside it, uncuffed Stewart, lifted her from the bicycle and, opening a door, threw her still unconscious body on to the back seat, together with the plastic bag which he had still been carrying. Hoisting the tandem on to the roof rack, he secured it with the clips that were there.

He looked at his watch one last time. *11:18. On time.* This evoked a sour grin of satisfaction.

Allowing himself a couple of seconds for one final quick look behind him to ensure that there was no pursuit, he got into the car, eased quietly out of the lay-by, and drove off into the night.

About twenty-five past eleven, Allen was a neurotic mess. "Chief, for God's sake! If there was something happening, the uniforms would have contacted us by now. Something's gone wrong. I know it. We need to get over there."

Sheehan's own psychic antennae were buzzing alarmingly. Although the plan demanded they give the killer until eleven-thirty to make an appearance, he had not expected that they would have to wait this long. Feeling as nervous as Tom now, and dreading that something terrible had gone wrong, he grunted, "Right. To hell with it! We'll go now. Radio Miller and McNeill to follow us."

A few seconds took them to the house. They stepped out of the car looking around. Everything seemed quiet, normal. Nothing appeared to be out of place. The door to Kelly's house was closed, and a light continued to shine behind the blind in the window. Nor was there any movement behind the fence at Owens's house. *You'd think they'd have come out when they saw us arriving,* Sheehan wondered. He called to Miller who was exiting the car behind him. "Go up to the Owens house, Simon, and see what the uniforms have to report."

Allen was already at the door of Kelly's house, knocking on it. Getting no answer, he went to the window and knocked there. Still nothing. His expressive face showed the depth of his consternation as he rushed back to the door, pounding on it this time.

"There's no answer, Chief," he said, desperation in his voice. "I'm going to kick the bloody door in."

Sheehan gave him a rigid nod. "Go ahead."

Allen had the door off its hinges in a couple of violent seconds. They rushed into the hall, to the sitting room, and stopped aghast at the sight that confronted them. Kelly was lying on his back on the floor, covered in blood, a large, ugly gash on his throat, obviously dead. There was no sign of Stewart.

Allen's hands flew to the top of his head and he turned away, his back to the body. "Jesus, boss," he cried, his voice anguished. "What have you done? Your shitty plan has got Denise killed."

Sheehan had a hand over his mouth, his normally placid demeanour ripped to shreds. "Christ, Tom ..." He didn't know what to say. Then he had a thought that threw him a faint hope. "Maybe she's upstairs. Maybe she's locked herself in a room or something."

Allen flew past him, taking the stairs three at a time. Miller came rushing in from the hall. "Chief," he panted, "the uniformed men are both dead. Their throats have been cut."

Sheehan put his hands over his face, almost reeling. "Oh my God," he moaned. "What have I done? What have I done?"

Miller heard and understood. He put a hand on Sheehan's shoulder and said forcefully, "You did nothing, Chief. It was a team decision."

Sheehan stared again at the dead body of Kelly, at the excess of blood, his face rigid with distress. "Dear God, I shouldn't have released Jones so early. I should have kept him on remand until tomorrow. Bloody hell! What a mess."

"Do you think it was Jones, sir?" Miller asked.

"I don't know, Simon. Go and find out where he is, will you? Search his house. He can't have had much time to ferret Stewart away anywhere."

"Right, sir. Where does he live?"

"Can't remember. It'll be in the charge book. Phone the duty sergeant and he'll give you the address. And tell him to get the coroner and the SOCO boys here ASAP." Sheehan's voice sounded utterly despondent.

"Okay, Chief. I'll get back to you when I learn anything."

Allen came back from rushing around the upstairs rooms. His face was contorted. "She's not in any of the rooms upstairs, sir." He swivelled around, desperation in his every move. "God, sir, where the hell is she?"

Sheehan could see that Tom was close to total panic. Pushing down his own sick self-condemnation, he said, "Try to stay calm, Tom. Panicking won't help. One thing seems clear. If she's not here, then he's taken her with him. Comfort yourself with the thought that in all probability she's still alive."

Tom was repeatedly punching his right fist into his left palm, anything but calm. "God, Chief, where the hell do we start to look for her?"

Sheehan stared at him helplessly. McNeill came into the room and stopped, appalled. "Holy God!" he said, shock killing his stutter. He looked at Allen. "Where's Denise?"

Tom looked at him, his face taut with misery. He was obviously near to tears, and McNeill went over and put his arms around him. "Don't lose it, Tom," he said, positively. "We'll find her." He turned to Sheehan. "Won't we, sir?"

Sheehan still had not recovered from the shock of the night's grim events and was unable to find an answer to Geoff's plea. At that point, Doctor Campbell entered the room, followed by Bill Larkin and a couple of SOCOs. None of Campbell's normal congeniality was evident. He just gave Sheehan a cold, offhand nod and said curtly, "Would you mind moving aside so that I can examine the body, please." Clearly he hadn't forgiven Jim for arresting Jones. Sheehan wasn't happy with Dick's attitude, and debated inwardly whether he should try to clear the air. But now wasn't the time and, anyway, he had more urgent matters to deal with.

He looked around and saw that Larkin and the SOCOs had swiftly and efficiently set about their normal analysis of the crime scene. Doors and handles were already being dusted; one officer was on his knees, painstakingly crawling on the floor, searching for anything untoward, however small; Campbell was now engrossed in his examination of Kelly's bloodied corpse; Larkin was wandering around the house doing his usual inventory.

Resolve flooded back into his brutalised psyche. He breathed a heavy breath out through his nose and said to Allen. "Right. These guys have this covered, Tom. There's not much we can do here. C'mon."

Allen's eyes lit up with sudden hope. "Where to, Chief?"

"Back to the station. Let's go." He strode from the room without further word to Campbell or any of the others, Allen following at his heels.

Sheehan drove back to the station, his mind racing. Allen was in the front seat beside him, silent, but fidgeting endlessly, constantly wringing his hands, rubbing his face with them, moving backwards and forwards, showing signs of deep, emotional distress. Sheehan was about to speak to him, to find some way to strengthen him, when his mobile phone rang. He pulled it quickly from his pocket and said, "Well, Simon?"

Allen could hear Miller's tinny voice at the chief's ear. "Chief, I found Jones at his home. He seemed well settled, as if he'd been there for hours and hadn't moved. He was studying, sir. Books all over the place. I didn't have a warrant, but I asked him if he would mind if I had a look around the house. He just told me to help myself and went back to his books. Ignored me after that. Didn't care where I looked, sir."

"You're sure you searched the whole place?"

"Count on it, Chief. Every inch. No way Sergeant Stewart is anywhere in that house. And I had a wee feel at the bonnet of his car when I was leaving. It was cold. If he was out tonight, it wasn't in that car. Honestly, sir, the whole scene looked absolutely kosher. I really don't think Jones is our man."

"Thanks, Simon. I'll talk to you later." Sheehan switched off and put the phone back in his pocket.

He attempted once more to speak to Allen, but again the phone interrupted. He looked at the screen. "Yes, Geoff?"

"Sir," McNeill's voice was hesitant. "Uniforms canvassing the area have just reported f-finding the strangled body of the old woman who lives in the house opposite K-Kelly. Apparently she's been d-dead for several hours."

Sheehan's eyes closed and the car drifted towards the pavement. He righted it quickly and said wearily, "Thanks, Geoff." He put the phone back in his pocket.

Allen said, "What was that all about?"

"The bastard's been hiding all day in an old woman's house across the road. His tone was bitter as he added, "And he couldn't just tie her up. He had to go and strangle her, too. This blackguard is utterly without mercy." His lips compressed. "Right, Tom. This bastard has had it. We catch him. We catch him tonight."

FIFTY-SIX

Sheehan and Allen entered the Serious Crimes Room, Allen still in a state of near panic. His fists were clasping and unclasping, his breathing was ragged, and his eyes were almost rolling in his head. "But how are we going to catch him, Chief? What are we going to do? We can't just sit here. We have to do something?"

"What do you suggest, Tom?" Sheehan's terse response revealed his own tension. "That we rush out into the night and start searching … anywhere? We need to think this through. Going off half-cocked will serve nothing."

"But, Chief …"

"Tom, this is a time for cool heads," Sheehan said. "Settle yourself somewhere. I need time to think."

"God, Chief, if ever we needed one of your famous hunches, we need one now. What are you going to do?"

Sheehan pointed to the whiteboard. "The answer's there. And I'm going to sit in front of the damned thing until I find it."

"Shit, sir. That's a bit iffy. Can we not brainstorm this, or something?"

"No, that's not the way my brain works. Look, Sherlock Holmes used to tell Watson to give him peace to think. He would indicate the amount of time he would need by saying that it was a one pipe, or two pipe, or three pipe problem. I think this is a two pipe problem, so go get yourself a coffee or something. I'll call you as soon as I get anything."

"Jesus, Chief. Maybe I should stay here. I mean ..."

Allen's panicked prattling was beginning to irritate Sheehan. "Tom, I can't afford the slightest distraction. Go away." And with that, Sheehan pulled a chair in front of the board, already studying it, already oblivious of his angst-ridden young colleague.

Tom went to the coffee table, made himself a cup, and went to his desk where he sat, his eyes fixed on the back of his chief's skull, willing him with all his mental strength to find a solution.

Sheehan calmed himself, found ways to still the trepidation and, yes, the guilt, he was feeling. He did not try immediately to find an answer or *the* answer. He quietly let his eyes range the board, waiting for something to impinge upon his consciousness, or to rise from his subconscious. He stared at the macabre photos of the dead bodies, tamping down any emotional response. He shifted his gaze to the photograph of the three young men. No thoughts entered his head. He continued to let his gaze roam. He studied the colour photograph of Lynda Bell. His mind was now beginning to wander free. No thoughts forced. As he stared at the photo, he thought casually that, with a different hairstyle, this photograph might well have been Stewart about seven or eight years ago. *Okay, Sheehan. Focus. No wool-gathering.* He looked at the newspaper clipping, at the photographs of the cufflinks, at other scene-of-crime photographs. Nothing was happening. He forced himself to relax. *Don't press. Don't press. Just keep ranging the ...*

His eyes shot back to the photograph of Lynda Bell. His body, electrified by incipient understanding, became suddenly rigid. His brain sizzled with the shock of a full and immediate epiphany. Bell? Stewart? Bell? Lynda Bell had been the key all along. He knew that he had the answer, but his brain had not yet articulated it. He stared at the board, his eyes now scurrying swiftly here, there, even staring blankly away from the board altogether as the pieces of the jigsaw began to fit swiftly together. Now he knew what subconscious thought had been triggered by Stewart's comment about Weir calling the ambulance *before* he beat up his wife. Jones's story flitted across his memory. Now he knew where the stalker fitted in, and why Nigel had been led to believe that he had been stalking Stewart for years. He knew, too, where Stewart's informant fitted in. How could he have missed it before? And now he knew why the three victims had been murdered, and why Stewart's informant had singled her out. And, loud as a siren, a comment sounded in his head that he had heard spoken but, given the circumstances, should not, could not have been made. How did he miss that?

He knew enough now. The rest could be fitted in later. He jumped from his seat so swiftly that the startled Allen, who was still staring at him, spilled the remaining dregs of his coffee over his desk. "Come, Allen," Sheehan shouted, echoes of Sherlock Holmes still lurking at the back of his brain, "the game's afoot. We have a long journey ahead of us, and we must get there with the utmost dispatch."

"W ... what?"

"Run down to the compound and get us a fast car, siren, lights. Hurry, Tom.

We've no time to lose. I have one phone call to make. I'll join you at the gate in two minutes."

Tom fled from the room as Sheehan dashed into his office. He dialled a number, and tapped his fingers on his desk with anxious impatience as he waited for a response. The voice of Declan Connors sounded on the line. "Hello?"

"Declan, it's DCI Sheehan here."

"You got something, sir?" Connor's voice radiated hope.

"I need you to find out whoever is in charge of the Land Registry Office and get him to find an address. And I need the full details, post code and whatever, to feed into the sat nav."

"Sir, it's after midnight ..."

"I don't give a shit, Connors. It's life and death. Drag him out of his bed. If he gives you any trouble, arrest him or something. But get that address. And I need it sooner than ASAP."

"What address, sir?"

Sheehan told him the details once, slammed the phone down, and bolted from the room.

Allen was waiting at the gate in the driver's seat of a 5 Series BMW, engine already idling, when Sheehan arrived. Sheehan rushed to the driver door, pulled it open, and shouted, "Move round to the other side, Tom. I'm driving."

Allen raced to the passenger seat without argument, anxious not to waste a second. "Where are we going, sir?"

Sheehan shot out through the gate, siren already wailing, scarcely stopping to see if his exit was clear. He had probably been betting on the fact the Dundella Avenue, quiet even in normal times, would be clear in the post-midnight darkness.

"Sir?" Allen prodded again.

"Gimme a second, Tom," Sheehan muttered, through clenched teeth. "I need to watch what I'm doing. Can't afford any accidents at this point."

He tore through the urban streets, heading for the B505. The road now was wider, and he was able to continue speeding with less tension. "See if you can get Ardboe on the sat nav, Tom, will you?"

Tom started pressing buttons. "Ardboe? Where the four by four was found? What the hell's taking us there?"

"A pure guess, Tom. If I'm right, Connors will be phoning through to confirm our direction. If I'm wrong, we'll have wasted a lot of precious time."

Ardboe, from the Irish Ard Bó, meaning 'height of the cows', is a small village in the north east of County Tyrone and is situated near the western shore of Lough Neagh. The area has its own interesting history. It had been a base for three thousand United States Army Airforce troops during the Second World War, and it had more than its fair share of unfortunate incidents during the Northern Ireland 'troubles' of the '70s and '80s. At the time Sheehan and Allen were speeding toward it, however, the little village boasted less than nine hundred inhabitants, and the entire area, for the most part, seemed to consist of countryside and uncultivated landscape.

When Allen entered the name of the town land, a female voice on the machine said neutrally, "Please continue straight on to the A2."

"What does the map line look like there, Tom?"

Tom pressed some more buttons. "Pretty much a clear run to the M3, off a short while later on to the M2, then another switch to the M22. Don't worry. I'll keep you right. It all looks pretty straightforward. There's a few miles on the A6 across the north shore of Lough Neagh toward Toome. Then pretty much south all the way after that."

Sheehan was scarcely waiting for instructions, driving almost faster than the robotic voice could issue directions. The headlights of the powerful car lit up the motorway in front of them, but driving was demanding since, even at this late hour, there were many other travellers who seemed to have reasons for being abroad. The screaming siren, however, continued to clear a path for the detectives as the other drivers pulled aside to let them pass.

More stressful minutes passed. Allen could only wring his hands, wishing to hell they'd already arrived at wherever it was that they were going. The female voice sounded again. "In one hundred yards, keep left on the M22."

Now that he was on the motorway, Sheehan was pushing the powerful engine to racetrack speeds. Other road users, sensing the speed and urgency of the police vehicle, gave them a wide berth. The speedometer was hovering around one hundred miles per hour and, while Allen still wanted to know where they were going, he decided not to be a source of distraction at these kinds of speeds.

Both men remained tensely silent, a silence rendered the more eerie because of the darkness, the obtrusive wailing of the siren, the desperate purposefulness of their chase, and the absurd contrast of the calm, disembodied voice from the sat nav as it continued to issue directional instructions. "Please take the B18 one hundred yards to your left, and continue towards Drumnagh."

Over half an hour had passed since they had left the station. "Tom, take my mobile out of my jacket pocket and check that it's switched on, will you?"

Tom did so. "It's on, Chief."

"Shit! What the hell's Connors doing?"

"What *is* Connors doing, Chief?"

"He's supposed to be phoning us with the address of the place I can only hope we're headed to."

As if on cue, the mobile sounded a tune from some classical symphony. Allen answered immediately. "What have you got for us, Declan?"

"Who's that?"

"It's Allen, for feck's sake. What have you got for us?"

"Oh, sorry! I was expecting the chief."

"He's driving like a lunatic here. He couldn't answer his phone. What's the address?"

While he listened to Connors, Allen entered the address and new post-code into the sat nav machine.

"So what's going on?" Connors half whispered.

"Damned if I know," Allen said with feeling, uncaring that the chief could hear him. "You know what he's like. He's clammed up for the time being."

"Tell him to follow us and bring backup," Sheehan instructed him.

"Chief says you're to bring backup," Allen told Connors. He listened a second. "Uh, yourself, Miller, McNeill ..." He looked over at Sheehan. "Anyone else, sir?" He held the phone closer to his boss so that Connor's could hear what was being said.

"Get Larkin. He's at Kelly's house. Tell him to bring a couple of SOCOs with him. God knows what'll be there in the way of evidence. And tell them to hurry."

Allen said into the phone, "Did you get that?"

Connors apparently did because Allen immediately switched off the phone and said, "Connors confirms that you are heading in the right direction. I've entered the new post code."

Almost immediately, the female voice intoned, "At Ballyonan, take the shore road to the B160 and continue past Derrycrinn."

Allen switched to the route map again. "Looks like the new input has us by- passing Ardboe and heading along a narrow road called the Killmascally Road."

"Is it far?"

"About six more miles."

Sheehan began to lean on the accelerator again. Tom pressed back in his seat, his feet pointlessly trying to push on brakes that weren't there. "Easy, Chief. We want to get there. These roads are getting very narrow."

Reducing speed only minimally, Sheehan said, "Look at the map again. What does that Killymathingy Road look like?"

"Killmascally. It's narrow, has some bends, nothing serious, but a couple of miles down, there's a severe left turn." He moved closer to the screen, peering at it. "Huh! The road seems to peter out after that."

"Hmmm. Makes sense."

Allen, tense and feeling powerless in the passenger's seat, muttered tersely, "Maybe to you." Then, more forcefully, "Isn't it time you told me where we're going, Chief, and why?"

Sheehan, eyes glued to the road, ever vigilant for an unexpected late traveller or perhaps some hapless animal wandering around in the night, increased speed to ridiculous levels, and said, tight-lipped, "I'll tell you in a minute."

Allen, hanging on to the dashboard and any other anchor he could find, was not anxious to disturb his boss's concentration, but he did say, "You think the guy we're looking for is there?"

"And Stewart, too, if my reasoning is correct."

Allen's heart tried to leap and constrict at the same time. "Who the hell are we looking for, Chief?"

Sheehan told him.

Allen sucked in shocked breath. "You're kiddin'. Are you sure?"

"Pretty sure."

"Bastard. Scheming, conniving bastard," Allen exploded. "When I get my hands on him, I'll kill him."

Sheehan, eyes still on the road as the car continued to hurtle forwards, suggested calmly, "It might be better all round, Tom, if we simply confine ourselves to an arrest."

Allen wasn't mollified. "I just hope he tries to resist arrest, that's all I have to say."

Bordering five of the north of Ireland's six counties, Lough Neagh is the largest freshwater lake in the British Isles. At eighteen miles wide and seven miles long, it is also the third largest lake in Europe. It has been for many years a popular tourist destination, offering everything from boat trips, award winning marinas, areas for exploration, gardens to view, and even numerous opportunities to listen to traditional music at the many thatched and atmospheric inns that populate its shores. Lough Neagh offers the traveller much to see and do, but neither Sheehan nor Allen were remotely interested in seeing and doing anything other than speeding to their destination.

The voice of the sat nav device in the car was beginning to sound somewhat harried, as Sheehan continued to urge the car forward at a speed totally unsafe on the narrow road, but he had the siren screaming and blue lights flashing as a warning to oncoming drivers. Allen, who was focusing on the sat nav voice, heard the lady say politely, "You have passed your turn. Turn back at next junction."

"For feck's sake, Chief!" he roared, in a tone far from his normal subservient respect, "you've missed the bloody turn. Go back! Go back! Go back!"

Sheehan jumped hard on the brakes. The car swerved and fishtailed on the narrow road as it skidded to a rasping halt almost in the roadside ditch. Sheehan wasted no time throwing the gear stick into reverse, almost repeating the same fish-tailed manoeuvre as he reversed at speed, the engine protesting with an injured roar.

Allen was searching frantically for the turn in the darkness, his head swivelling this way and that. "There it is, Chief. Over there."

Sheehan saw the turn about the same time as Allen. It was little wonder that they had missed it. It was not much more than a track, hidden from any oncoming driver behind a grassy bank that spilled out on to the side of the road. Sheehan reversed back far enough to make the turn, and roared up the track at his previous breakneck speed. There was no further protest from Allen, whose emotions were in turmoil as he stared desperately ahead, his fists clenched to whiteness.

Clouds covered the sky, preventing any moonlight from seeping through. Visibility was very limited. The polite lady on the sat nav device informed them, "You have reached your destination." Sheehan braked, and they looked around, uncomprehending. Vague silhouettes of trees, dark humps which might have been grassy knolls, and a stygian blackness beyond that, were all they could see, although the shimmering surface of Lough Neagh was visible a few hundred yards to their right.

Allen was frantic. "For Christ's sake, boss, where the hell is it?"

Sheehan climbed out of the car. "It's got to be here somewhere." Faint moonbeams struggled to help them. Their light revealed a shadowy wooded area. "Let's look in those trees."

Allen took off like a greyhound, leaving Sheehan struggling in his wake. After they had been chasing around fruitlessly in the trees for some minutes, the moon emerged from the clouds full and clear, and they found a small, rutted track winding through the wood. A rusted metal gate hanging on dilapidated posts indicated that this was a driveway to a residence. They rushed back to the car and eased it along the track, driving without lights or siren and with a great deal more caution. If Stewart was here, they didn't want to warn her abductor of their presence. The wheels were crunching on the half-hearted gravel surface but there was little they could do about that. There were no lights on the narrow road, nor could they see any in the direction they were headed. With only the sidelights on, passage was proving difficult, the darkness amplified inevitably by the trees around them. Eventually Sheehan stepped on the brakes. "This is no good, Tom. We'll have to walk, or we're going to wreck the car and warn our suspect that we're here."

Allen didn't argue. As before, he was out of the car almost before Sheehan had finished speaking, striding down the track, driven by an overwhelming dread that something terrible might have happened to Denise, and by an irrational hope that he still might get there in time to prevent it.

At the end of the road, standing on a gravel-covered clearing, was a two storey house, its stone walls covered in ivy. To its right was a separate two-car garage, now locked, and close by was a small motor launch, mounted on a trailer with four wheels.

"It would be interesting to see what's in that garage," Sheehan muttered, "and I think I know what we'd find."

Allen couldn't have cared less. His heart was constricting to the point where he could scarcely breathe as he became conscious of the fact that there were no lights either in the upper or lower storeys at the front of the house. There seemed to be no sign of life anywhere. His hope disintegrated with a deadening physical sensation. Had the chief blown it? His insights were normally so reliable. *Ah, holy shit, Chief! What a time to get it wrong.*

His eyes darted wildly back and forth as he struggled to quell the panic that was rising in him, but nothing prompted any possibilities for action. He took off at a run to search around the back. Sheehan, now caught up, whispered urgently, "Easy, Tom. You're making an awful racket on the gravel."

Tom barely slowed, unable to force himself to caution, and Sheehan followed, struggling to keep pace. But his sciatic hip, a nuisance at the best of times, was subjected suddenly to a severe wrench as he inadvertently trod on a block of hardwood, invisible in the gloom, the type normally found squeezed under the tyres of old vehicles with unreliable brakes. His ankle twisted, and he lost his balance, falling heavily sideways. He emitted an agonised grunt, gritting his teeth and holding his breath against the severity of the pain. He lay there for a tortured moment, panting jerkily, trying to massage his right hip and thigh.

"I think I might have twisted something, Tom," he gasped. "I'll need a minute or two to …" Pain stabbed him again. "Uhh! Christ! Tom, you'll have to go on alone." Tom, oblivious to his chief's pain, was already moving, but Sheehan continued to hiss after him, "And use your head, Tom. Bulling in and getting caught won't help Stewart. This guy might be insane, but he's cunning and vicious. So, watch yourself. I'll catch up in a couple of minutes."

As he lay on the ground gasping and massaging his hip, he muttered with a great deal of fervour, "Please, God, don't let anything happen to him … to them. Please protect them both." And the ever-present little voice said, *Oh, so now we're praying, are we?* And again aloud, Jim said testily, "We'll talk about this some other time, Lord, okay? Just protect them, will you?"

Allen, half running, half tip-toeing, on the gravelled surface, hurried around to the back of the house. Light, an oddly pink light, was streaming from a window on the second floor. *Holy shit! The chief was right. There is somebody here.* He searched around in the gloom. There was sufficient moonlight to show him a back door. He tried the handle and, to his surprise, the door opened easily. Way out here in the middle of nowhere, the guy probably wasn't expecting guests. Sucking in a tense breath, he went through the door into what seemed like a small washhouse. There was another door in the opposite wall. He went through that as well into a dark hall. A pale light from a partially open door on the floor above was spilling on to the top of a flight of stairs. That allowed Tom to ease forwards in the darkness to where he guessed the foot of the stairs to be.

As he stood there, virtually blind, not breathing, his heart palpitating wildly, he thought he could hear voices, or a single voice maybe. He strained to hear.

"… been so careless? Jones was supposed to go down for the killings. But no, you had to mess it up with your fancy deductions about his left hand." There was silence for a while, and then the voice again, louder, frustrated. "We were supposed to be the golden couple, for God's sake. Could you not see that?"

Tom didn't wait to hear any more. Denise was in that room. He was sure of it. He started gingerly up the stairs, clinging to the banister, one slow step at a time, while the murmuring from above continued to filter down to him. About half way up he was brought to a heart-stopping halt by a rasping creak. One of the boards under his foot was loose. He stopped dead, his face scrunched tight, hoping the sound had not carried to the room above. He listened in the darkness, praying that he hadn't been heard. The muttering in the room had ceased, as if the speaker, too, was listening.

Allen had begun to fear the worst but expelled the breath he had been holding when the speaker began talking again in the same hectoring tone as before. "But it doesn't matter. We were meant to be together and together is what we'll be."

Allen edged forward again, this time placing his feet on the outer sides of the steps. He was at the top of the landing now, and he moved swiftly on the carpeted floor to the room from which the light was spilling. He pushed at the door quietly, staying in the hall, but opening it enough to allow him to peer inside. His first sight of the room was a shock to his eyes. It was an extraordinary room. Pink walls, pink carpet, pink window curtains, pink dressing table, pink bedcovers. Only the rare white border here and there relieved the awful monotony of the blowsy décor. *"Like a bloody cat house in New Orleans,"* he was thinking, even as his eyes drifted to Stewart who was lying on the bed, naked, her mouth covered by grey metallic duct tape. Her arms were spread, a wrist handcuffed to each of the pink metal posts of the bed head. He took a tentative step forward, trying to see if anyone was standing to one side of the door.

Stewart noticed his entry and began shaking her head frantically from side to side. Her eyes were rolling madly as she tried to warn him of danger, but Tom, misinterpreting her signals as signs of fear and panic, rushed forward to release her.

He succeeded in taking two steps before he was felled by a fifty-thousand volt charge from the taser held in the hand of the man who had been standing just behind the door. Tom didn't lose consciousness, but the vicious jolt of electricity fed directly into his muscle fibres causing them to contract uncontrollably. The reins of his central nervous system were hijacked as well, overriding his brain's control of his body. He was able to focus blearily on the man standing above him but, although the man was speaking clearly, Tom had difficulty making sense of what he was saying.

"Welcome, Detective Allen," Robert Turner sneered down at him. "I don't know how you were able to figure out where to find us, but I definitely expected you, you ever-present piece of shit."

Groaning with the pain of the electric shock, Tom shook his head, trying to clear his brain. His ability to remember things, even to process information, had been seriously impaired by the heavy burst of electricity. Strong as he was, Tom was severely disoriented. He had no idea where he was or what had happened to him. His eyes roamed the room, vaguely seeking some point of reference. His gaze fell on Denise who was staring at him helplessly, her eyes distraught.

Still uncomprehending, but recognising his colleague, Allen wheezed, "Denise? Wha' …?"

Turner bent down and slapped him heavily across the face. "Take your eyes off my woman, you snivelling bastard. You think I don't know that you've been trying to weasel your way into her life since she arrived at Strandtown?" He stood up and gave the young detective a sour grin. "But, no matter. You won't be weaselling for much longer." He put his hand behind his back and, from his belt, withdrew a wicked-looking knife with a broad blade that looked to be about five inches long. Allen's cognitive faculties were starting to kick back into life. He knew something about knives and recognised this one as a Jack Pike Bushcraft knife. Not that that was a matter for self-congratulation. Turner was approaching him with a venomous scowl on his face, caressing the edge of the blade with a thumb. "You cheated death twice, you bastard, but no luck required for the third effort. You're helpless now. This time I won't fail."

Tom tried instinctively to retreat, but he still had no control of his muscles and was unable to move. He gazed helplessly at Stewart who was gyrating furiously on the bed, moaning and whimpering, struggling to plead for Tom's life.

Turner took another step forward, raising his arm, but without warning he crumpled to the floor like a marionette that had had its strings suddenly cut. Sheehan, behind him, was standing there with a pained expression on his face, shaking his right hand, clasping and unclasping it as he did so. As middle weight boxing champion at the police academy, he had struck many a blow that had earned him victory, but none had given him anything like the satisfaction he felt now at flooring Turner. *Beautifully timed,* he thought. *Full weight of the body at impact. Lovely.*

He threw his jacket over Stewart, and pulled open the doors of a built-in wardrobe near the bed. It was full of women's clothes. *And I bet they're all Stewart's size,* he thought grimly. He selected a pair of jeans and a woollen sweater, threw them on the bed, and pulled the duct tape from Stewart's mouth as gently as he could. Using his master key, he released her from the cuffs.

Stewart couldn't speak. She was afraid she would start blubbering the minute she opened her mouth. As it was, her eyes were already beginning to fill with tears, but she managed to give Sheehan a look of gratitude before grabbing the clothes and scuttling into the en suite, clutching Sheehan's jacket around her.

Sheehan, meanwhile, used the cuffs to manacle the still unconscious Turner's hands behind his back before helping Tom on to the edge of the bed. Tom's muscles were beginning to react and awareness was returning. He looked up, then frantically around the room. "Denise?"

"It's okay. She's getting dressed in the bathroom."

Allen saw Turner on the floor. "Bastard," he said, and seemed to move towards him.

Sheehan placed a hand on his arm and stopped him. "Leave him. He's got punishment aplenty coming to him."

Stewart came back into the room, stopping at the en suite door. Her face was tight as she tried to exert some control, but it was clear that she had been severely traumatised.

"Tom," Sheehan said. "Back-up's on its way. Could you go round the house and turn on all the lights to let them know where we are? And maybe you'd check to see if Turner's navy Mercedes is in the garage."

Tom seemed to demur, glancing at Denise and then back to the chief, his face pleading.

Sheehan read his thoughts. "Oh," he said, retrieving his jacket from Denise. "Okay, I'll go myself."

He had barely left the room when Denise rushed forward into Tom's arms, shaking like a leaf and crying uncontrollably. Tom just held her, not knowing what to say, letting her tears flow until they were spent. When her sobs diminished, Tom said, "God, Denise, when we broke into that house and found you missing, I thought I'd lost you. Jesus, if we hadn't found you, I would have … oh, God, it doesn't bear thinking about."

Denise looked up at him, her eyes still brimming. "I knew you'd come," she said simply and laid her head on his shoulder, still clinging tightly to him.

Tom shook his head. "It was the chief …" he started.

"I don't care," she cut in, still sobbing. "I knew you'd come." She began to cry again. "Oh, God, Tom, he was terrifying. He was going to …"

"It's all right. It's all right," Tom said, rubbing his hand on the back of her head. "It's over now. You're safe."

There was a moan from the floor and a hoarse voice snarled, "What the fuck are you doing, Allen?" Turner struggled to his knees. "Get the hell away from her."

Tom got up, wordless. A step brought him to the kneeling man. A single, sharp jab from his massive fist to the side of Turner's jaw rendered him unconscious again. Tom came back to Denise and took her in his arms once more. Grinning down at her, he said, "Don't tell the chief I did that."

A noise at the door caught their attention. Sheehan had come back. "I hear sirens in the distance. Backup will be here in a minute."

Allen looked at the prone Turner. "We need backup?"

Sheehan grinned. "Somebody needs to take this place apart for evidence. And I was right. The garage was interesting. Turner's smashed up Mercedes is out there, and there's another car in there, too, with a tandem on the roof rack. That's how the devious bastard was able to slip past us this evening." He looked at Denise. "You all right, Stewart?"

"Yes, sir, I'm fine. Thank you so much for ..."

He waved a hand to cut her off. "Forget about it." He dragged the groggy Turner to his feet. "Come on down to the front of the house, Mister Prosecutor, and we'll wait for some of your ... teammates ... to come and get you." He pushed the snarling man towards the bedroom door.

Turner struggled to resist, turning back towards Stewart. "You're mine, Lynda." He was almost yelling, and flecks of foam began to appear on his lips. "You're mine. I'll beat this petty rap, and we'll be together again. You'll see."

Stewart looked at him, at the raging face. This half-insane creature bore no resemblance to the urbane barrister she had dinner with. She shuddered as Sheehan pushed him on through the door. "God, I hope I never have to see him again."

The sound of shrill sirens shredded the peace of the night as police cars began pouring into the clearing. Sheehan said back over his shoulder, "I'll just have a quick word with Larkin. He can look after the clean up here. Then we're off. Follow us down to the car now and I'll drive you home."

Turner's voice, still strident but now pleading, came back to them from the stairs. "Wait for me, Lynda. Don't worry. I'll find a way. Wait for me."

Tom stared at Denise, his head shaking from side to side. "The guy's completely off his rocker. What's this Lynda stuff?"

Denise turned away towards the wardrobe, hands raised to either side of her head. "Don't know. Don't want to know." Among the many designer shoes on the lower shelves - pumps, boots, sandals, high heels, low heels, flats, straps, suede loafers, more variations than her eyes could take in - she found a pair of sensible shoes and put them on. "Turner must have gone on dozens of shopping trips to fill this wardrobe with all these clothes and shoes my size," she said, shaking her head in wonderment. "Did he think I was just going to live with him here?" She shivered as if she was cold, and with Tom's arm around her, they went downstairs.

FIFTY-SEVEN

Sheehan drove back to Belfast at a speed considerably slower than the heart-stopping velocity that had brought him to Ardboe. Allen, in the back seat, had his arm around Stewart who was snuggling against his chest, happy never to move.

"Okay, Chief. Time to tell us what you saw when you were studying the whiteboard."

Sheehan took a minute to gather his thoughts. "All during this case, I kept thinking that any theory that didn't include the stalker, the informant, the three victims, Lynda Bell and, yes, you, Stewart, was not going to lead us to the killer. But I just couldn't see the connections. For sure, my brain would get little jolts when somebody said something. My subconscious probably knew these things were significant but my upper mind couldn't see anything. But I was in desperation studying that board, and I tried to clear my mind in the hope that something would click. I noticed the resemblance between Lynda and Denise, but at first I thought it was only a distracting thought. But after a few minutes I suddenly realised this resemblance was the key to everything. And I could now see that what looked like a series of separate events actually all fitted into someone's personal plan. Everything began to fit. I could see it was all connected … the three victims, Lynda, Denise, the stalker, the informant …"

"What informant?" Allen said.

"Stewart had a mystery informant. We kept that a secret."

Denise said, "I'll tell you about it later. Go on, sir."

"Well, that was pretty much it."

"Oh, well. That clears it all up then," Allen said, his tone close to sarcasm.

Sheehan grinned. "I had the advantage of having listened to Greenwald spouting in my ear for an hour the other night. Some of the things he said were very relevant. For example, he said that the level of the stalker's violence indicated that he'd been stalking Stewart for a couple of years at least, yet Stewart maintained that she had only become aware of a stalker a few days ago. There was a serious contradiction there until I saw that resemblance. But listening to what Greenwald said, and hearing Jones's story about Lynda's stalker, I was able to figure out …"

"Transference," Stewart almost shouted.

"Exactly. In Turner's mind, you had virtually become Lynda. So the stalking wasn't new to him. He was just continuing from where he'd left off."

"That explains why he looked at me in court as if he owned me, at a time when I had just met him. I thought it was because I was his star witness. But he was already seeing us as a couple."

"Yes. The serious point is that for twelve years a deranged rage festered in him. He clearly was already on the way to being psychotic when he started messing with Jones and his property at Queen's, but over the years he'd have been reliving the events, wishing that he'd been a lot more aggressive. Now all of a sudden he has a second chance. Any moral sanity he might have had would be long gone by now. Violent lashing out would be his action of choice. When he saw you with Denise, Tom, leaving her home, chatting with her, his demented jealousy would allow him only one course of action. You had to be removed. He'd have thought no more about it than swatting a fly. Hence the two attempts on your life."

"Feck! I said the guy who was driving the car was nuts but, my God, he really was nuts." He stopped, arrested by a sudden thought. "But he could still deny involvement in those attempts."

"He can try. But we've got those couple of hairs forensics found in the four by four. They're his. No question."

"You were very lucky, Tom," Denise said, with a palpable shiver. "So he was really after a relationship with me from the word go?"

"Uh huh!"

"But what made him think that I would go along with it? And he filled that house with all those clothes. Did he think I would just quietly join with him and his deluded fantasies?"

"He would have absolutely believed that you would. From his warped perspective, you were in love with him. His obsessive love, as Greenwald called it, wouldn't allow him to contemplate any other possibility."

"But he seemed to need more. He seemed to be doing everything in his power to build me up."

"He was. With his ego, he had big plans for you and him. I could see that he was trying to push you into promotion. In his mind it was to be you and him, the handsome prosecutor on the rise, and the beautiful new star of the PSNI photographed by his side in all the papers."

"That would be you," Allen smirked.

Stewart said, "When he had me tied up, he was shouting something about us being the golden couple."

"Yes. It had to be that way in the scenario he had devised for you. That's why he kept saying things like, 'When you solve this case,' even though the whole team was on it."

"Yeah," Stewart said. "He annoyed the hell out of me every time he kept doing that."

"And that's why he became your mystery informant and kept phoning you with clues as to how you should proceed. He wanted you to be the key figure in the finding and arrest of Jones."

"I got a call from him on Saturday night. He was as mad as hell because we let Jones go."

"Yes, that was a serious spoke in his plans. He carried his manic resentment all through those twelve years. Killing Fitzpatrick and the others was their punishment for raping Lynda and driving her to suicide. Jones was to go down for life for attempting to come between him and the person whom he saw as his girl, Lynda. You, now in Lynda's place, were to get huge media attention for finding Jones, and Jones was to be paraded as a mad serial killer. Instead you got Jones off. Turner must have been spitting teeth."

"But what put you on to him, sir?" Allen asked.

"A few things. Early on I could see he was coming very strongly on to Stewart, but I just put that down to hormones. But Stewart and I were talking about timelines outside Weir's house the night he beat up his wife, and she suggested that the timing would fit if Weir had called the ambulance first and then beat up his wife while he was waiting for it. That set me buzzing, but I didn't know why. I know now that what was niggling at me had nothing to do with the ambulance. It was about the false time thing. What my subconscious was playing around with was the thought that Turner could well have reported his car stolen several days before it was involved in that attempt on your life, Tom. He just reported the fictional theft, with the hit and running of you on his mind, in case the car might be recognised when he took his shot. The car, already reported stolen, would give him an alibi. So when Bill said at the debrief that Turner couldn't have been driving the car when it tried to run Tom down, we all just accepted it."

Sheehan negotiated a narrow turn, watching for any unsuspecting vehicle that might be approaching. Then he said, "And there was another even more obvious clue that just slipped by me. I don't know how I missed it. At one of our debriefs, Turner was pretty much chastising Stewart for wasting her time with Mrs. Weir, that she should be at Queen's trying to find the other student in the photograph. Feelings were running a bit high at that point, and we were all edgy. I suppose that's why we didn't notice. Turner said something like, 'It's fair enough if your informant comes up with something new.' But he should never have known about the informant. Only Stewart and I knew about him."

"You're right, Chief," Stewart breathed. "In the heat of the moment I completely missed that, too."

"But he was agreeing with me all over the place that Denise should not be used as bait tonight," Tom said. "What was all that about?"

"Camouflage, basically. But I think he also knew that the more he tried to dissuade Denise from taking part in the plan, the more she would resist him. He wanted her there. And he knew she would be stubborn enough to get her way."

There was a grunt of sorts from Stewart in the back, but Sheehan ignored it. "But the biggest clue of all was sitting in front of us the whole time and we all completely missed it."

"What was that, sir?" Tom asked, stifling a yawn. It was after three o'clock in the morning, and sleep was tugging at him.

"It took another one of Stewart's perspicacious remarks to put me on to it."

"Oh?" Stewart said. "Perspicacious?"

"Yes. You remember on Saturday I was kicking myself because I didn't make the connection between the fact that Lynda's boyfriend was a snappy dresser and the fact that Jones, too, was very elegantly dressed."

"Yes, sir. I thought you were being hard on yourself."

"Do you remember what you said?"

"Em, something about young middle class professionals all tending to dress well. I think I said that Turner was about the same age as Jones, and he dressed immaculately, too, but that you weren't kicking yourself for not suspecting him."

"Exactly."

This remark elicited only silence. After a moment, Stewart said, "I don't get it, Chief."

"Me neither," Allen said.

"You'll be kicking yourselves when you hear how obvious it is."

"We'll take the risk," Allen said. "Fire away."

"You said that Turner was about the same age as Jones, Denise. And he is. So Turner must have gone to Queen's the same time as Jones, and Fitzpatrick, and Shaw, and Kelly, and Lynda. Jones said that he was in the medical faculty and didn't have any need to be around the arts faculty, but Turner, a law student, would have been in and out of arts all the time. The story of Lynda's suicide, and the rumours surrounding it, must have been flying around the campus. He couldn't have missed them. If he had been an ordinary student, why didn't he mention this fact at our meetings? What was he hiding? He didn't even mention that he had been at Queen's during the time we were investigating. Why not?"

Sheehan felt some thuds against the back of his seat. "What's that?" he asked.

"That's me kicking myself," Allen said, annoyed that he had missed something so obvious.

Sheehan grinned and drove on in silence.

"What about all that Lynda stuff he was shouting?" Allen was nowhere nearly finished with his questions.

"Well, as things stood before tonight, Turner was walking a fine line between sanity and madness. He was clever and self-aware, and was able to maintain that smooth, cultivated persona as long as his plans were progressing. But we smashed his plans to bits tonight. My guess is that the trauma of that has driven him over the edge. Stewart is now Lynda to him. I'm not even sure that he'll be in our reality anymore when the police doctors come to examine him."

"Whoa! I hope that's not right. I need that guy to face his disgrace, to fully feel the punishment that's going to land on him."

"Well, maybe the court psychiatrists can do something about that."

That set them thinking, each pondering possible scenarios for Turner's future. After some moments listening to the sound of the car's engine and watching the hedges fly by, Allen said musingly, "So it was all Turner. Weir and Duffner were just two innocents caught in this lunatic's slipstream?"

"Hardly innocents. But, yes, they had nothing to do with these crimes. Looked like they had motive enough for a while but they were just a distraction."

"How did you know to go to Ardboe to look for Denise, Chief?"

"Just a chance remark Turner made to me. We were chatting a week or so ago about how we spent our spare time. He told me he had a cottage, yeah, that big house was his 'cottage', at the edge of Lough Neagh and he liked to go boating when he could, to clear out the cobwebs. When you were asking where we should start looking for Denise's abductor, I remembered that the four by four had been abandoned near Ardboe which is very close to Lough Neagh. I got Connors to check out with Land Registry where Turner had bought his cottage, but I took a mad chance to save time and headed straight for Ardboe. Saved almost forty minutes."

Tom sucked in a spooked breath. "Thank God you did, sir. That forty minutes made all the difference. God knows what he might have done to Denise in that amount of time."

"The way you explain it all makes it seem very simple, Chief," Denise said, "but I know it was anything but simple. The situation would have defeated all the rest of us put together. I can't thank you enough, Chief, for saving me."

"Ah, give over, will you."

Silence descended upon the group. Stewart clung to Tom, almost terrified to let go. The trauma she had experienced still had a strong hold on her psyche. The powerful car droned on into the night, the humming of its tyres soporific. Sheehan had now left the side roads and had reached the motorways. Even at that hour of the morning there were many cars and lorries travelling in both directions. *Wonder where they could all be going at this time*? was Sheehan's perplexed thought.

Dawn was beginning to pull the edges of darkness away from the sky when Sheehan said, "Right, folks, we're back in the city. I'll drop you off first, Denise ..."

"Oh, no, sir." The words were out of her before she could stop them. She went on in a rush, "I don't want to be alone tonight, sir. I ..."

"I'll stay with you, Sergeant," Allen offered. "I can sleep on the couch."

"No, I've a couple of spare bedrooms. A big lump like you couldn't sleep on that wee thing."

"All right. That's settled then." Sheehan said, yawning. "And take a lie on in the morning. I intend to."

After Sheehan had dropped them at Denise's house, they stood in the hall looking at each other. Suddenly Denise said, almost in accusation, "You saw me naked."

Tom was nonplussed. "No, I didn't," came his instinctive reply.

She punched him on the arm. "You saw me naked."

"Ouch! How could I? I was writhing on the floor."

Another punch. "You saw me naked."

"No. All I saw was that awful pink, the handcuffs, the duct tape."

She punched him again, harder this time. "You saw me naked."

"Ow! Hey! Well, I sort of a little bit saw you naked."

She stopped punching. "What? How could you a little bit see me naked?" she scoffed. Then, a punch accompanying each word, she said, "You ... saw ... me ... naked."

"Ow! Ow! Okay. I saw you naked. So?"

She gave him an authoritarian look. "That demands reciprocity."

"Re ... see what? Jeez, Denise, sometimes I just don't know what you or the chief are talking about." He was grinning down at her, staring at her lovely face, searching her eyes. Suddenly he bent down and kissed her. It was just a touch, a simple peck, a question, a minor exploration. He moved back, and saw that she was waiting for him to kiss her again. He put his lips on hers, softly, moving slightly, trying to learn, trying to sense who she was, trying to find intimacy. Their lips met, separated, met again. This time the probing took longer, their lips became the focal point of their existence. All the terrors of the night sped away. The walls of the hall, of the house, moved from them in all directions. Nothing else existed. There were only their lips, lips that filled their being, lips that became their entire world. Now they were fused together. No more separating. The softness became pressure, became longing. They pressed harder, harder, lips melded together for an emotional eternity, until need grew, until desire filled their lips, filled their bodies.

Gasping, Tom pulled back and stared into eyes six inches from his own. There he saw desire, yes, but he also saw love. He bent and picked her up in his arms as if she weighed no more than a child. With her arms still around his neck, he carried her up the stairs to her bedroom, whispering, "Tell me a wee bit more about this reciprocity."

THE END

Dear Reader,

If you enjoyed this book, I would appreciate it if you please take a few moments to write a short review of it and post it online.

Thank you for taking the time to read it.

Kindest regards,

Brian O'Hare

About the Author

Because of a childhood disease that required a liver transplant, Dr. Brian O'Hare took early retirement in 1998 from his post as Assistant Director of the Southern Regional College in Newry in Northern Ireland. He now enjoys full health, plays golf, and travels. He is author of several academic works as well as two memoirs, and three award winning fiction novels, as well as Crimson Cloak's Inspector Sheehan mystery series.

http:/brianohareauthor.blogspot.co.uk/

https://www.facebook.com/inspectorsheehan

https://www.facebook.com/brian.ohare.96

twitter: @Brian O'Hare26

Also by Brian O'Hare:

The Miracle Ship, conversations with John Gillespie

Fallen Men

A Spiritual Odyssey (a memoir)

Inspector Sheehan Mysteries:

The Doom Murders, book 1 of the Inspector Sheehan Mysteries

Murder at Loftus House, Murder at the Roadside Café, and *Murder at the Woodlands Care Home* (Inspector Sheehan short stories)

Coming soon: ***The Coven Murders,*** an Inspector Sheehan Mystery

Fiction

Fallen Men (Contemporary Romance/Psychological Drama.) This novel won the Amazon IDB Award in January, 2013.)

A young priest's life spirals out of control when long-submerged memories of childhood abuse begin to surface. Fallen Men touches on some dark themes but it is ultimately a novel of redemption. It is also a heartrending love story.

Great story … I could not put it down when I got to the second half. Well written, great characters. The psychological aspects are key. Stephen Frankini, Publisher, Tumblar House Books.

O'Hare has a pleasant, easy-to-read writing style. I have written five books and edited five others, so I realize the hard work and effort that go into writing a full length novel ... There are aspects of this book that I thoroughly appreciated. The topic of sexual abuse is dealt with sensitively. There are no attention-seeking graphic descriptions. The flashbacks of child sex abuse and the depictions of the depression, guilt and breakdown after a rushed abortion are particularly well done. I found the court sequences to be believable and compelling. This is definitely an author with natural storytelling ability. Ellen Gable Hrkach, Reviewer, Catholic Fiction (USA)

A story that is both current and gripping. It has distinctive and credible dialogue and beautifully forged characters. It is clear that the writer is a keen observer of human nature. John Anthony, Publisher, Pink Cloud.

THE DOOM MURDERS by Brian O'Hare is book 1 of the Inspector Sheehan Mysteries. It was awarded The Indie Book of the Day Award, March 2014, in recognition of the Author's valuable contribution to the Indie Writing Community.

The New Apple Book Awards for Excellence in Independent Publishing is pleased to announce that **The Doom Murders** was chosen as the Official Selection for the "Mystery" category of the 2014 New Apple Book Awards.

Reader's Favourite Bronze award winner, 2015.

Non Fiction

A Spiritual Odyssey [A Memoir by Brian O'Hare]

A Spiritual Odyssey is the compelling story of a six-year journey on two converging paths - a burgeoning spirituality, and a dramatic physical degeneration that took the author to the doors of death. It is essentially a witness to the miraculous grace of God, and how it reaches into both soul and body. The author describes in detail his medical journey to a liver transplant while, at the same time, struggling with questions of a theological nature. These questions, however, are not academic. They emerge from the practical, often confusing, circumstances in which the author finds himself as he copes with dying and tries to understand his growing spirituality.

Some of the medical descriptions chill the blood but the religious explorations are heart-warming, ranging from reading theologians as different as Sean Fagan and Basil Hume, to a meeting with the sensible and down-to-earth Sister Briege McKenna, and to a pilgrimage through the holy places of France, all of which makes this a fine exposition of the riches of the Catholic tradition.

[David McLaurin, I]

Intelligent and sensitive...very moving...gives a graphic account of suffering and anguish...gives us wonderful vignettes of people he met on his journey. His description of Lourdes is truly evocative and marvellous.

[Anthony Redmond, *The Irish Catholic*]

The Miracle Ship *was awarded Top Medallist Honours in the non-fiction category of the 2015 New Apple Awards for Excellence.*

Do you believe in miracles? Do you believe in demonic possession? Do you believe in exorcism? John Gillespie has been gifted with a most extraordinary power. This true account of his life and ministry, of the miracles and deliverances that follow his prayers, will amaze you. If you read and liked Miracles Do Happen, you'll love The Miracle Ship.

The Miracle Ship was chosen as the Medal Winner for the "Religion Non-Fiction" category of the 2014 New Apple Book Awards for Excellence in Independent Writing.

Like the prophets of old, every so often God raises up a special person to address the needs of their generation. John Gillespie is a man for our times. [Eilish Cummins, daughter of Larry Cummins]

This is a fascinating story of an incredible man. His journey has been fleshed out in an understandable, yet thought-provoking manner through the able pen of O'Hare [Luana Erlich, author *of One Night in Tehran, When Camels Fly*, etc.]

Spoke directly to me and forced me to re-assess myself, my beliefs, my faith, my spirituality, and just about everything I thought I knew {Joy Nwosu Lo-Bamijoko.author of Mirror of Our Lives, etc.}

Printed in Great Britain
by Amazon

75777626R00225